T E
J
Techniques

By the same author:

Making Silver Jewellery (1982)

THE ENCYCLOPAEDIA OF Jewellery Techniques

Peter Bagley

B. T. Batsford · LONDON

© Peter Bagley 1986
First published 1986

All rights reserved. No part of this publication
may be reproduced, in any form or by any means,
without permission from the Publisher

ISBN 0 7134 4255 7

Typeset by Tameside Filmsetting Ltd
and printed in Great Britain by Anchor Brendon Ltd, Tiptree, Essex

for the publishers
B. T. Batsford Ltd.
4 Fitzhardinge Street
London W1H 0AH

Introduction

The tried and tested techniques in this book should be within the scope of the serious amateur or individual professional jeweller.

Many of the techniques are traditional and have been practised by jewellers for centuries. Examples of many of these established techniques can be seen in museums throughout the world. Other techniques are applications of processes more associated with industrial production, and some, such as the use of plastics, resins and electroforming, are relatively new in the making of jewellery.

In all the techniques, and in particular those involving heat, chemicals and machinery, adequate safety precautions should be taken to protect the operator from injury.

None of the techniques, even the traditional ones, is fully exhausted and the reader is encouraged to develop the techniques further for personal satisfaction and the benefit of the craft and the customer.

Abrasive blasting (see also Finishing metal pieces)
Metal components may be finished by blasting with a variety of materials.

Abrasive stick (see also Finishing metal pieces)
A slim wood stick to which is glued sheet abrasive paper over one end. These may be purchased or made.

Acids (see also Pickle)
Acids are used to change the condition of the surface of metals. Acids are used in diluted form with water; always add acid to water.

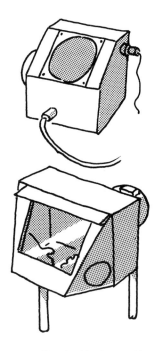

Diag. 1 *Abrasive blasting machines*

Adhesives (see also Peg setting of pearls)
Jewellery components can be joined by adhesives. The type of adhesive selected will depend on the materials being joined, the type of joint and the rigidity of the material.

Adhesives may adhere to a surface either by filling the tiny surface irregularities, in the way epoxy adhesives adhere to metal, or by chemically changing the surfaces to be joined, as with polyester cement.

Air-gas torch (see also Heating methods)
This hand-held torch has a separate gas and pressurised air supply. Available from needle point to melting capacity, this design of torch produces a hotter and more controlled flame than torches which have no pressurised air supply.

Albert bar
A cross bar attached to the end of a watch chain enabling it to be fastened through a button-hole.

Diag. 2 *Abrasive stick*

Alloy (see also Raising and reducing gold quality)
Metals can be combined by melting to produce alloys or combinations with new properties.

Alum (see also Pickle)
An alternative to sulphuric acid-based pickle, a 'safe pickle' can be made by dissolving alum in water until no more will dissolve. The solution is not so aggressive as acid pickle but is somewhat safer to handle.

Aluminium
A silver-coloured metal produced from bauxite.

Aluminium oxide
A polishing and cutting compound frequently bonded into wheels.

Annealing (see also Drawing wire)
When metal is cold-worked by such processes as forging, drawing or rolling, the material becomes hard and will crack with further forming. To prevent this

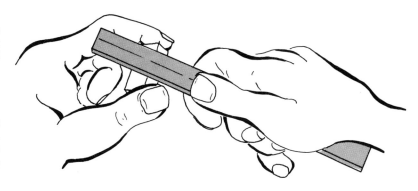

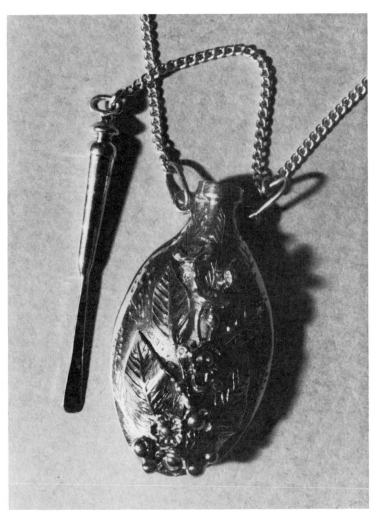

Fig. 1 *Perfume flask pendant formed from sheet silver and decorated with forged and engraved elements*

cracking, the material is heated to relieve the stresses, and cooled. This is the process of annealing.

Gold and silver may be quenched in *pickle* to both cool and remove oxides. Steel must be cooled slowly.

Anodising
The surface treatment of aluminium alloys. The surface can also be coloured during the same process.

Antique finish (*see also* Oxidising)
A finish particularly applied to silver items. It simulates the finish which occurs on silver items with age when the piece is polished only on the higher parts. To antique a piece of silver, it is first finished, polished and degreased. The piece is then swabbed, brushed with or dipped in an oxidising solution. When the desired colour is reached, the piece is rinsed to halt the oxidising action. The high points are then carefully polished with a swansdown mop or coated polishing cloth. This will create a contrast between the dark hollows and polished heights.

Anvil (*see also* Forging)
A shaped steel form over and on which metal is formed. Smith's anvils range in weight from 25kg to 100kg ($\frac{1}{2}$cwt to 2cwt) or over. For jewellery work a jeweller's anvil or bick iron is used for *forging* small flat, curved or bent pieces. An alternative for flat forging is a bench block and, for larger pieces, stakes and mandrels.

In use the jeweller's anvil is solidly set on a rigid bench; the smith's anvil is set on a short length of tree trunk, and stakes and mandrels are held either in a leg vice or in a bench socket.

Anvils can become damaged by hammer blows which miss the piece being formed and hit the anvil. Being a mass of metal, anvils tend to rust when stored in unheated areas. Lightly rusted surfaces can be restored with a rubber bonded abrasive block.

Appliqué
The technique of applying individual pieces to a background or main body, typically by sewing. In Elizabethan times pieces of jewellery were attached to clothing by sewing. The use of sequins, *beads* and buttons is the present-day comparable practice.

Aqua regia (*see also* Streak testing)
A mixture of two parts nitric acid and one part hydrochloric acid, it is used to test gold of 18 carat and above. If a small amount of aqua regia is put on a sample of gold, there will be no effect if the gold is 18 carat or above. Below this quality the metal will discolour.

Arbour
A spindle, generally for fitting into the chuck of a lathe or drill. Arbours come in a variety of shapes and sizes and are constructed to accept cutting tools, abrasive wheels and paper or small components.

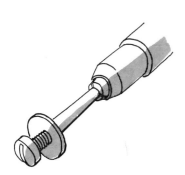

Diag. 3 *Arbour for pendant drill*

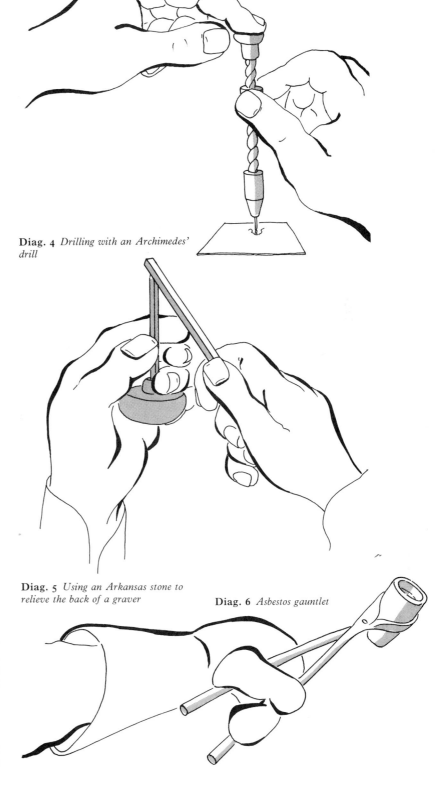

Archimedes' drill *(see also* Drilling)

A small hand-worked drill, it consists of a central screw along which moves a free nut. At the end of the screw thread is a small chuck to hold, generally, a spear point drill. At the other end of the thread is a freely rotating knob. In use, the point of the drill is put on the centre mark and, with the drill vertical, the knob is held in the left hand. The right hand moves the free nut up and down causing the drill to rotate in alternate directions, making a hole.

Diag. 4 *Drilling with an Archimedes' drill*

Arkansas stone *(see also* Sharpening tools)

A fine, hard, nearly white stone used for final sharpening of steel cutting edges. Arkansas stone is available in various shapes: flat boxed pieces for sharpening blades and *gravers*, as well as small hand-held pieces for working around intricate cutting edges or other parts of hardened steel tools.

Diag. 5 *Using an Arkansas stone to relieve the back of a graver*

Diag. 6 *Asbestos gauntlet*

Asbestos gauntlet

A piece of protective clothing for the hand and lower arm. Used when handling hot metal, the gauntlets are sold singly and fit either hand.

Ashfeltum *(see also* Etching)

A bituminous material, dark brown in colour which, when

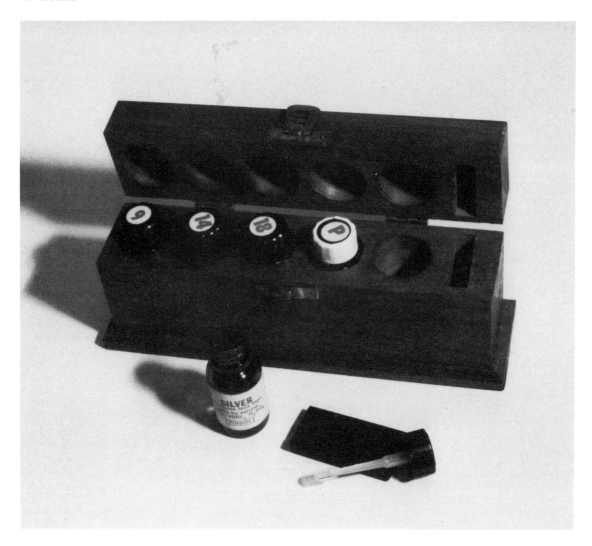

Fig. 2 *Acid testing kit for precious metals*

mixed with turpentine, can be painted on metals as a resist for etching.

Assay (*see also* Hallmark tab)
Platinum, gold and silver pieces are assayed or tested for the precious metal content by an assay office before they are hallmarked. There are assay offices in London, Birmingham, Edinburgh and Sheffield. There were assay offices in many cities, notably Chester, Newcastle, Dublin, Glasgow and Exeter, which are now closed. The precious metal content of pieces of jewellery or raw material can be estimated by *streak testing.*

Assay mark
An assay mark defines the quality of the metal on which it is stamped. It forms part of the hallmark.

Astrological stones
Certain stones are associated with the signs of the zodiac and birthdays.

Automatic centre punch
(*see also* Punching)
A round pointed centre punch with a triggered sprung internal hammer. The amount of impact can be adjusted by twisting the top barrel. The point is centred on the spot to be marked. With the punch held vertically, a downwards pressure is exerted by hand. As the top hammer is depressed, a spring is compressed until the trip point is reached, at which point an internal hammer is released which drives the point into the material being marked.

—B—

Back painting

A painting technique frequently used to decorate bottles and jars by painting the inside. The technique is also applied to flat glass. In jewellery small pieces of back painted glass can be set as stones or cameos. Watch glasses are available in a wide range of sizes; the curvature adds to the presentation. Oil or acrylic paint can be used, and wide variations of the technique are possible, but the following technique covers basic requirements.

The design is produced actual size in reverse. The painting is built up from foreground to background in layers which should be allowed to dry before the next layer is put on. Highlights can be put in by scratching through with a sharp needle and the highlight colour painted over the scratch line. The last layer of paint covers the whole area.

The technique can be extended to include the use of coloured foil shapes and other materials.

Back saw (*see also* Sawing *and* Bench hook)

A hand saw with deep blade held rigid by a grooved back to which is fitted an in-line handle. The main use is for cutting soft materials of deep section where the deep blade helps keep the cut straight. The blades are interchangeable.

Baisse-taille (*see also* Enamelling)

A form of enamelling.

Baker's fluid (*see also* Soft soldering)

A liquid flux used in the soft soldering of metals.

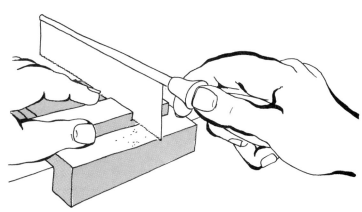

Diag. 7 *Sawing a large section with a back saw on a bench hook*

Balance

A measuring device used for weighing. Designs vary and include those incorporating a fixed weight, which creates a variable moment by varying the distance from the fulcrum. Other designs employ variable weights at a constant distance from the fulcrum. In this later design the pans may either be suspended or set up on a parallelogram arrangement.

Bangle

A piece of jewellery which fits around the wrist or arm. Generally circular inside, it slides over the hand and is not fitted with a fastening. Bangles are frequently worn in groups.

Baroque pearl (*see also* Peg setting of pearls)

Naturally occurring pearls, asymmetrical in shape.

Barrelling (*see also* Burnishing)

A finishing process in which steel shot is tumbled over small pieces of metal jewellery. The pieces are given a *burnished* finish by the continuous rolling-over action of the shot. The piece and shot work in a mixture of water and soap or other lubricant or polish. The shot used will depend on the intricacy of the piece. Plain pieces with no intricate recesses require plain spheres. Belt drive, open bucket arrangements set at an angle between vertical and horizontal can be loaded and emptied without having to open and close sealed covers.

Very small pieces can be more quickly sorted from shot after working by removing the shot with a magnet. Intricate pieces passed over a small magnetic compass will indicate if any shot is trapped in the piece. For finishing beads the shot may be omitted and the pieces finished by burnishing against each other. This is particularly useful for finishing silver shot.

Diag. 8 *Forms of steel shot used for barrelling*

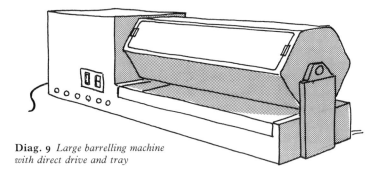

Diag. 9 *Large barrelling machine with direct drive and tray*

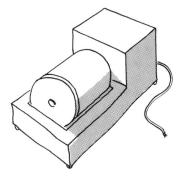

Diag. 10 *Simple barrelling machine driven by friction rollers*

Barrier cream
Used to protect the hands when carrying out dirty and wet operations.

Base metal
A term generally used to describe material used in jewellery made from non-precious metal but which imitates precious metal. Typically brass, plated steel and plated zinc and aluminium-based castings.

Bastard cut files (*see also* Files)
A very coarse cut file used for roughing operations.

Bead (*see also* Found materials *and* Glass beads)
Any small component with a through hole can be considered a bead. Materials frequently used are shell, glass, metal (both precious and base), ceramic wood, plastic, pearls and seeds.

Bead loom (*see also* Weaving)
A simple frame loom for weaving small glass beads into braids.

Beading (*see also* Fion)
A technique in which small spheres are raised on a metal surface. The beads can be simply decorative or, more commonly, used to retain a stone in its setting.

Diag. 11 *Bead linking methods*
a *Plain threading*

b *Threading with knots*

c *Linked wires*

d *Linked wire loops*

e *Linked bars*

Diag. 12 *Beads rolled from triangular paper*

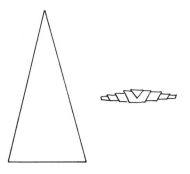

The process involves raising a small shaving using a graver. This creates a V groove leading to the shaving which is then cold formed into a small bead using a hand-beading tool with a rocking motion.

Where a line of beads is required, wire can be formed into a continuous length of linked beads which can be soldered in position.

Beading tool
Hand-held tool similar in proportion to a graver. The tip is interchangeable and terminates in a small hemispherical indentation. Various diameters of tip are available.

Beeswax (*see also* Sawing)
Available in small blocks, beeswax can be used as a lubricant. Typical applications are draw plates and saw blades.

Bellows (*see also* Heating methods)
A pair of hinged panels joined by a flexible skin. One of the panels is fitted with a one-way valve creating an air entry. An air exit to suit a small bore hose is fitted to one of the panels. For providing air for a *gas torch*, bellows are foot-operated. A more steady air stream is provided by a double-action unit.

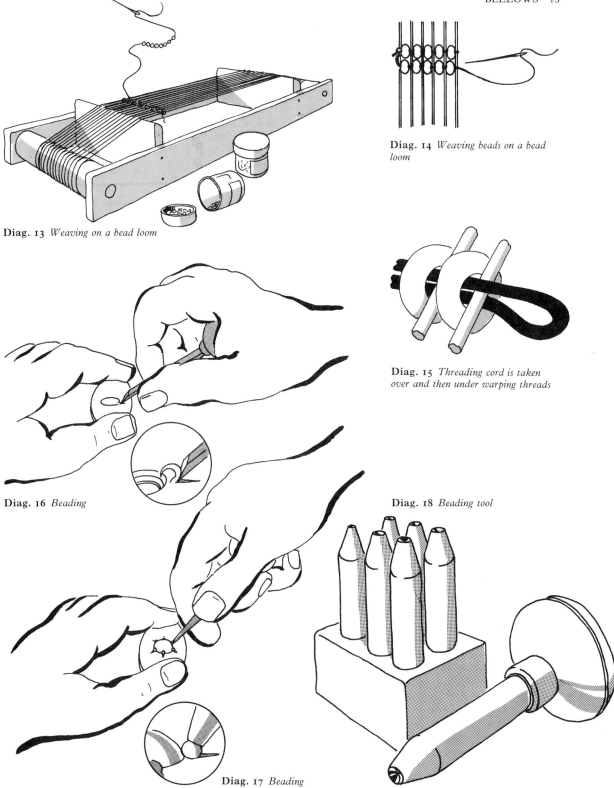

Diag. 13 *Weaving on a bead loom*

Diag. 14 *Weaving beads on a bead loom*

Diag. 15 *Threading cord is taken over and then under warping threads*

Diag. 16 *Beading*

Diag. 18 *Beading tool*

Diag. 17 *Beading*

Bench (*see also* Jeweller's bench)

The principle work station used in jewellery making. For metal jewellery the traditional jeweller's bench has a semi-circular cut-out which accommodates a skin or tray. This tray or skin is used to catch scrap and dropped items as well as for holding tools in use. The sides can form useful arm supports for delicate operations.

Fixed at or near the centre of the cut-out is a *bench pin* or peg for sawing and filing on.

For assembly work and non-metal jewellery making, a plain table or bench is suitable. It is preferably plastic laminate faced and should be higher than a desk or dining table to bring the work nearer to the operator. This can also be achieved by adjusting the height of the stool or chair.

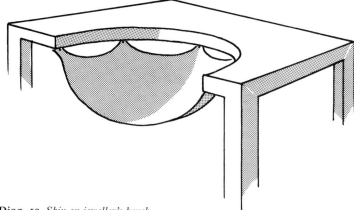

Diag. 19 *Skin on jeweller's bench*

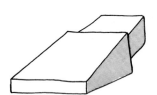

Diag. 20 *Bench peg*

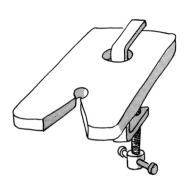

Diag. 21 *Bench peg with clamp*

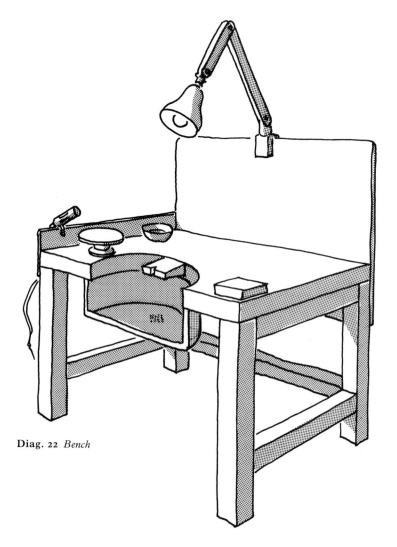

Diag. 22 *Bench*

Diag. 23 *Bench block*

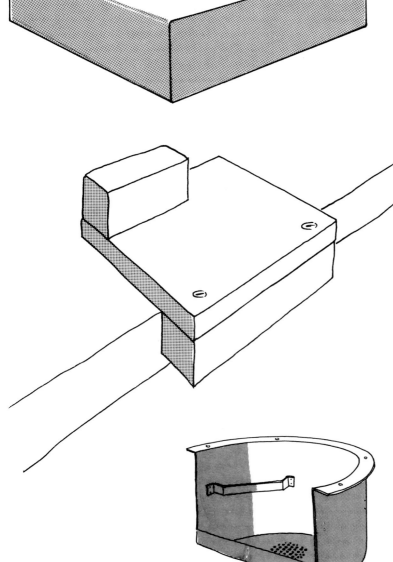

Diag. 24 *Bench hook*

Bench block

A hardened steel block with a polished face about 75mm × 75mm × 25mm (3in × 3in × 1in). It is used for flattening sheet metal and light *forging*. If protected by a sheet of brass, copper or hardboard, it can also be used for light *punching* operations.

Bench hook (*see also* Bench)

A wooden block guide which hooks over the edge of a bench to protect it and provide a stop to locate material being sawn.

Bench tray (*see also* Jeweller's bench)

A metal tray, semi-circular in plan ... bars to hold hand tools and a sieve in the bottom with a removable cup to retain filings. An alternative to the older style skin, bench trays are generally made of galvanised steel and are more resistant to hot metal.

Diag. 25 *Bench tray with lemel collection and tool rack*

Bending block

Rectangular blocks used in folding machines when making box constructions; or blocks with V grooves used in box making.

Bending metal

Simple smooth curves in wire and thin section can be bent by hand. A drawn shape is useful with which to match the formed piece. For thicker sections, more rigid methods of holding and forming are required.

A simple right angle bend in sheet metal can be achieved by holding the larger part of the piece in the smooth jaws of a chuck and forming the projecting piece over with a *drift* and *hammer*. In order to avoid marking the piece, protect it or the vice with self adhesive clear plastic.

More controlled bending is achieved by using a bending machine which grips the metal and forms the projecting part using a moving pivoted arm. Alternatively, and more appropriate to jewellery needs, a range of forming tools can be used in an arbour press. This is a low force press ideal for simple forming.

Bending strips into curved shapes can be achieved by using round bending tools on an arbour press or by bending around pegs. In a simple arrangement the pegs can be held in a vice set at a distance to suit the tightness of the bend. For really heavy sections, a piece of steel tube fitted over the piece being formed can increase leverage and assist bending. More mechanised bending tools use eccentric forming bars or bars which revolve around a central peg while a clamp secures the piece.

Bezel (*see also* Collet)

A hoop of metal used to contain a stone or similar element. Bezels can be integral in a cast piece, formed from a wall of thin material soldered to a backing or formed from bezel strip.

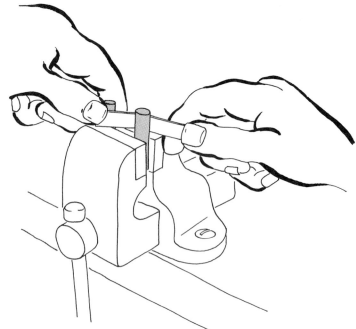

Diag. 26 *Bending metal*

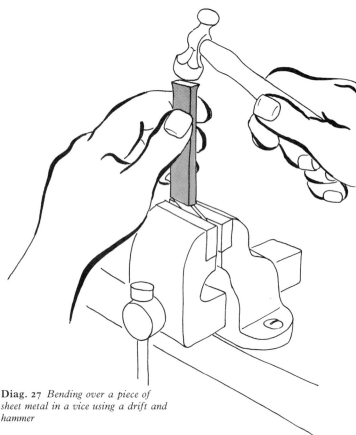

Diag. 27 *Bending over a piece of sheet metal in a vice using a drift and hammer*

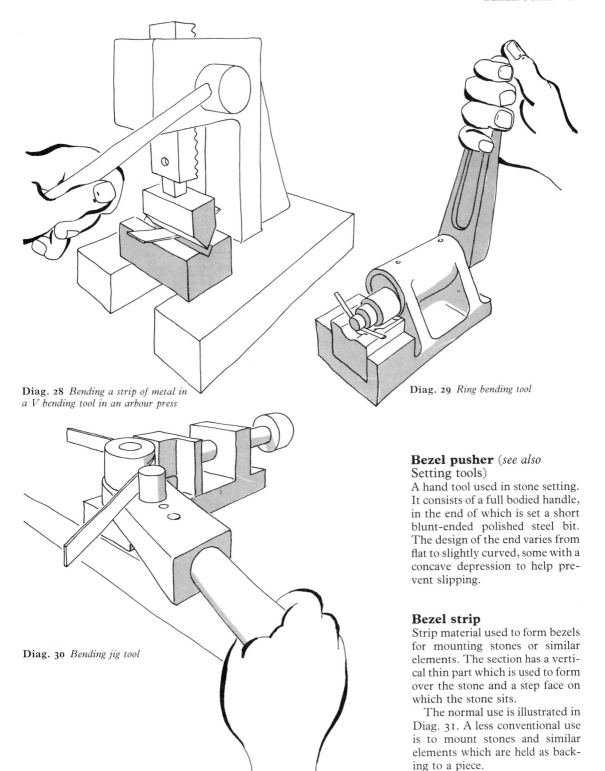

Diag. 28 *Bending a strip of metal in a V bending tool in an arbour press*

Diag. 29 *Ring bending tool*

Diag. 30 *Bending jig tool*

Bezel pusher (*see also* Setting tools)

A hand tool used in stone setting. It consists of a full bodied handle, in the end of which is set a short blunt-ended polished steel bit. The design of the end varies from flat to slightly curved, some with a concave depression to help prevent slipping.

Bezel strip

Strip material used to form bezels for mounting stones or similar elements. The section has a vertical thin part which is used to form over the stone and a step face on which the stone sits.

The normal use is illustrated in Diag. 31. A less conventional use is to mount stones and similar elements which are held as backing to a piece.

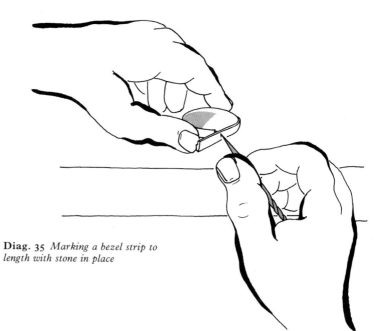

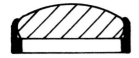

Diag. 31 *Cabochon set stone – bezel strip*

Diag. 35 *Marking a bezel strip to length with stone in place*

Diag. 32 *Open bezel*

Diag. 33 *Cup bezel collet*

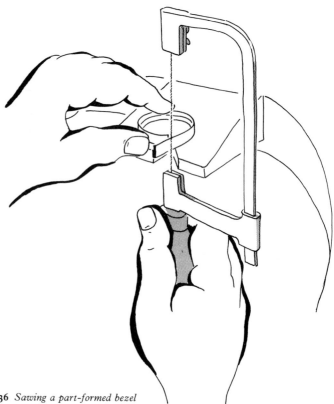

...collet

Diag. 36 *Sawing a part-formed bezel to length*

Bick iron (*see also* Anvil)

A tool used in forging and forming metal. It consists of a circular cast metal base on which is set a double horn-shaped polished steel head similar in shape to a smith's *anvil*.

Bidri work

Bidri work is a decorative process practised in India in which silver wire and sheet are inlaid into the surface of blackened zinc alloy cast pieces. The technique relies for its effect on the contrast between the sharply defined silver decoration and the black background. The Bidri alloy consists of 93 per cent zinc, $3\frac{1}{2}$ per cent copper and $3\frac{1}{2}$ per cent lead.

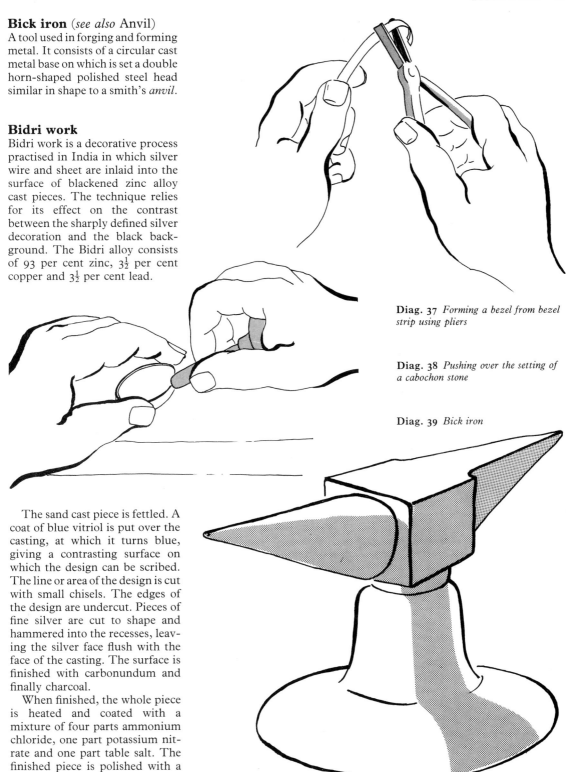

Diag. 37 *Forming a bezel from bezel strip using pliers*

Diag. 38 *Pushing over the setting of a cabochon stone*

Diag. 39 *Bick iron*

The sand cast piece is fettled. A coat of blue vitriol is put over the casting, at which it turns blue, giving a contrasting surface on which the design can be scribed. The line or area of the design is cut with small chisels. The edges of the design are undercut. Pieces of fine silver are cut to shape and hammered into the recesses, leaving the silver face flush with the face of the casting. The surface is finished with carbonundum and finally charcoal.

When finished, the whole piece is heated and coated with a mixture of four parts ammonium chloride, one part potassium nitrate and one part table salt. The finished piece is polished with a cloth and a small amount of oil.

Binding (*see also* Soldering)

Component parts of metal can be held together with iron binding wire during hard soldering. Generally the solder will not adhere to the wire. Any components thus bound should not be quenched in pickle, as the chemical action will cause copper to be deposited on the surface of the metal. Binding components with iron binding wire can also keep down the temperature of delicate pieces.

Binding can be used to terminate braids and twists made from threads and fine wire. For heavier threads a loop is initially made over the length of the binding, through which the end of the thread is threaded, and is finally pulled back under the binding. For very fine threads, the end can be terminated by sewing it back into the binding.

Binding wire

Iron wire supplied on reels or cards and used to hold metal pieces in place when *soldering*.

Binocular headband

An optical magnifier allowing closer working, leaving the hands free.

Birmingham side light

(*see also* Heating methods)
A bench-mounted gas torch used with a blow pipe or compressed air.

Birmingham wire gauge

(*see also* Measuring)
A measuring system of gauge numbers used to specify the thickness of sheet metal and the diameter of wire.

Blank (*see also* Punch and die)

The piece of material removed by a punch passing through a die.

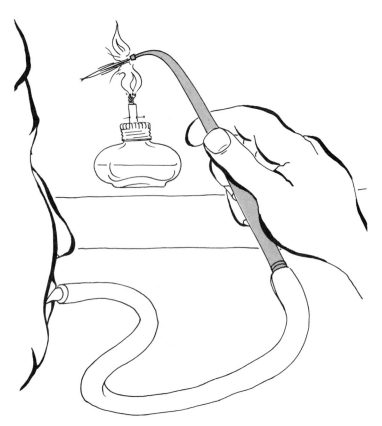

Diag. 40 *Blow pipe in use with a spirit lamp*

Blanking (*see also* Punch and die)

The process of removing a flat-shaped blank from a sheet of material using a punch and die, generally in conjunction with a press.

Blood stone

A semi-precious stone, dark green with red blotches.

Blotting paper (*see also* Pickle)

Can be used to dry parts after quenching in pickle and washing in water as an alternative to sawdust.

Blow pipe (*see also* Heating methods)

A small bore tapered tube generally of brass, bent at one end with a fine hole. Connected to a mouthpiece by flexible rubber tube, it is used to create a fine soldering flame by blowing into a soft flame such as produced by a spirit lamp or *Birmingham side light*.

Blow torch

Gas-powered torches with an air supply. The air intensifies and shapes the flame. Sizes vary from melting capacity down to needle point.

Blued metal (*see also* Hardening metals)

Steel pieces can be given a deep blue-black finish by quenching in oil after heating.

For mild steel the piece is heated to a dull red and immersed in the oil. Carbon steel and case hardened mild steel is first heated to a bright red and quenched in water. It is then heated to the appropriate temperature and colour and *quenched* in the oil.

Chemical colouring of steel is possible by using the materials available from gunsmiths.

Bluing has a beneficial effect in helping prevent rust.

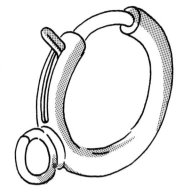

Diag. 41 *Bolt ring*

Boiling out (see also Pickle)

After hard soldering and other hot operations on precious metals, *oxides* and hard flux can remain on the surface. These can be removed wholly or partly by boiling the piece in pickle. This is carried out in a copper pickle pan or a heated container. The *acid* is kept hot but not boiling, which would cause excessive splashing. After treatment in acid, the piece should be washed in hot water to remove all traces of acid. Light brushing and the addition of a little bicarbonate may assist.

Bolt ring (see also Findings)

A polular fastening device for neck chains. It consists of a metal tube formed into an incomplete circle. Inside is a small coil spring which holds a wire bolt shut to complete the circle. The bolt ring is attached to the chain by a small jump ring attached to the outside tube. These jump rings can be closed or open. The open jump rings can be twisted open to fit the chain. The closed rings require an additional jump ring to be used to link the chain to the bolt ring. This can be advantageous where the chain is very light and a jump ring of intermediate gauge can be used. If this intermediate jump ring is soldered closed, extreme care is required to prevent the bolt ring overheating, which will weaken the spring and render it ineffective. A good compromise is to use a heavy-gauge small-diameter jump ring to join bolt

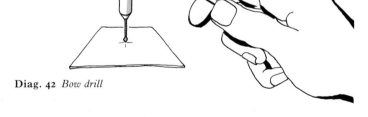

Diag. 42 *Bow drill*

rings with solid jump rings to chains. The linking of bolt rings to chains can also incorporate a hallmark tab.

Bolt rings can also be attached to cords and thongs as an effective means of fastening.

Bolt rings are available in base metals with a gold or silver colour finish as well as precious metals in various qualities. Sizes range from 5mm to 12mm ($\frac{3}{16}$in to $\frac{1}{2}$in).

Bone (see also Carving)

Animal bone, when correctly prepared, provides a low-cost yet attractive material similar to ivory and suitable for carving and inlay work. Bone from normal meat joints can be prepared by boiling in dilute sulphuric acid after scrubbing, followed by washing in household bleach and then washing in clean water. It is then left to dry.

Borax brush (see also Flux)

A brush constructed with no metal parts and used to mix and apply borax paste as a flux.

Borax slate (see also Flux)

A piece of slate or unglazed ceramic on which a borax cone is ground with water to produce a paste used as flux when soldering precious metal.

Boring (see also Drilling)

Large holes can be made by boring on a *lathe*. The piece of material is held in the chuck and a pilot hole is drilled using a twist drill mounted in a chuck set in the tail stock. This pilot hole should be large enough to accept the boring tool.

Bow drill (*see also* Drilling)
Probably the earliest form of drill. A central shaft fitted with a drill one end rests in a hollow cap at the other end. A simple wood bow has its string making a complete turn around the shaft. Holding the cap in one hand, the bow is moved to and fro causing the drill to rotate. Spear drills are used. Alternatives are the Archimedes' drill or drill stock.

Box chain (*see also* Chain making)
A chain formed by interlinking strips of metal formed initially up into a U shape and finally into a full box, the butting edges being soldered.

Diag. 43 *Box chain*

Box snap (*see also* Developed shapes)
A form of clasp used to join bracelets and chains. Any soldering to the tongue should be carried out before forming so that it can be work-hardened prior to forming, retaining the spring quality.

Boxwood (*see also* Dopping *and* Doming)
A tough close-grained wood used to make doming punches and similar tools for forming precious and other soft metal. Boxwood can be easily formed into special shapes and has the advantage of minimising surface marking. Resin bonded fabric and other plastics can be used as an alternative.

Bracelet
A piece of jewellery which fits around the wrist or arm. It is a close fit on the wrist with a means of opening and fastening, unlike a bangle.

Diag. 44 *Box catch and snap*

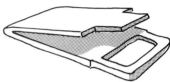

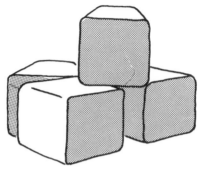

Diag. 45 *Brazing cubes*

Braid (*see also* Weaving)
Threads of various materials such as silk, cotton, wool and synthetic materials can be woven and twisted into braids, to form neckpieces, bracelets and bangles.

Brass (*see also* Drift)
A metal alloy formed from copper and zinc. The proportions are dependent on the qualities required.

Brazing (*see also* Soldering)
A jointing technique, similar to soldering, in which a brazing rod melts onto the joint under the heat of a torch. The process is essentially the same as hard soldering.

Brazing cubes (*see also* Soldering)
Ceramic cubes used to support metal during soldering and brazing.

Brazing hearth (*see also* Melting)
An area set aside for soldering and brazing. The design depends on the size of pieces being worked and the heating methods.

For precious metal jewellery much work can be carried out on the surface of a jeweller's wig or a charcoal block. For melting prior to casting and heavier work, an

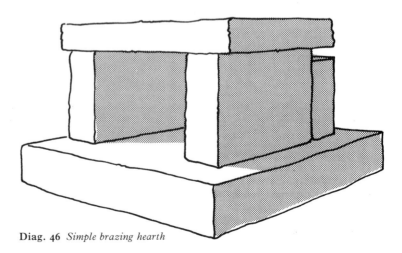

Diag. 46 *Simple brazing hearth*

unbonded arrangement of fire bricks is adequate. A gap at the rear at the top allows for the passage of hot gasses and assists with heating.

An alternative design employs ceramic chips in a shallow tray and the air spaces underneath assist in heating larger pieces.

Bright dip (*see also* Acids)
Oxides and traces of base metals can be removed from the surface of precious metals by dipping the piece in a solution of aquafortis.

Broaches and broaching
A tool for removing metal or other material. The description is used to describe two different forms of tool. In jewellery making the term describes a tool used to enlarge small holes. The tool is a tapered shaft with flat sides generally four or five in number. There is a wide range of sizes from 0.33mm to 5.77mm. In use, the broach is held in a pin chuck or similar holding device. Inserted in the hole to be enlarged, the broach is rotated by hand and gently pushed forward. The cutting edges of the broach will remove fine shavings of material. A light cutting and lubricating oil may assist. For enlarging larger diameters, an engineering tapered reamer should be used.

The term broach is also used to describe a cutting tool used for enlarging holes but one where the shape of the hole can be other than round. The cutting teeth are at right angles to the axis of the tapered shaft. Typically the cross section varies from circular to the cross section of the hole required.

In use, a hole to accept the circular end of the broach is drilled in the piece. The broach is fitted in an arbour press or similar press capable of steady pressure. With the drilled piece set on the press, the broach can be forced through the hole cutting the circular hole to the final cross

section of the broach. It is generally convenient to allow the broach to pass all the way through the piece rather than withdrawing it.

Brooch
A piece of jewellery for attaching to clothing, with a pin which fastens.

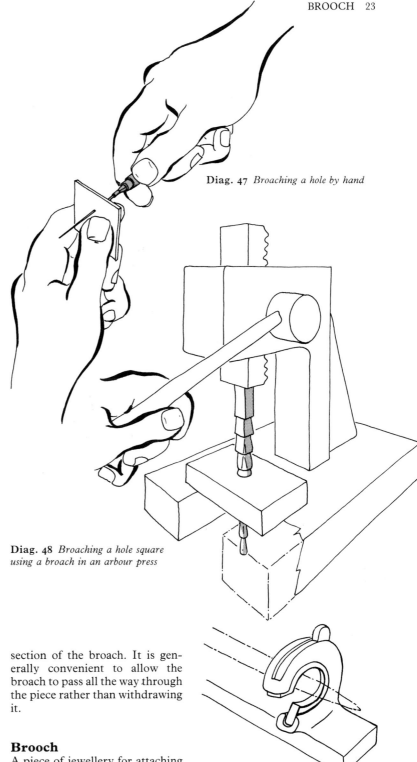

Diag. 47 *Broaching a hole by hand*

Diag. 48 *Broaching a hole square using a broach in an arbour press*

Diag. 49 *Brooch safety catch*

Brooch pin

Brooches are attached to clothing with pins, and some designs are shown in Diag. 50. Pivoting pins require a stop set near to the pivot point to cause the pin to spring. The degree of spring can be set by adjusting the height of the stop.

For brooches made of silver, the pin, if used as a spring, can be made from base material and need not be part of the piece submitted for hallmarking.

If pins are made from silver or low carat golds, they will require work-hardening. This is achieved by drawing or, if the hinge piece is soldered on them, light hammering.

Buckle

The rigid fastening piece of a belt. Designs are single- or double-sided, where the belt is threaded through, or in the form of a clasp.

Buff (*see also* Polishing)

A rotating polishing wheel carrying a polishing compound.

Buffing

Before use, any long or loose threads should be trimmed from the buff and the buff dressed with *polishing* compound.

Having ensured that the wheel is securely fitted onto the pigtail and is moving true, the motor is switched on. A block of polishing compound is held against the wheel until it is adequately charged or dressed with compound. The piece to be buffed can now be held against the rotating wheel.

Burnisher (*see also* Barrelling)

A hand-held tool used to burnish metal. It consists of a substantial handle set into the end of which is a metal or stone tip which is hard and highly polished. The shape of the tip varies from a rounded cone

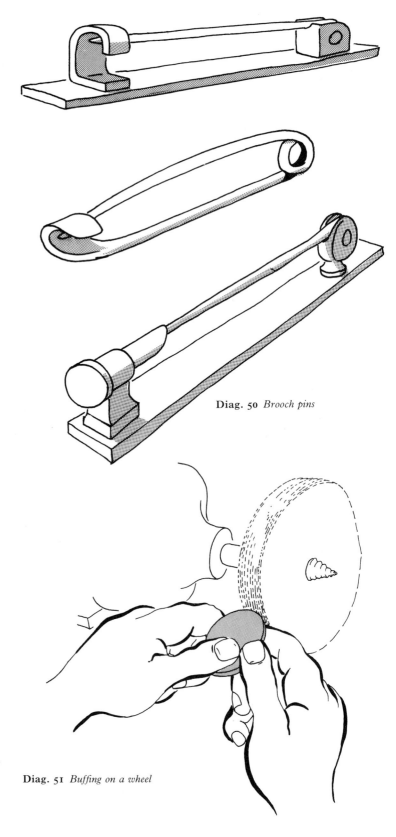

Diag. 50 *Brooch pins*

Diag. 51 *Buffing on a wheel*

to a flattened and curved form. Some burnishers have tips both ends of a handle.

Burnishers have to withstand substantial pressures in use, and in selecting one, attention should be paid to strength of construction and comfort in holding.

Burnishing (*see also* Barrelling)

A finishing process carried out by either hand or machine. Machine burnishing is barrelling. In hand burnishing a hardened and polished steel tool or a polished hard stone tool is drawn over the surface of the material. It is generally applied to finish precious metals but can be used on any metal which is softer than the burnisher. The process is carried out using a small amount of lubricant. Traditional lubricants are spittle, cold beer, and seaweed water. Readily available and equally effective is a 50/50 mixture of liquid detergent and water.

Burnishing can be applied to almost any piece of metal jewellery but is particularly suitable on intricate parts which cannot easily be polished on rotating mops.

The piece to be burnished should first be finished to a uniform matt finish with an abrasive such as water of Ayr stone. All traces of abrasive must then be removed by washing and brushing. A small amount of lubricant is smeared over the part of the piece

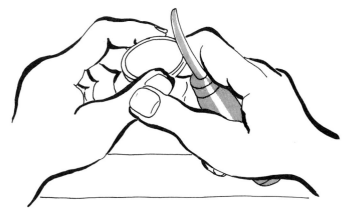

Diag. 52 *Burnishing the edge of a stone setting by hand*

to be burnished. The piece can be hand-held, but the process does involve pressure from the tool, and so holding the piece in the jaws of a ring clamp or similar holding device may be more comfortable. The holding tool can be conveniently located in the V slot of the bench pin, further steadying it. The burnisher is grasped in the right hand with the thumb parallel to the burnisher and behind the piece which is held in the left hand. The burnisher can now be applied to the piece using reasonably heavy pressure, subject, of course, to the strength of the piece. The tool is drawn with a paring stroke across the surface of the piece.

The action of the tool smooths and flows the surface of the metal, giving a high polish without removing metal. The pattern of strokes imparts a shimmery quality unique to burnishing.

Burr (*see also* Sharpening tools)

When metal is cut, a small, generally sharp, edge is thrown up. This burr will tend to be larger with blunt or worn cutting tools.

Butt joint

A joint in which two faces come together. There is no strength to the joint other than the bonding agent.

Buying precious metal (*see also* Commodity market)

Precious metals are traded and the price varies daily. More economic buying can be achieved by following the market.

— C —

Cabo

the point where the surface curves over. Excessive height past this point will both hide much of the stone and be difficult to form over evenly.

Before the wall is burnished over, the edge must be finished. It cannot easily be finished after the stone has been set.

The wall is initially formed over using a pusher working progressively around the edge and correcting the corrugation thus formed. It is convenient to have a resilient face supporting the setting against which to push. The final stage is to burnish the retaining wall to a smooth continuous face.

Cadmium

A metal used to alloy with other metals.

Calibrated stone

Stones supplied to specific sizes and shapes. Stones to random sizes and shapes are described as native cut.

Calico mops (see also Polishing)

Available in various diameters and hardnesses for attaching to motors for polishing. A good general-purpose mop is 150mm (6in) in diameter and 25mm (1in) thick.

Callipers – fastening (see also Findings)

A form of fastening consisting of two pivoted hooks which overlap and engage in a loop.

Callipers – measuring (see also Measuring)

A measuring instrument consisting of a pair of arms hinged together at one end. The arms taper down from the hinge. The other ends are turned in.

Callipers are used to compare the size of two pieces or one piece with a measured length.

Cameo (see also Shell)

A decorative carved plaque generally set in a metal frame. Shell cameos use the different coloured layers of sea shells to contrast the raised parts of the design with the background. The helmet shell, Cassis cameo, is a popular material.

Cameo carving was started in southern Italy.

Cane

Split cane can be woven using basket making and corn dolly techniques into low material-cost jewellery.

Capillary attraction (see also Soldering and Fillet)

The force which causes a fluid to flow into narrow gaps away from a normal fluid level. The phenomenom is employed in soldering.

Carbide tools

Metal cutting tools such as burrs, drills and mills in which the cutting parts are made from tungsten carbide. The resultant tools are suitable for cutting harder materials than can be cut with normal carbon steel tools, and on normal materials tool life is greatly extended.

Diag. 53 *Calliper fastening*

Carbon transfer (see also Marking out)

Carbon paper can be used to transfer designs from paper to metal or other materials. For a clear image, metal faces should first be coated with a thin coat of white emulsion or acrylic paint. If the design is made on tracing paper, the design can be reversed to produce symmetrical patterns.

Carborundum

An abrasive material in wheel or slab form used for grinding and sharpening steel tools.

Carving

Soft to medium hard materials can be carved to shape. The cutting tools will depend partly on the hardness of the material being cut. Carving is traditionally a hand operation, but powered tools such as *pendant drills* will speed the removal of material. Hand and powered techniques can be combined.

Casting (see also Cuttlefish casting and Lost wax casting)

The process of shaping metal by persuading molten metal into a shaped cavity.

Casting plaster (see also Gravity casting)

Also called plaster of Paris and dental plaster. It is not suitable for investment in lost wax casting. It can be used for slip casting clay and for making small plaques and beads in low cost jewellery. Water-colour and acrylic paints can be used for colouring.

Cellulose acetate (see also Plastics)

An acetic ester of cellulose available in sheet form. It can be shaped by heat and joined by the use of solvents. It is highly inflammable.

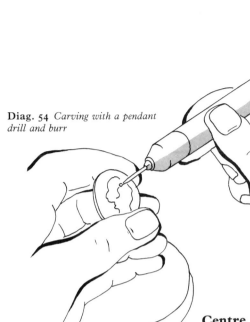

Diag. 54 *Carving with a pendant drill and burr*

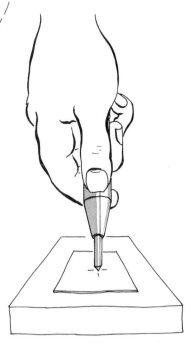

Diag. 55 *Automatic centre punch*

Centre punch (*see also* Punches)

A simple steel tool pointed at one end and used with a hammer to punch an indentation in metal. The indentation can be used to mark the position for drilling a hole and assists in centring the drill.

Automatic spring-loaded ver-

Cellulose lacquer

A quick-drying lacquer. It consists of either cellulose acetate or cellulose nitrate together with a volatile solvent and pigments.

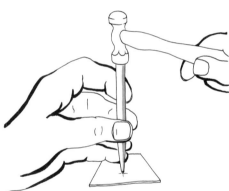

Diag. 56 *Using a centre punch*

sions are available which incorporate a spring-loaded weight which impacts on the pointed end when the outer end is pushed down.

Centrifugal casting (*see also* Casting)

The force created when a mass rotates about a centre acts to force the mass away from that centre. This can be illustrated by swinging a weight around on the end of a

Fig. 3 *Steam casting equipment*

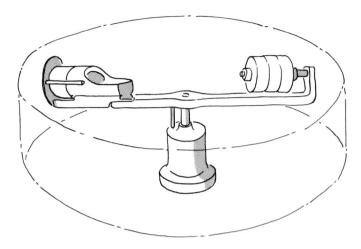

Diag. 57 *Centrifugal casting machine*

string. If the mass is molten metal in a crucible with a small hole in the base and at the base is a cavity, then rotating this unit will force the molten metal from the crucible into the cavity. This is the principle of centrifugal casting.

The most simple centrifugal casting system is easily constructed by the craftsman. Detail of design can be varied. The essential components are a small platform supported by three or four arms. The arms join together at right angles to a spindle on which is set a freely rotating handle, the overall length being approximately 800mm ($31\frac{1}{2}$in). The cavity in the form of the desired shape is produced by the lost wax process in a short squat casting flak using investment material. The top surface is carved into a shallow depression linked to the sprue hole. The flask is wired to the platform.

The whole casting operation should take place in a low lit, well ventilated room with adequate room to swing the casting unit. Practice swings with an unheated unit should be made to ensure adequate space and safety.

To cast using this equipment, the metal to be melted is placed in the shallow cavity in the top of the flask together with some flux.

The unit is held by the handle in the right hand and a torch for melting in the other. There should be a convenient place to hang the torch after use.

The torch is used to bring the metal to a fully molten state, at which point the torch is put aside and the unit is swung with both hands with a lifting action. Swinging is continued until the glow from the sprue has gone. The flask is removed with tongs and pliers and dropped into a metal bucket of water.

The sudden cooling will fracture the investment and free the casting. This system is limited to small castings.

Mechanised centrifugal casting machines are available which give better control and are less hazardous in operation. They consist of an arm which rotates in either a vertical or horizontal plane and around which is or can be fitted a protective wall generally of sheet metal.

At one end of the arm can be inserted a purpose-made fire clay crucible. This is cup-shaped with a side hole which feeds a face onto which the base of the invested flask is clamped. The other end of the arm has an adjustable balance weight. The hub is fitted with a spring or motorised drive which can initiate the arm spinning and then disengage to allow it to spin freely.

For spring-driven units the arm is cocked and the trigger set. To cast, having prepared the flask with a sprue hole to locate in the crucible, the required volume of metal is put in together with some flux. The counter-weight is set to balance the arm.

A flame of sufficient heat is directed at the metal in the crucible bringing it to a fully melted condition. When this is reached the flame is withdrawn and simultaneously the arm triggered. The acceleration of the arm causes the melted metal to flow into the cavity in the flask. When the arm has ceased to spin, the flask is removed with flask tongs and quenched in a metal bucket of water, thus freeing the casting.

Centrifugal casting is a process suitable for casting most types of metal.

Cerium oxide (*see also* Polishing)
A polishing powder used for the final polishing of stones.

Chain making
Individual links are interlinked to form a continuous flexible chain. Machine made chains in precious metal are made from wire with a solder core. The cut ends of the wire are joined by heating the interlinked formed chain to *soldering* temperature.

An infinite variety of chains can be assembled from an equally infinite variety of links. Diag. 58 shows some possibilities.

For tapered chains, the links should enlarge progressively. This can be achieved either by winding wire around a tapered mandrel or by cutting a wedge out of a parallel wound coil. Square, rectangular, triangular and oval links can be formed by winding wire on appropriately shaped mandrels. To minimise spring back the wire should be in an annealed condition.

a *Serpentine*

b *Foxtail*

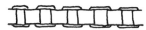

c *Box*

d *Trace*

e *Belcher*

f *Curb*

g *Rope*

h *Fancy*

Diag. 58 *Chain types*

The wire used to form the links can be of any section such as is commercially available or can be drawn or rolled. For example, in a belcher chain, the links are from *D section* wire.

In forming links from square wire, there is a tendency for the wire to bend across the diagonal

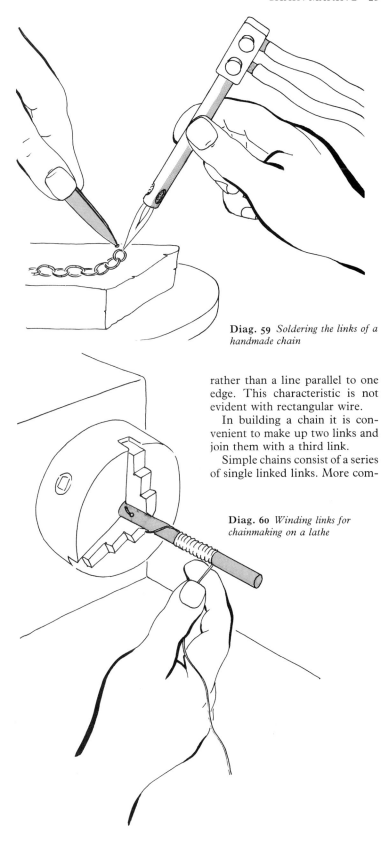

Diag. 59 *Soldering the links of a handmade chain*

rather than a line parallel to one edge. This characteristic is not evident with rectangular wire.

In building a chain it is convenient to make up two links and join them with a third link.

Simple chains consist of a series of single linked links. More com-

Diag. 60 *Winding links for chainmaking on a lathe*

plex chains can be made by building the chain in pairs of links. Another more solid chain is made by threading oval links through the ends of a previously formed up oval link.

When formed, a chain may have its section changed by twisting, as in curb chain. A complete chain can also be changed in section by drawing it through a draw plate or passing it through the flat or square rollers of a mill.

Links can be more elaborate than simple loops and manufactured from pressings, casting and forgings. Some of the many possible variations are illustrated. By convention, chains are made from metal, but there is adequate scope to employ other materials.

Champleve (see also Enamelling)

A form of enamelling in which the enamel is fired into etched recesses. Typically, the enamel forms a background to larger areas of engraved flat metal. The

Diag. 61 Chasing a piece set in a pitch bowl

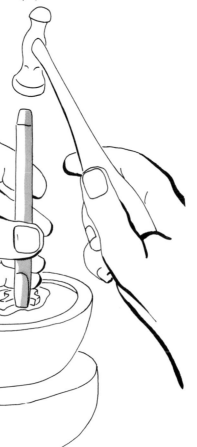

method of charging the recesses is as with cloisonné enamelling. The process should only be used on heavy gauge metals greater than $1\frac{1}{2}$mm ($\frac{1}{16}$in) thick.

Charcoal (see also Soldering)

Charcoal is produced by burning material, such as wood, imperfectly. Blocks of charcoal are used as a support for pieces being soldered and for small melting jobs.

Charcoal absorbs little heat, resists flames at melting temperatures, can be shaped for simple supports and does not adhere to molten metal. It is available in natural or reconstituted blocks size $12 \times 7 \times 3$cm ($4\frac{3}{4} \times 2\frac{3}{4} \times 1\frac{1}{4}$in). Both materials have similar properties although reconstituted blocks have a tendency to burn and can easily be reduced to a small heap of ashes overnight. Natural charcoal is the more expensive.

Blocks degrade with use but surfaces can be recovered by scraping or filing. There is a tendency for blocks to crack in half and this can be reduced by winding binding wire around the outside. Alternatively, the whole block can be set in plaster in a shallow tin.

Chasing (see also Repoussé)

A finishing process using hammer and punches. It is the second stage in the production of low relief in sheet metal, the first stage being repoussé. It is also used to finish castings. The process is described in full under *repoussé*.

Chemical bonding of grains and granules (see also Granulation)

Fine grains and granules can be set on a base piece without the use of solder, which would flood the piece and detract from the crispness of the spherical shapes.

The technique is particularly suited for gold granulation work but can also be applied to silver. The bond is achieved by allowing copper to diffuse into the contacting surfaces.

Various processes offer variations on a theme, but the essentials are as follows. The surface is coated with a mixture of gum tragacanth or secotine glue and copper hydroxide or other copper-based salt. On this are set the grains or granules in the desired pattern. The piece is brought to a temperature of about $890°C$ with a reducing flame, at which point a chemical action takes place between the gum and the copper hydroxide forming a pure copper bond at the contact point. As soon as a bond is achieved, the flame should be removed and the piece pickled. Only light polishing is carried out so as not to lose the quality of the spheres.

Chenier (*see also* Tube making)

The term is used to describe small-diameter tubing of precious metal.

Seam free chenier can be purchased and is made from drawn down deep drawn billets. It is more expensive than the same weight of sheet or wire.

To make chenier from sheet, a parallel strip of sheet $3\frac{1}{7}$ times the required diameter in width is needed. The material should be in a fully annealed condition and the end should have a blunt point cut on one end to allow it to be gripped by draw tongs.

The strip is formed up into a U shape using a swage block and dowel. The U shape is formed over the dowel into a full tube, which is then drawn through a round draw plate to shape. It can now be soldered and then drawn down further. To prevent collapse, a rod should be kept inside the tube. Excessive drawing down will require a range of rod sizes, and during drawing stages the material may require annealing and resoldering.

Diag. 62 *Chisel*

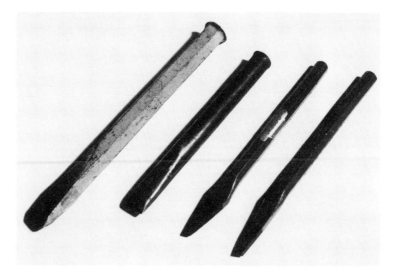

Fig. 4 *Chisels*

Chisels

A cutting tool used to cut or carve. It is made to cut by being struck on the end. Chisels to cut wood are fitted with a wooded handle and are struck with a mallet. Chisels to cut metal are of all metal construction and are struck with a hammer. Related tools are gravers and carving chisels which are forced into the material by hand.

The cutting edge is varied depending on what cutting or carving action is required.

Chromium plate

An electroplating technique which can be given a satin or high polished finish.

Circle cutter

Materials can be cut into circles with a variety of tools. Thick materials such as wood and plastics are cut with cylindrical saw edge cutters in a pillar drill. These are available in discrete increments. Thinner rigid materials can be cut with a trepanning tool. Used in a pillar drill, it consists of a shank which fits in the chuck and carries a cross arm which is formed over and shaped to a cutting edge. Some trepanning tools are equipped with two cutting arms allowing washers to be cut out. Stone slabs can be cut into circles with diamond-tipped cylindrical tube cutters.

Clasp (*see also* Findings)

A fastening used to join chains and necklaces. The most popular form of clasp is the bolt ring.

Claw (*see also* Stone setting)

Part of the setting for faceted stones. A number of claws hold the stone in position.

Claw setting (*see also* Setting tools)

Gem stones are frequently claw set to maximise the amount of light reaching and leaving the stone. Three, four or more *claws* may be employed, dependent on the size and shape of the stone.

A claw setting is essentially the same as a collet setting but with much of the material removed.

Settings may be purchased or made and various methods of manufacture may be employed. Commercially made settings are lost wax cast but frequently require the seat cutting on which the stone sits. This consists of remov-

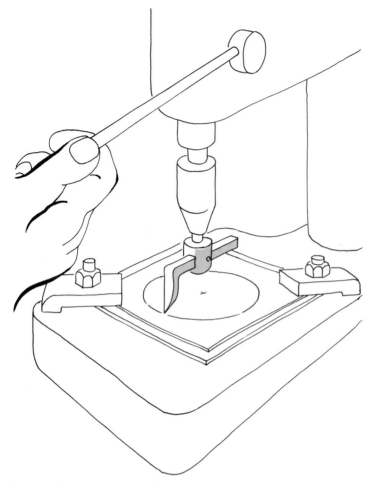

Diag. 63 *Cutting a circle from sheet metal using a trepanning tool*

Fig. 5 *Circle cutting tool*

Diag. 64 *Claw setting*

ing metal from each claw on the inside, allowing the stone to sit evenly on each small face, and reducing the claw in section so that it can be formed over more easily. This thinning may not extend all the way up the claw, giving strength to the end of the claw.

The setting is traditionally made from sheet material by laying out the developed shape, sawing to size and forming up. The ends are then butted and soldered, forming a truncated cone. The fabricated piece is formed true with a collet punch and die. With this approach it can be convenient to cut the seat for the stone with a setting burr before removing metal by sawing or filing to form the claws.

A quick and efficient method of forming the basic *collet*, particularly in the higher carat golds, is to melt a small bead and tap it with a flat ended punch into a tapered collet punch. After annealing, the shaped bead is replaced and the collet punch driven into the centre, causing the metal to flow into a cup shape in which the seat for the stone can be cut and the claws formed by sawing and filing. This method has the advantage of eliminating soldered joints.

Cleaning

Various forms of contamination are removed by differing methods (see table opposite).

Cloisonné enamelling (*see also* Enamelling)

A form of enamelling in which

single colours of enamel are enclosed within small shaped areas defined by a shallow and thin wall of metal. Gold, copper and silver are popular materials suitable for this process.

To produce a cloisonné enamel plaque, the established design should be scribed on a piece of material larger than the finished piece. As a guide, a 1mm thick backing piece is suitable for large pieces and 0.8mm thick piece for smaller pieces. A frame is first formed from rectangular section metal. Again as a guide, 1½mm wide and ½mm thick is suitable. This material can be cut from sheet or formed by rolling round wire between parallel rollers – a process which gives gently rounded edges to the strip and receives the solder when the piece is fitted. The strip should be annealed and clean. It is shaped to the outline of the piece and soldered in place using high melting point enamelling solder. It may be necessary to hold the outside frame in place with iron binding wire during soldering. The solder should be fed from the outside to minimise the amount of solder on the inside face of the backing.

Any excess solder inside the frame should be removed and the piece pickled and washed.

The walls which form the cloisonné can now be formed up using a thinner strip but of the same height. A 0.3mm or similar

thickness is suitable. It is convenient to join the ends of these pieces before final shaping and fitting. Again, enamelling high melting point solder should be used. To heat the backing adequately and prevent overheating of the walls, it is convenient to support the piece on a tripod applying most of the heat from underneath. Stick soldering or the use of paillons is appropriate.

When complete, the edge should be trimmed and any attachment pieces fitted. The piece should now be finished. It is important that all traces of flux and polishing compound are removed. The lustre of gold and silver may be heightened by use of a glass fibre brush when transparent enamels are being used. Final pickling and washing will prepare the piece for enamelling, which should be dried with blotting paper tissues or sawdust and placed on a clean sheet of paper. The selected, well washed enamel powder is mixed with water to a slurry with the addition of a little gum tragacanth, gum arabic or a trace of one of the modern wallpaper pastes. The enamel should be well mixed to eliminate lumps and allowed to settle to remove air bubbles.

Watercolour pallets make ideal mixing bowls for enamels. Mixing can be done with wooden spatulas shaped with a penknife for fine work.

With the enamels mixed, the cloisonné can be filled, taking care not to let one colour contaminate another. A spill of blotting paper can be used to lift out mistakes. The cloisonnés must be well filled, pushing the enamel well down into the corners and eliminating air bubbles. An eye-dropper filled with water can be used to refresh mixed enamels as they dry out.

When the filling is complete, the piece can be left to dry thoroughly. When completely dry, it can be fired. This will cause the colours to sink and the effect may be desirable and left. The traditional method is to refill the cloisonnés with more enamel and repeat the process. The final layers are ground flat and, after washing, quickly fired to regain the gloss. Any fire stain on silver or oxidisation of copper should be removed and the piece finish polished taking care not to damage or overheat the enamel.

As an alternative to soldering the walls in place, the soldered shapes can be set on a thin layer of clear flux which fires them in place. This technique is useful for fine detail where there could be a danger of melting the small pieces of metal.

Cloths for polishing
Impregnated cloths are used to carry polishing compounds for final polishing of precious metals.

Cloths are available ready impregnated or can be made by impregnating a good quality and weight of non linting flannel with the following mixture dissolved in a litre of hot water:

Ground chalk 250g (8¾oz)
Magnesium carbonate 250g (8¾oz)
Powdered rouge 100g (3½oz)
Detergent liquid 5ml (⅓cu.in)
Diglycol-stearate 1kg (2lb 3oz)

Coiled wire frame and thread
Simple jewellery can be made

Contamination	Material	Cleaning method
Hard solder flux	Silver	Pickling in dilute sulphuric acid
Hard solder flux	Gold	Pickling in dilute nitric acid
Oxide	Silver	Silver dip, hotel dip, de-oxidiser
Polishing compound	Precious metal	Detergent, water and hard brush; steam cleaner; ultrasonic cleaner; barrelling
Investment	Precious metal	Barrelling; ultrasonic cleaner

from tightly coiled wire over which is wound coloured threads. The wire, preferably hard drawn copper, is wound around a former and then stretched. Cut into appropriate lengths, it can be formed into frames which are subsequently assembled by soft soldering.

The 'notches' on the stretched coil allow thread to be wound around the frames without slipping off.

Fastenings and supports in base metals can be soft soldered in place prior to winding the thread.

Variations in coil size and degree of stretching, together with the selection of threads, allow for a wide variety of low cost jewellery to be made with a low material cost.

Coin mounts

Coins can be set as pendants without damage by mounting the coin in a prepared frame which is

Diag. 65 *Coiled wire and thread construction*

fitted with a suspension loop. Diameters and shapes are available commercially in gold and silver for most popular coins. A typical design consists of a shallow channel formed in a circle or other shape to fit the coin with the ends butting together. The ends of the channel are fitted with small rings which overhang the ends of the channel and overlap each other when the channel fits around the coin. A heavy jump ring passed through these rings secures the channel to the coin and provides a suspension point. The small loops can be made more elaborate and decorative.

An alternative method is to make up a mount to encircle the coin, to which is attached the suspension device. After finishing the mount the coin is inserted and the overlapping edge of the mount burnished over the coin. A variation of this system is to claw set the coin inside a flat rim.

Cold shut (*see also* Casting)

A fault in castings and mouldings. It is caused by the material flowing from different directions and cooling or setting before meeting. The result is a fracture line.

Collage

The assembly of individual pieces to form a whole. All normally used materials can be used to form a collage. For contrast and interest, different materials can be combined and techniques such as embroidery, basket work, tapestry

Diag. 66 *Coin mount*

Diag. 67 *Open coin mount*

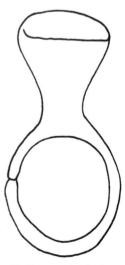

Diag. 68 *Open casting fault*

and weaving can be employed on a miniature scale as a background for the applied items.

Metal jewellery can be created by assembling pressings, castings and forging onto a backing. Fastening can be by soldering, riveting and screw threads.

Collet (*see also* Bezel)

A continuous metal frame with or without a backing, used to hold *cabochon* stones and similar items. The edge of the metal is *burnished* over to fix the stone in position. The stone sits either on a backing or on a ledge around the inside of the frame.

Collet blocks and punches

Collets for stone setting can be accurately sized by driving the approximately shaped material into a tapered hole with a matching punch.

Collet blocks with specified angle holes in various shapes cover the range of normally available calibrated stones.

Coloured glass (*see also* Moulding glass)

Supplied in flat sheets either through coloured or surface coloured. Glass can be incorporated into jewellery in the same way as stones.

Commodity market (*see also* Buying precious metals)

Silver, tin and other materials are traded on the commodity market. The price charged by a supplier will depend on the price at which the basic material is traded. Silver price is fixed twice a day. Commodity prices are published daily in some newspapers.

Compounds for polishing (*see also* Polishing)

Polishing wheels are dressed by pressing a block of polishing compound against the rotating wheels.

Compounds consist of a carrier and an abrasive. Carriers are typically hard fats or tallow. The abrasive may be naturally occurring, such as tripoli, lime or chalk, or man-made, such as aluminium oxide or silicon carbide.

Compounds can be divided between those for coarse cutting and those for finishing. They are available for precious and non-precious metals, plastics and other non-metals.

Compounds	Application
Tripoli	Coarse compound for removal of material. Used on most metals.
Platinum green	Used on platinum and white gold.
White diamond	Silica-based compound used on non-precious metals.
Crocus	Cutting compound for brass, copper and aluminium.
Rouge – hard and soft	Finishing precious metals.
Plastic	Hard plastics, ivory, bone, amber.
Green	Stainless steel, chrome, platinum finishing.

Cutting and polishing compounds in powder form can also be applied by hand with cloths, felt, orange sticks etc.

Loose powder mixed to a paste with water can be used to dress rotating felt discs when static.

Compounds	Application
Rouge powder	.Metal finishing.
Cerium Oxide	Polishing stones.
Tin Oxide	

Compressor

A motor-driven pump or high-pressure fan. Used to provide air for gas torches or to power spray guns and presses.

Coolant

A liquid used during cutting processes. The flow of liquid takes away heat and waste material from the cutting face. Specialised coolants are produced for cutting different materials.

Cords and cord making

Cords, purchased or made up, can be used to form neckpieces, bracelets, bangles and to suspend pendants. Cords made up from two or more threads can first have a ring or fastening threaded on, requiring only one end to be bound.

Ready-made cord is attached to jump rings and fastenings by binding.

For cords with a large bead or other tube piece at the centre, the cord can be twisted back from two places, each passing through a ring or fastening leaving the ends to be bound at the centre and thus covered.

To make a cord, threads are wound around two thin pegs set at a distance approximately $2\frac{1}{2}$ times the required finished cord length. The actual length is dependent on the degree of twist. Enough threads to half the thickness of the finished cord are required. Threads of different colours can be combined, and to link them the whole group of threads should be knotted together at the ends. Any rings or fastenings should now be threaded over the threads.

One end of the threads is now looped over a hook held in the chuck of a hand drill. The threads are now twisted with the threads held taut. Over-twisting will cause random knotting and thread breakage. With sufficient twist the fastening or ring is centered and held from twisting. The two ends are brought together, keeping the threads taut. The ends are now allowed to rotate and the two elements will twist together. The open ends should be knotted for security.

Diag. 69 *Initial twisting in making cord*

Core drill (*see also* Drilling)
A hollow cutting tool used in a pillar drill. It removes a thin wall of material and is used in thin materials such as shell and plastic sheet to produce discs. Used in thicker materials, it is used to cut around a core which in blind holes is removed by fracturing.

For softer materials core drills are made from hardened steel. Harder materials require diamond-coated tools.

Cork
Taken from the outer bark of the corkoak the material is easily cut with a craft knife and can be incorporated in simple jewellery.

Cotton thread (*see also* Cords *and* Cord making)
Normally sold for embroidery, coloured cotton threads can be

incorporated in jewellery by winding into cords or knotting into tassels and other macramé-based designs.

Cotton thread for embroidery is sometimes sold as 'embroidery silk' and should not be confused with real silk.

Couching
A decorative technique in which shaped wire is held by finer wire to a surface. Annealed wire is used and may be either fully preformed or part preformed and part formed *in situ*.

Counter enamelling (*see also* Enamelling)
When flat sheets of metal are enamelled on one side only, there is a tendency for the unequal expansion of the materials to cause the enamel to fracture and flake off. This can be reduced or eliminated by covering both sides of the piece with enamel; the back covering is called counter enamelling.

Laid on a clean sheet of paper, the prepared piece of metal is first brushed with a thin coat of gum tragacanth, gum arabic or a trace of modern wallpaper paste in water, and dusted with enamel, then lifted onto a stainless steel

Diag. 70 *Twisting a first twist back on itself*

trivet which touches only at the edges. Lifting is done with a steel spatular or palette knife. When dry, the piece can be fired and when cool turned over and the front enamelled as desired.

Enamel for counter enamelling should be similar to the front enamel but can, if not easily seen, be made from recovered enamel which is contaminated by other colours.

Countersinking (see also Drilling)

Enlarging a hole into a conical shape at one end. Normal twist drills can be used but this tends to produce chatter and an uneven face. Conical burrs and rose bits are preferred. Countersinking is used to accept the formed over head of a rivet, allowing a flush face, or to accept countersunk screw heads.

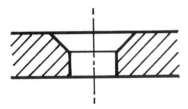

Diag. 71 *Section of a countersunk hole*

Craft knife

A short bladed knife with replaceable blades used to cut soft materials. Many designs of both handle and blade shape are available.

Craft material

Various forms of mouldable materials similar to clay which air dry and can be finished by painting and varnishing. The material is very suitable for making beads and small plaques; instructions for the latter follow below.

A master is made by rolling, carving and modelling a knob of plasticine set on a smooth hard

Diag. 72 *Cutting a straight edge with a craft knife*

surface. A wall (plasticine) is set around the master and the whole cavity is filled with a smooth mixture of plaster of Paris. This will set and the surface will warm. When this cools, the plasticine can be peeled away and the mould thoroughly dried. The face of the mould should be treated with a soap solution and is then ready.

A knob of moulding material is pushed into the mould, the surface smoothed and left to dry. When dry, the moulded plaque is removed and finished with paint and varnish.

Beads are easily made by rolling small balls and threading them onto a needle and coarse thread. The surface of the beads can be decorated by impressing the surface with shaped stamps. When dry, the depressions can hold a contrasting colour to the body colour. Larger beads can be made by winding a thin roll of material around a cocktail stick or needle.

Crimping

Materials such as cords and thongs can be attached to metal components by crimping.

In essence a light gauge metal tube with the cord or thong inserted is indented from the

Diag. 73 *Crimped thong*

outside, thus forcing the metal into the centre material. The indenting can be with a pattern of centre punches carried out with the tube supported in a half round swage block. Alternatively, a pair of normal cutting pliers can be modified by filing or grinding two matching half round and blunt edges; this is gripped around the tube with a clamping and rotating action producing a circular groove on the outside of the tube.

Crocus paper

A very fine abrasive used for finishing prior to final *polishing*.

Crucible (see also Melting)

Containers made from refractory materials and used to contain metals during melting. Sizes from 70g (2½oz) to 17kg (37½lb) are readily available.

Tall crucibles are used in kilns and melting furnaces. Flat fletchers are used for smaller quantities of metal melted by torches.

Cultured pearl
Pearls produced in living oysters by inserting a bead made from mother of pearl. The oyster deposits a pearlescent coating over the bead in the same way in which a natural pearl is formed.

Cupric oxide
The black surface layer which forms on alloys containing copper.

Cuprous oxide
The pinky red under-surface layer which forms on alloys containing copper.

Curb chain (see also Chain making)
A design of chain which is made with repeated links as trace chain but which is twisted so that the links lie flat.

Cushion punch (see also Repoussé and chasing)
A flat-ended punch also called a matting punch. It is used to force down the retaining burrs in metal inlay.

Cut off tool (see also Turning)
A lathe tool used to cut through a bar to remove the turned part. Also called a parting off tool. It is tongue-shaped and is relieved on both sides.

Cutlery – discarded (see also Found materials)
Interesting jewellery can be con-

Diag. 74 *Bracelet made from a discarded fork*

structed from discarded cutlery. In particular, forks and spoons can be formed into bracelets and bangles.

Cutting
Different techniques are required for cutting the various materials used for making jewellery.

Metal sheet
Metal sheet, both precious and non-precious, can be cut in intricate shapes using a jeweller's saw, with the material resting on a bench pin. Powered saws which will accept similar saw blades are also available. The saw blade is selected dependent on the material thickness.

Sheet metal can also be cut in straight lines with a guillotine. This has the advantage, particularly with precious metals, of not removing any material. The edges are also more clean and burr free.

Jeweller's snips are used for cutting small pieces of metal, but long cuts can show burrs and edge marks. They are available with straight or curved blades. Holes can be produced by drilling. Small circular blanks, and holes, can be cut using sharp edge punches on a resilient surface. More intricate shapes can be cut with a matching punch and die. Simple matching punches and dies are readily available for circular blanks.

Small intricate shapes with few restrictions on the degree of complication can be cut from various sheet materials using the RT blanking system.

Heavy sections can be cut by hand with a hacksaw or by machine with a band saw.

Shell
Shell can be cut using normal metal cutting tools, although thick sections are best cut using a diamond saw. Carbide-tip tools give significantly longer tool life.

Bone and ivory
Bone and ivory can be cut using normal metal cutting tools. Carbide tip tools give significantly longer tool life.

Wire rod and section
For precious metals and metals of similar hardness, side or end cutters are used; for very fine wires, jeweller's snips are best. With harder metals, or where the end face must be square and flat, as well as for heavier sections, saws are used. A chenier cutter is used both to guide the saw and for repeating pieces of the same length.

Variations in diameter and axial holes can be made in rod using a metal cutting lathe.

Hard steels, such as those employed in cutting tools, are cut by the above methods when in a soft condition before being hardened or by grinding after being hardened.

Wood
Seasoned wood is prepared for sale in rectangular sections by sawing and finished by planing. Thin sections can be cut in intricate shapes by jeweller's saw and thicker sections by band saw. Straight sections are cut with a tenon or back saw. Three-dimensional pieces can be carved with penknives, called whittling. For finer work, wood carving chisels are used. Very fine work can be carved with a craft knife.

Stones

Rough stone is cut on a diamond saw, although some of the very soft stones can be cut with metal cutting saws. Holes are cut using diamond drills, although high production ultrasonic methods are used in industry.

Paper and card

Intricate cut-out shapes can be produced using a craft knife, with the paper or card resting on a piece of hardboard or similar resilient surface. Straight edges are cut using a metal straight edge and repeat shapes using shaped sheet metal templates.

Plastics

Flexible plastic sheet can be cut with scissors or craft knives. Rigid plastic sheet can be cut with metal working saws. A coarse blade used slowly should be used or there will be a tendency for the cut edges to reunite with many thermoplastics. Cooling lubrication can assist.

Rigid plastics can be turned and drilled on metal cutting lathes. Over-fast feed speeds can cause melting or even ignition.

Large circles and holes can be cut in rigid plastic sheet using a trepanning tool.

Cutting with punches (*see also* Punches)

Sheet metal can be cut with hand punches and hammer. Circular holes are most easily cut with sharp-edged hollow punches. A solid bench or heavy anvil is necessary to achieve clean bounce-free cutting. The sheet metal to be cut should rest on a resilient surface. Brass or aluminium sheet is suitable, but repeated use can raise burrs which will mark the lower surface of the metal being cut. A disposable alternative is thick cardboard or layered paper such as discarded magazines or scrap pieces of hardboard. The end of sharp-edge cutting punches have a hemispherical hollow. The softer the

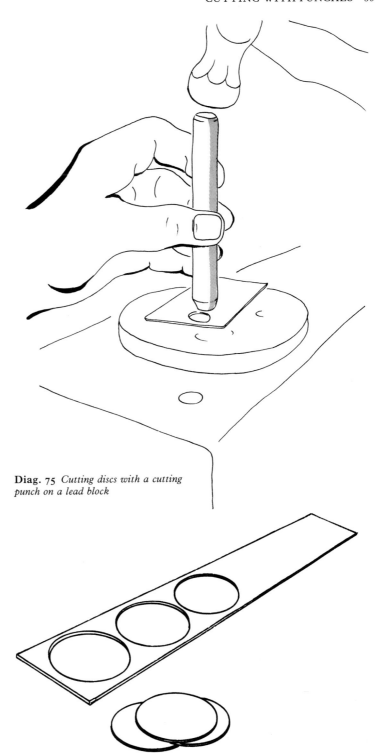

Diag. 75 *Cutting discs with a cutting punch on a lead block*

Diag. 76 *Discs blanked out from a strip*

resilient layer on which the material is cut, the more hemispherical the blank which is removed will be. If a very resilient material is used and the blank is forced well up into the punch, it can be removed by tapping the side of the punch on the anvil. The doming effect on the blank can be used to create bead halves requiring only light subsequent forming in a doming block.

Precious metals up to about $1\frac{1}{2}$mm ($\frac{1}{16}$in) thick and harder metals up to $\frac{3}{4}$mm ($\frac{1}{32}$in) thick can be cut by this method.

With the support metal and punch in position, and keeping the face of the punch square and pushed against the metal face, the punch is given a single heavy blow. This should cause a clean cut through the metal. If a complete cut has not been achieved, ensure that the punch is located in the first cut before a second blow is given.

Where non-circular blanks or very small holes are required in thin precious metals, an alternative form of hand punch developed by the author can be used.

The required shape is formed by filing the end of a length of silver steel. It is essential that the edges are crisp and sharp. The sides of the punch should taper away from the cutting face and the punch should be hardened and tempered. To use the punch, the material should be placed on a solidly supported pad of scrap paper at least 8mm ($\frac{5}{16}$in) thick. Discarded magazines make an ideal pad. A single heavy blow with a heavy hammer will push the punch through the material. The blank is recovered from between the layers of the pad.

Small holes can be cut with vice-mounted screw punches. Turning the screw forces a circular punch through the material and into a matching diameter.

Larger holes can be cut with a die block and punches, forcing the punch through the material and into the die with a hammer.

Cuttlefish bone (see also Cuttlefish casting)

The remaining skeleton of a cuttlefish. It has unique qualities of heat resistance to molten metal, ease of shaping, and provides a low cost means of *casting* metals.

Cuttlefish casting (see also Casting)

This technique provides a simple casting method for one-off pieces without the use of patterns, wax or investment. It can also be used to produce small ingots from precious metal scraps ready for rolling and drawing.

The molten metal is forced into the cavity by the mass of the sprue, and the air in the cavity is allowed to escape along fine channels scored in the face of one piece of cuttlefish. To facilitate an adequate head of metal, the cavity in the shape of the piece to be cast is positioned low down on one face.

Two pieces of cuttlefish bone of similar shape are selected and the thin ends cut away to give two equal length pieces. The soft faces are cut roughly flat and the two pieces rubbed together in a figure of eight shape to give two flat faces. A hollow in the shape of the piece to be cast is cut into one piece and a funnel shape feeding into this cavity is cut in both pieces. Deep shaping can be done with a penknife or craft knife, and shallow recesses made by pressing a blunt tool into the surface. Very fine detail is not possible due to the ribbed structure of the mat-

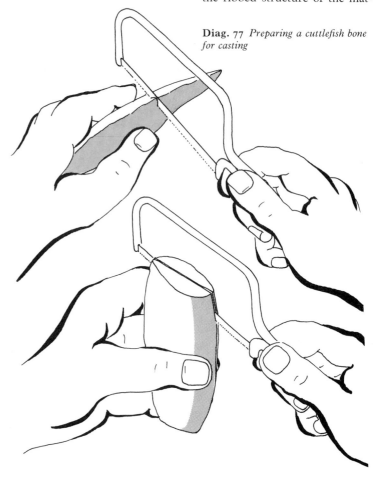

Diag. 77 *Preparing a cuttlefish bone for casting*

Diag. 78 *Cuttlefish casting*

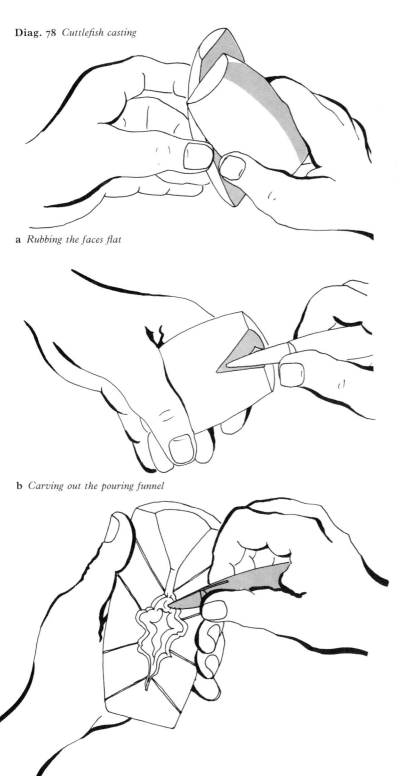

a *Rubbing the faces flat*

b *Carving out the pouring funnel*

c *Carving the recess*

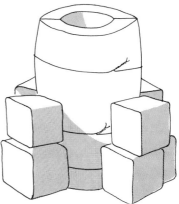

Diag. 79 *Cuttlefish mould ready for casting*

erial. This can be improved a little by dusting the face with carbon dust made from ground charcoal. It is possible to cut cavities in both pieces, and small pegs should be inserted to align the two pieces. By dusting one shaped piece and putting the two pieces together, the image of the dusted piece will be transferred to the other piece, allowing better alignment of the two cavities. All of the cavity should be below the sprue, and return shapes are undesirable. When the cavity is finished, venting passages are scored from the cavity to the outer edge.

The two pieces of cuttlefish can now be placed together and held in place with iron binding wire. This assembly is set on a heat-resistant surface and held upright with ceramic blocks, metal retort stand or similar support.

The metal to be cast is melted in a crucible or fletcher and, when fully melted and freely spinning, poured with one continuous movement into the top of the cuttlefish assembly.

When the glow has gone from the metal the whole piece can either be opened using pliers or dropped into a metal bucket of water.

The piece can be finished as required. The characteristic ribbed pattern can be incorporated in the finished piece.

D

D section (see also Wire and Chain making)

Wire, frequently used for making rings, with a cross section shaped with a flat back and curved front as a D.

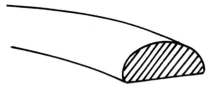

Diag. 80 *D section*

Damascene

The inlaying of contrasting metal into a base material. The Japanese name for this work is *zogan* and the various Japanese methods comprehensively describe the processes.

Honzogan
Sheet or wire set in undercut grooves and hammered flat

Senzogan
Round wire set flush in grooves

Hirazogan
Sheet metal set flush

Takazogan
Raised pieces set in base material

Hira shizukuzogan
The inlaying of dots finished flush

Shizukuzogan
Domed dot inlay – toad skin finish

Dapping (see also Doming)

Dapping block (see also Doming block)

Dapping punches (see also Doming punches)

De bubbleizing (see also Investing)

When investing wax in lost wax casting, small bubbles can form on the surface of the wax which, if not removed, will cast as small spheres.

De bubbleizing consists of vibrating the investment both prior to pouring and when in the flask to release the bubbles. Brushing the wax model with a weak detergent solution will also assist, as will evacuating the air under a bell jar.

Deburring (see also Burr)

Most metal cutting processes raise a burr on one edge of the material in the cutting process. These burrs need removing both for visual requirements and safety.

Burrs raised by drilling can be removed either by light countersinking, or by a surface cutting action such as abrasive paper used flat across the hole. Edge burrs on sheet can be removed by filing or abrasive paper.

Deep drawing (see also Forming)

Container-shaped pieces can be formed by drawing sheet down through a die by pushing it through with a rounded punch. The top of the die has rounded edges, and a pressure plate allows the material to flow without crinkling. The formed piece is pushed right through the die and recovered below it. Well annealed material, suitably lubricated, helps ensure uniform unpunctured results.

Deep drawing can be used for forming deep lockets and boxes. The same process, but dispensing with the pressure plate, can be used for producing collets.

Degreasing

Cutting fluids, *polishing* compounds and finger prints can deposit grease on metal surfaces which needs to be removed before such operations as soldering or enamelling.

Degreasing tanks employing volatile fluids are used for high-volume production.

For small-scale degreasing of metal components, the process of heating, quenching in a pickle suitable to the metal followed by washing in water and drying is quick and effective.

Density of materials

The relative density or specific gravity of a material is a measure of the mass of a given volume of a material when compared with the same volume of water.

Units of measurement may be grams/cc or lbs/cub.ft.

Design

The creation and specification of all the elements of a product, and the recording of this so that the product can be produced.

Designing jewellery (see also Functional design)

Designing is a creative process.

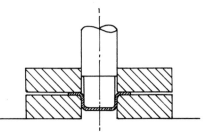

Diag. 81 *Deep drawing – cross section of a tool*

All design projects must have an objective; such objectives may vary from exploring the qualities of a material to meeting a specific product brief.

Designs can be worked out with pencil and paper or made up with low cost materials such as paper, card or plastic.

In producing and developing a design, the major factors to be considered are method of manufacture, suitability for use and aesthetic qualities. Awareness of fashion and the designer's own identity need consideration.

Developed shapes

Three-dimensional pieces can be formed up from sheet material by folding along bend lines which link the flat areas and form the faces of the three-dimensional final shape.

Some typical developed shapes are shown in Diags. 82–85.

Diadems

A decorative piece of jewellery worn on the head. Frequently associated with weddings and other ceremonies.

Diamond milling

Diamond milling produces highly finished repeating patterns on precious metals. The milling machines can provide a range of feeds and mounting angles to produce an infinite variety of faceted patterns. Diamond-tipped tools create a high-quality finish requiring no further work.

Small milling machines or lathes with milling attachments and fitted with an indexing head can be used to provide a lower cost machine, but with limitations on the range of possible designs.

Diamond tools

For cutting stones and hard metals, tools with diamond-coated cutting faces are required. Diamond tools cut due to their hardness rather than being due to ground cutting faces as with conventional cutting tools.

Die casting (see also Casting)

Casting in metal dies is termed die casting. The metal is formed into the die under either gravity or pressure and is termed either pressure die casting or gravity die casting.

In jewellery making, die casting is primarily used for casting base metals.

Die stamping (see also Drop forging)

Die stamping is the process in which a pair of matching tools are used to blank out or shape metal parts. Die stamping can be achieved by hammer blow, under a hand press such as a fly press, or under a power press. Tools

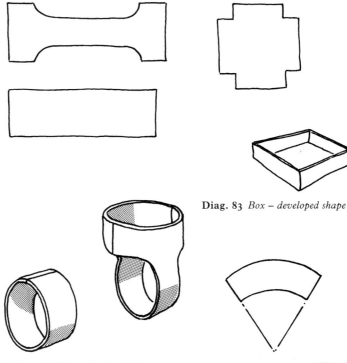

Diag. 82 *Ring – developed shape*

Diag. 83 *Box – developed shape*

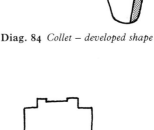

Diag. 84 *Collet – developed shape*

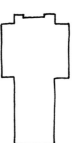

Diag. 85 *Box catch development*

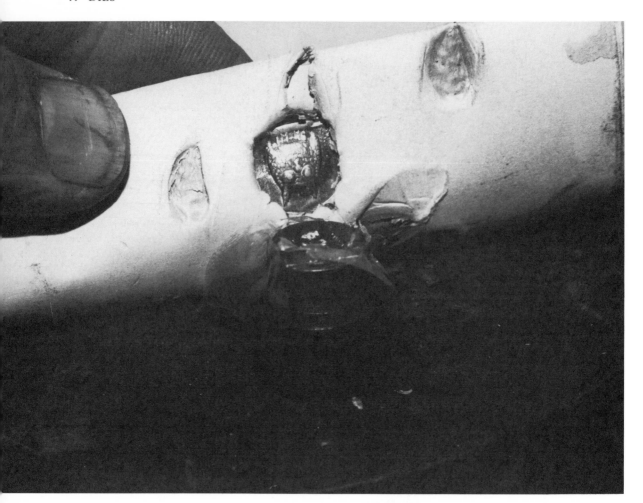

Fig. 6 Die stamped sheet using layers of paper to forge the sheet into the die under the blows from a hammer

can be arranged individually or in succession, producing a piece incorporating more than one operation.

Dies (*see also* Drawing wire)

Dies are pieces of shaped material, frequently steel, onto, over or through which a softer metal material is shaped.

Punch and die sets consist of a pair of matching tools used in a press: a moving shaped punch and

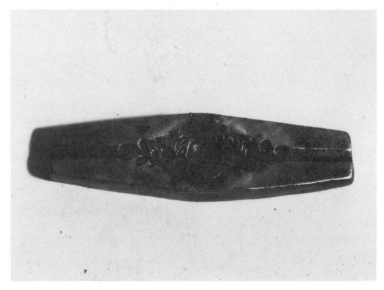

Fig. 7 Indian brass die for forming a sheet metal ring in thin gauge metal

a fixed die into which the punch fits. Sheet metal placed between the two will have a hole cut and produce a blank in the shape of the punch and die. A punch and die with rounded edges and set with larger clearances can be used to draw down shapes such as collets.

Collective graded dies for drawing wire are draw plates. Designs cut into steel blocks are termed dies when used to shape metal driven into the design.

Threaded blocks or plates relieved to create cutting faces for forming threads on rods are also termed dies.

Display

Finished jewellery has to be displayed to potential buyers in a way which promotes its qualities. Jewellery also has to be packaged for the point of sale and this may be the way in which the piece is displayed prior to sale.

Lighting is a critical element of display and can be used to enhance aspects of a piece.

Distilled water

Distilled or deionised water is used in enamelling where salts and other impurities could impair the qualities of the enamel.

Dividers

Dividers are *measuring* tools used to scribe radii when marking out or in comparing measurements.

Dome block

A metal cube or slab in which are cut a range of hemispherical recesses.

Dome punches

Punches of steel or tough hard wood of a range of diameters used in conjunction with doming blocks to shape sheet material.

Doming (*see also* Punching)

Discs of metal can be formed into dome shapes using a doming block and punches. The disc of metal is laid in a domed recess just larger than the disc. A punch at least two material thicknesses smaller than the recess is selected and, with a hammer when using metal punches, or a mallet for wooden punches, the disc is formed to the shape of the recess. The process is repeated using progressively smaller punches until the desired degree of doming is achieved. As the material work hardens, annealing is necessary.

Diag. 86 *Dividers used to scribe a radius*

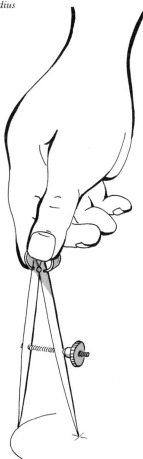

Diag. 87 *Doming a disc*

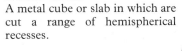
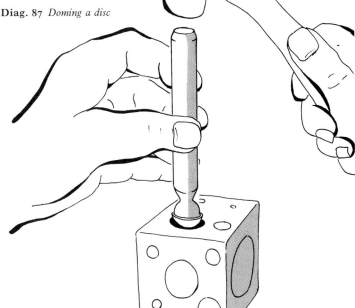

Larger shapes can be formed using dome headed hammers in shaped recesses. Alternatively, free forming using a dome headed hammer or a lead block can be used, particularly where asymmetrical shapes are required.

Dop stick

A short stick, frequently of wood, on which a rough stone or saw cut slab is set, enabling it to be held when grinding and polishing.

Diag. 88 *Dop stick*

Dopping (*see also* Stone cutting *and* Grinding)

Dopping is the method of securing rough rock to a holding stick during shaping and polishing.

Dopping sticks consist of short lengths of round section dowel wood, smaller in diameter than the finished size of the stone. The end is coated in dopping wax on which the stone is set.

To set a stone, the dopping wax is melted, avoiding burning, and the end of the stick dipped in and rotated to give an even coating, initially overlapping the end. While hot, the end is partly flattened by dabbing the end squarely on a flat face.

A back face is ground on the piece of rock, or one face of a sawn blank is selected as being the back. The stone is warmed and the back face is coated with dopping wax. While the stone is still hot, the flat face of the wax on the stick is heated to just on melting point, and the two brought together, ensuring that the stone is set squarely on the stick. Small adjustments to the shaping of the wax, using fingers, finally positions the stone. A bowl of cold water is useful for cooling hot fingers.

Before grinding, the wax must be left to cool naturally.

Dopping cement

Pitch-based cement used to fix rough rock or slab sawn stones temporarily to dopping sticks for *grinding* and *polishing*.

Dot inlay

Visually contrasting inlay can be simply produced by drilling blind holes and driving in short lengths of material. The projecting pieces are cut flush and the surface finished. Some combinations of material may require the addition of an adhesive. Silver in ivory or wood is typical.

Doublet

Thin layers of precious stones backed by less precious material with a cemented joint are termed doublets. The practice is particularly employed with opals.

Dowel

Lengths of round section material of specified diameter. Dowels are used to position accurately one component relative to another and provide some degree of restraint.

Draw bench (*see also* Drawing wire)

Smaller gauge wire can be drawn by hand, but heavier gauges of wire and heavier work drawn through a draw swage require the mechanical advantage of a draw bench. A typical construction consists of two parallel steel channel sections, some $1\frac{1}{2}$ to 2m (5 to $6\frac{1}{2}$ft) long and set on legs at bench height. At one end are set stops against which rests the draw plate. Between and above the channel sections run the draw tongs. The tongs are moved along the channel sections by a chain to which the tongs are linked. The chain passes the full length of the channel sections, passing over cogs at each end. At some position along the length a side-mounted gear hand drive is mounted.

The draw tongs are designed to increase grip with increased pull.

Home-constructed draw benches using such equipment as trailer winches of pulley systems offer alternative methods of drawing heavy sections.

Draw filing (*see also* Filing)

Filing is generally done by moving the length of the file at right angles across the piece. This process is effective in removing material but can leave unacceptable marks. Draw filing is a process of finishing a filing operation and imparts a uniform texture.

The file is held at right angles to the piece and moved to and fro along its length. The process is effective but tends to clog the file more quickly which thus requires more frequent cleaning.

Draw plate

Used for reducing or changing the cross section of wire, draw plates consist of a series of tapered holes in a metal plate. The holes are graded in size so that wire drawn through them in sequence is progressively reduced.

Draw plates are available with a wide variety of hole shapes enabling wire of section ranging from round, square, triangular and D section to teardrop, star crescent and knife edge to pass through. Most of the sections available are symmetrical in section.

Draw plates can be made and the process is as follows. A tapered punch is made with cross section in the form required and tapered over the range of hole size required. The punch is polished, hardened and tempered. A series of holes is drilled in a silver steel plate, each smaller than the section required. The holes are countersunk on one side and the tapered punch is progressively driven in, creating the sequence of tapered holes. The plate is then hardened and tempered.

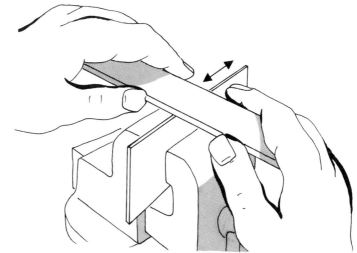

Diag. 89 *Draw filing*

Fig. 8 *Draw plates*

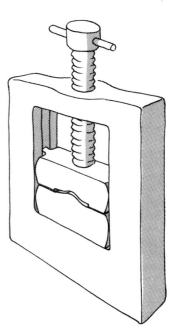

Diag. 90 *Simple draw swage with die blocks*

Draw swage
A tool for shaping strip material by drawing. Designs vary, but in essence a draw swage consists of a frame which can be securely mounted, for example in a vice, and which can hold shaped blocks between which the material is drawn. It is necessary to arrange for one block to be fixed and the other block to be adjustable to vary the gap and hence the degree of forming.

The diagrams show typical shapes of forming die blocks. The die blocks should be highly polished as any imperfections will show on the drawn material.

Draw swages are used in a similar way to draw plates.

Draw tongs (*see also* Drawing)
Heavy tongs used to draw wire through draw plates or draw swages.

Tongs used with draw benches are of 'lazy tongs' design so that the force of the pull clamps the material. Hand draw tongs have heavy flat textured jaws and one arm is formed into a hook to help prevent slipping.

For light work by hand, draw plates and normal short nose hand pliers with ribbed jaws can be used.

Drawing wire
Ductile wire in materials such as silver, gold and copper can be reduced or changed in section by drawing. The process consists of

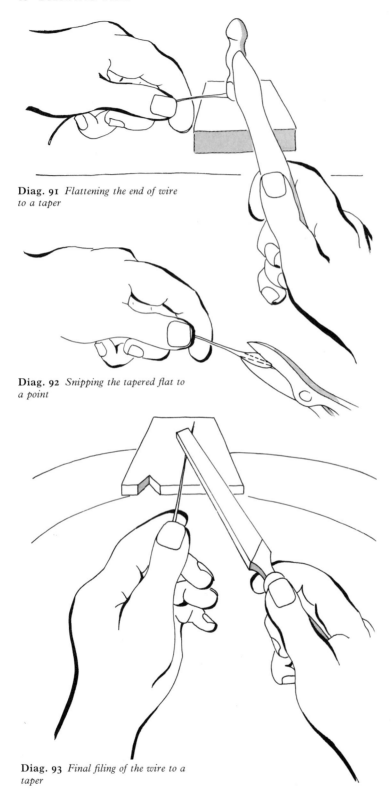

Diag. 91 *Flattening the end of wire to a taper*

Diag. 92 *Snipping the tapered flat to a point*

Diag. 93 *Final filing of the wire to a taper*

pulling the wire through tapered holes of progressively smaller size.

Starting with clean scrap material or casting granules, a roughly square or round section ingot is made. This is rolled through a mill to reduce the section and make it uniform (see *rolling*). The ingot is reduced to a square section larger than the finished section. After annealing, the material is ready for drawing. With sections below about 2mm ($\frac{3}{32}$in) this is possible by hand. For larger sections a draw bench is required.

To draw by hand the end of the wire is tapered. This is easily achieved by first flattening a taper by hammering and then cutting the taper to a square section with snips. Edges are filed round. The wire is now ready for drawing. A draw plate of the required section and range is securely mounted either in a vice or behind support pegs. It must be positioned so that there is adequate space to move back from the draw plate the full length of the wire to be drawn.

The draw plate is mounted with the larger end of the holes away from the operator. The tapered end of the wire is fed into the large end of a hole in the draw plate, the size of which is just smaller than the wire. The projecting end of the wire is firmly gripped with draw tongs and, with a steady pull, drawn through the plate. The process is repeated reducing the section of the wire and increasing its length. The surface is burnished to a high polish. Repeated drawing will work-harden the material and it should be *annealed* to prevent fracturing. A little beeswax will assist drawing and help improve the surface finish. Where long lengths are being drawn, care must be taken to prevent kinking of the wire prior to passing through the plate.

A draw bench is used in a similar way except that larger sections can be drawn and the gear reduction makes the work easier, although the lengths which can be drawn are shorter.

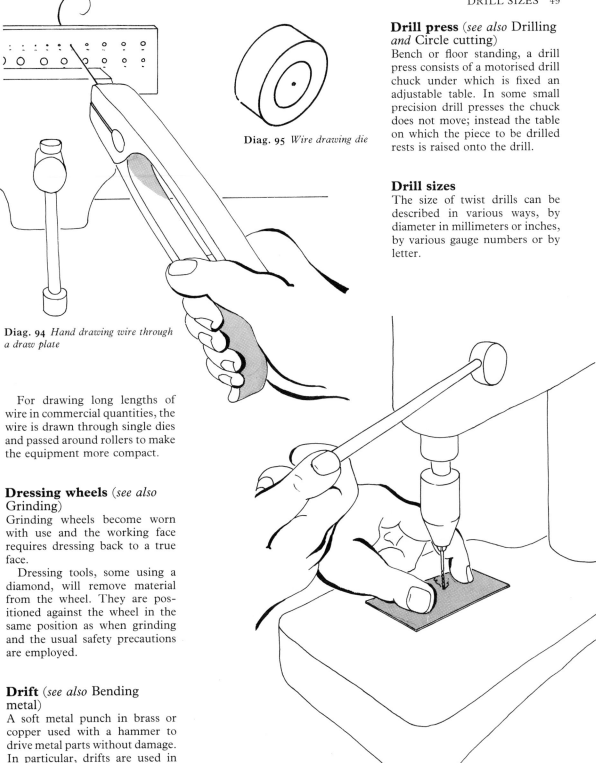

Diag. 94 *Hand drawing wire through a draw plate*

Diag. 95 *Wire drawing die*

Diag. 96 *Drill press with twist drill bit*

Drill press (*see also* Drilling *and* Circle cutting)
Bench or floor standing, a drill press consists of a motorised drill chuck under which is fixed an adjustable table. In some small precision drill presses the chuck does not move; instead the table on which the piece to be drilled rests is raised onto the drill.

Drill sizes
The size of twist drills can be described in various ways, by diameter in millimeters or inches, by various gauge numbers or by letter.

For drawing long lengths of wire in commercial quantities, the wire is drawn through single dies and passed around rollers to make the equipment more compact.

Dressing wheels (*see also* Grinding)
Grinding wheels become worn with use and the working face requires dressing back to a true face.

Dressing tools, some using a diamond, will remove material from the wheel. They are positioned against the wheel in the same position as when grinding and the usual safety precautions are employed.

Drift (*see also* Bending metal)
A soft metal punch in brass or copper used with a hammer to drive metal parts without damage. In particular, drifts are used in setting up large tools and bending metal.

Diag. 97

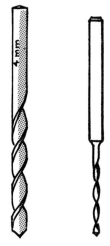

a *Twist drill*   **b** *Pivot drill*

Fig. 9 *Drill stock*

Drill stock (*see also* Drilling)

A drill stock or jeweller's drill consists of a vertical metal rod at the end of which is mounted a drill chuck. A horizontal wooden bar with central hole fits freely over the vertical rod. On the metal rod and fitted near the chuck is a circular flywheel. From the ends of the wooden bar to the top of the rod is a strong cord.

To use the drill stock a drill is fitted in the chuck. The drill stock is used single handed, allowing the material to be held in the other hand. The drilling hand holds the wooden bar with two fingers each side of, but not touching, the metal rod, with the thumb underneath. The rod is rotated, twisting the cord around the rod and causing the bar to rise up the rod. A downward pressure on the bar holds the drill bit in place and causes it to rotate. The energy in the flywheel causes the rod to keep rotating and rewinds the cord up the rod with a lessening of the downward pressure. The process continues until drilling is complete.

Drill types
Spear drill
One of the most simple drills. It is suitable for use on soft metals such as gold and silver and on other materials such as ivory and plastics. Spear drills are only suitable for use at slow speeds of rotation and their use is generally confined to hand powered operation in bow drills, Archimedes' drills and jeweller's drill stocks. Spear drills

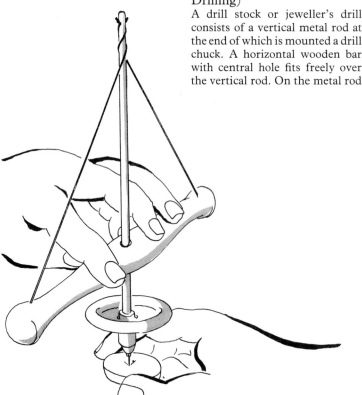

Diag. 98 *Using a drill stock*

are formed by flattening one end of a piece of steel whose diameter is less than the diameter of the hole to be drilled. The flattened portion is pointed by filing. If the flat portion is quite thin then the drill may be hardened and tempered and is then ready for use. If the flat portion is thicker, then opposite cutting edges are bevelled before the piece is hardened and tempered. Silver steel ground stock is a suitable material for spear drills.

Twist drills

The most common form of drill and available in sizes from tenths of a millimeter up to many centimetres. Some of the smaller sizes are available with fixed diameter shanks suitable for pendant drills. Some of the larger diameters have reduced diameter shanks to suit smaller capacity chucks. Twist drills are suitable for use in hand and motor powered tools. Where a large amount of material is being removed, a liquid lubricant is desirable. Twist drills are also available with carbide cutting faces which give extended life.

Diag. 99 *Spear drill*

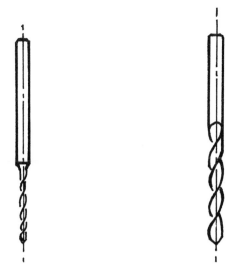

Diag. 100 *Twist drill with step shank*

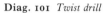

Diag. 101 *Twist drill*

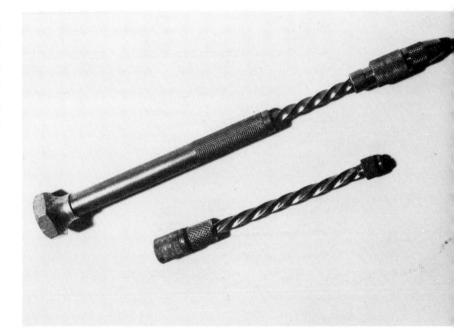

Fig. 10 *Archimedes' drills*

Diamond drills

Suitable for cutting hard materials including stones, diamond drills do not have a shaped point but rely on the cutting qualities of the coating of diamond chips which cover the cutting faces.

Drilling

Prior to drilling, the position of the intended hole should be marked, normally by scribing two crossed lines. On metals, plastics and similar materials, a centre punch is used to indent the surface at the intersection. For accurate positioning, the centre mark should be viewed under a mag-

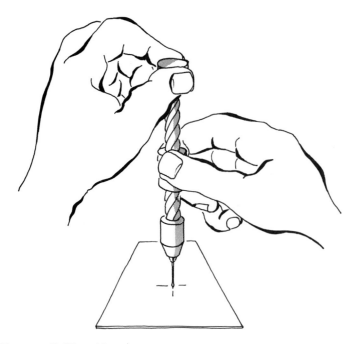

Diag. 102 *Drilling with an Archimedes' drill*

nifying glass. Any slight misplacing can be corrected by angling the punch and moving the mark.

If the hole is to be drilled with a one-handed jeweller's drill stock, Archimedes' drill or light pendant drill, then the piece can be handheld on a bench pin or piece of scrap wood. When using a pillar drill or other drill of similar pairer, then the piece should be held in a drill vice which must be bolted to the drill platform.

Small holes below about 1mm may not require the use of a cutting fluid, but, where more material is being removed or when it is being removed quickly, then a cutting fluid will remove heat and waste material. The speed of the drill will depend on the diameter of the drill and the feed rate: in general the smaller the size, the higher the speed.

Some pieces such as beads and tubes require jigs to hold them in a correct position for drilling.

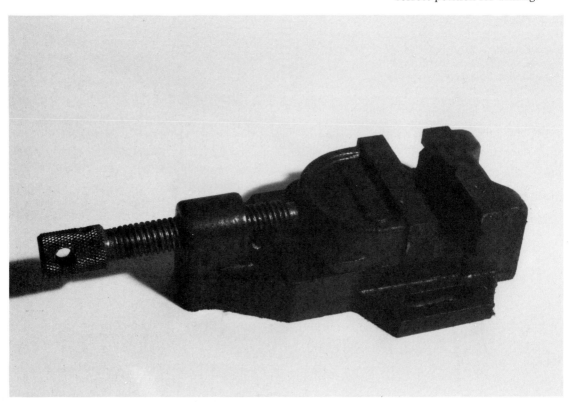

Fig. 11 *Drill vice*

Drop forging (*see also* Forging)
Metal blanks and billets can be shaped between dies under the action of a drop hammer.

Although the process is more associated with shaping heavier pieces than jewellery, the process is particularly effective in forging otherwise difficult to produce shapes in medium run quantities.

Dross (*see also* Melting)
The term used to describe the materials that form on the surface of metals when molten. It is lifted off or away from the pouring lip prior to pouring.

Dryer
When parts have been pickled and washed, they need to be dried before being used with tools, or corrosion and rusting of the tools will occur. Individual small flat pieces can be dried on blotting paper or pads of tissue paper. Larger, more three-dimensional pieces are traditionally dried in boxwood sawdust.

An alternative is to use a small warm air dryer. For small quantity work a simple dryer can be constructed by mounting an electric lamp in a metal food-can in which are cut air entry holes, and over the top of which is set a perforated or woven metal tray. The qualified electrician can construct higher wattage designs.

Dyeing
Many non-precious materials such as wood, feathers, bone, ivory and threads can be dyed to introduce alternative colours. For most materials commercial fabric dyes are suitable but some improvisation will be required.

Ear rings
Pieces of jewellery for attaching to the ears. Designs can be broadly divided between stud types, dangling types and loop types.

There are also three popular methods of attaching the piece to the ear. They are: through wires, with either retaining scrolls or formed in a hook, for pierced ears; and screw and clip types for non-pierced ears.

Diag. 103 *Ear findings*

a *Hook with bead*

b *Hook with safety catch*

c *Hook with pearl peg and cup*

d *Hook with swinging catch*

e *Screw with bead and open jump ring*

f *Screw with pearl peg and cup*

g *Wire, scroll with open jump ring*

h *Wire, scroll with pearl peg and cup*

i *Hinged ring*

Ear wire (*see also* Findings)

That part of an ear ring which passes through the wearer's ear. Ear wires may be straight, as from the centre of a stud ear ring, or hooked for pendant ear rings.

Easy solder (*see also* Soldering)

Low melting-temperature hard solder. Easy solders are available for carat golds and silver. Easy solders melt at between 705°C and 723°C. Excessive use of easy solders may cause a piece to be rejected for hallmarking.

Ebony

A hard, heavy, black wood used for small carved plaques and beads in jewellery.

Elastic

In the construction of beaded jewellery, round section elastic can be used for theading. This enables the piece to be extended, as with a bracelet or choker, without the need for fastenings.

Electric soldering machine (*see also* Heating methods)

Metal pieces can be heated to hard soldering temperatures using the heat generated by an electric current and the resistance of the piece. The machine supplies an adjustable voltage with footswitch control.

The piece to be heated is clamped to one electrode and a flexibly connected carbon rod completes the circuit.

Rapid heating with a minimum of heat discoloration is claimed, and some models are available with gem ring clamps which support and protect the piece.

Electroforming

An extension of electroplating, electroformed pieces dispense

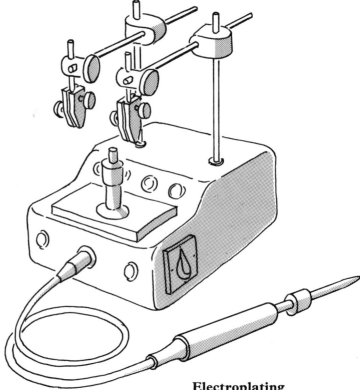

Diag. 104 *Soldering machine for hard soldering precious metals*

with the base and consist only of electrodeposited material. The texture of the material when built up to any thickness becomes noticeably crystalline.

The model is conveniently made from a non-metallic material such as expanded polystyrene (styrofoam), wax, and papier-mâché. This is coated with a conductive paint, to the underside of which is fixed, at an unobtrusive point, a copper or silver wire from which the piece is supported in the plating bath.

The plating may be composite, for example a heavy copper base finished with a coating of silver or gold.

After plating the core is removed, typically by burning out. The resultant shell can be strengthened and completed by fabricating.

Electroplating

Metal components can be coated with a thin layer of other metal by electroplating. Frequently a base metal is coated with precious metal.

The essential of electroplating is a plating bath which holds a quantity of fluid, the electrolyte. A variable low-voltage DC supply is available at the tank. To the − ve (cathode) line is attached the piece to be plated, and to the + ve (anode) line is attached a piece of the metal to be plated onto the piece. Both are suspended in the electrolyte. The current flow between the cathode and anode causes a flow of positively charged ions from the anode, the metal to be plated, to the cathode, the piece to be plated.

The DC power should be variable, and models from 10 amps to 50 amps at 10 volts will cover the needs of the jeweller. The plating baths may be simple Pyrex beakers or part of a system complete with heaters and bus-

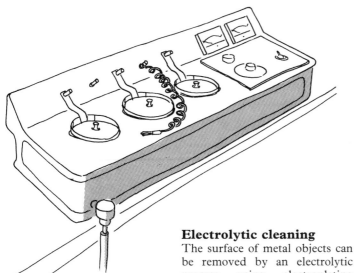

Diag. 105 *Electroplating bath*

bars (anode and cathode) from which to suspend the anode material and the piece.

The electrolyte fluid is selected dependent on the material to be plated. Many of these fluids contain cyanide and, as such, must be handled with extreme care. Adequate precautions must be taken to prevent contact with the skin, eyes and inhaling air from the bath or container. The need for adequate safety cannot be overstated.

Electrolyte fluids can be purchased ready made up or prepared from the basic chemicals.

Prior to plating, the piece must be chemically clean and highly finished. Any imperfections will show after plating. The cleaning is best carried out by electrocleaning.

Plating is carried out by attaching the anode and the piece to the busbars and setting them below the surface of the electrolyte.

The current, the thickness of plating and the size of the piece will determine the time taken.

Electrolytic cleaning
The surface of metal objects can be removed by an electrolytic process using electroplating equipment.

The piece to be cleaned is made the anode and the tank is used as the cathode. A hot alkaline solution is used as the electrolyte. The process should be complete within a few minutes.

Embossing (*see also* Repoussé)
The raising forward to varying heights of sheet material in a decorative form, also called repoussé.

Embroidery
Small pieces of embroidery can be set as jewellery. Mounted on a thin support, the piece can be set in a frame of bezel wire in which is set a watch glass by burnishing.

Emery cloth (*see also* Finishing metal pieces)
An abrasive material used for smoothing and light shaping of metals. A cloth backing creates a tough flexible support, and the cutting face is coated with a range of abrasive powders containing corundum and iron oxide in the form of magnetite or hermatite. The cutting face is black and the backing blue.

Torn into strips, emery cloth can be pulled through holes for finishing and deburring.

Emery paper
Constructed as emery cloth but with a paper backing. Emery paper is most suitable for using flat on a smooth hard backing, such as a surface plate or sheet of plate glass, cutting side up for smoothing flat pieces or the ends of large sections.

Emery powder
Used for finishing metal, it is particularly useful for reaching awkward places, which can be worked with a short length of soft wood using a little water.

Emery stick
Purchased or made emery sticks consist of a section of wood of various sections on which is glued emery paper.

Enamelling
The process of facing a layer of glass based powder, generally coloured with metal oxides, to a metal base.

The method in which the areas of colour is defined describes the form of enamelling. *Cloisonné, champleve, basse taille, plique a jour* and *Limoge* or painted enamel are the most popular methods. Small discs of metal slightly domed can be enamelled and set in jewellery as stones.

The most common base materials are copper and silver. It is practical to enamel on other metals such as steel, but additional surface preparation is required.

Enamel, as purchased, is essentially a form of powdered glass of a composition making it compatible with metal and coloured with metal oxides. Fired at high temperatures onto the surface, it forms a smooth shiny surface. There is a vast range of colours

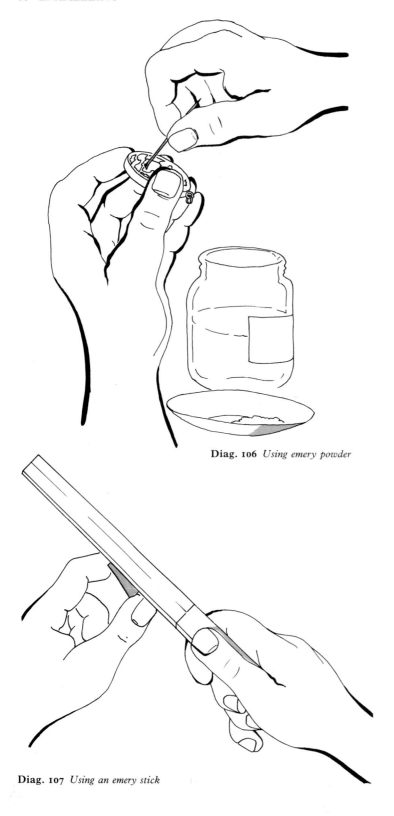

Diag. 106 *Using emery powder*

Diag. 107 *Using an emery stick*

available: opaque, which lets no light through; translucent, which will let some light pass; transparent, which lets more light pass; and opalescent, with its opal-like qualities. Variations in hardness and viscosity when hot have particular applications. Threads, beads, miliflori and metal lustres offer contrasing effects, and the ability to paint in fine enamels with all the subtleties of watercolour should satisfy the artist.

Design for enamel

Enamels are fired above the melting point of medium silver solder, so any fabrications must be made with enamelling grade, high melting point solder. Apart from finishing and fabrications not employing heat, all construction should be carried out before enamelling.

Enamel can be applied direct onto the piece or onto a component such as a plaque, which is subsequently mounted on the piece. The enamel can be applied over a whole surface, or contained within a definite area. The method of defining the area dictates much of the visual quality of the piece and the technique.

Preparation

Silver to be enamelled must be chemically clean and free from oxides, grease, polishes, flux, acid and, of course, dirt. Boiling in pickle followed by thorough washing in clean water is effective.

During all stages of enamelling cleanliness is essential. Any speck of dirt can contaminate the enamel and spoil the piece. Work on clean sheets of paper laid on the bench, with a very large container of clean water and supply of tissues, or a kitchen roll, for cleaning and drying tools and pieces. Once clean, it is a useful precaution to keep the piece under water until it is needed, and handle it only with clean tools, not fingers.

The enamel is best stored in an airtight container in a dark, dry place.

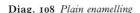

Diag. 108 *Plain enamelling*

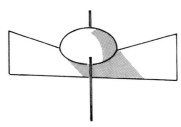

Diag. 109 *Stainless steel support for counter enamelling*

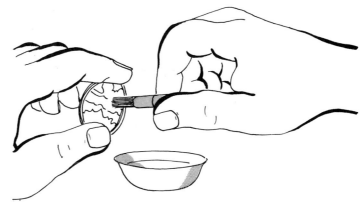

Diag. 110 *Using a glass brush to clean a piece prior to enamelling*

enamel by sieving it through a fine sieve (tea-strainer) to give a uniform coat all over.

The piece is then set on a nichrome mesh formed for easy lifting, or set on a tripod for flame firing.

When dry, the piece is ready for firing.

Cloisonné enamelling

Cloisons, small enclosed areas, allow colours to be placed in close proximity, divided only by a thin wall of silver.

Silver for the dividing wall is rolled from wire, or cut from sheet. A typical size is 2mm ($\frac{3}{32}$in) wide by 0.4mm ($\frac{1}{64}$in) thick.

A strip is formed to the outside shape, the ends soldered together, and, after final shaping, the frame is soldered to the back plate, all with enamelling solder.

In true cloisonné enamelling, the rest of the design is similarly formed and soldered in place. As an alternative, the formed design is set in place and the bottom of the enclosure covered in a thin layer of clear enamel. When fixed, this holds the internal design in place and provides a base for subsequent enamelling.

As an alternative to vertical thin walls, square or round wire may be used, giving more prominence to the silver, but requiring particularly good joints.

The enamels to be used are mixed with a little water and gum. Water-colour mixing palettes are good for enamel preparation. The enamel is lifted onto the cloisons with a very fine water-colour brush, or wooden orange sticks (toothpicks). The enamel should be well pressed down, filling the space, care being taken to prevent any colour spilling over and contaminating the rest.

When fired, the enamel will sink down. This effect can be retained

Enamelling a complete area

Small pieces associated with jewellery do not generally need counter enamelling, that is enamelling on the back of a piece to even out the stresses created by the different contractions of metal and enamel.

The clean piece is set either on a sheet of clean paper or in a tray, to aid recovery of enamel powder. The surface to be enamelled is painted with gum, either the traditional gum tragacanth, or a thin mix of cellulose wallpaper paste. This is then dusted with

Diag. 111 *Loading a piece into an enamel kiln*

Diag. 112 *Cloisonné enamelling*

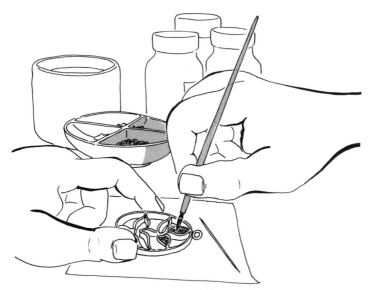

Diag. 113 *Placing wet enamel in cloisons*

Diag. 114 *Champleve enamelling*

Diag. 115 *Basse taille enamelling*

Diag. 116 *Plique a jour enamelling*

or the cloisons can be refilled and refired. The top edge of the silver is stoned down either just short of the level of the enamel, retaining the slight curve, or right down all over.

A rapid firing will revive the gloss.

Champleve enamelling

Larger areas of silver appear in champleve enamelling, in which the background is etched away and subsequently filled with enamel. The raised silver may be engraved, further contrasting with the enamel. One disadvantage of this technique is that quite heavy gauge material must be used – at least $1\frac{1}{2}$mm ($\frac{1}{16}$in) – to provide sufficient depths of enamel.

Basse taille enamelling

Similar to champleve, basse taille is enamelling with transparent enamels over engraved, repoussé and chased, stamped, punched or carved surfaces. Hollows hold more colour and the three-dimensional effects are dramatic. Well-supported thin gauge silver can be used.

Plique a jour enamelling

One of the most delicate and attractive enamel effects, but one of the most difficult. Plique a jour enamel has no backing; it is held in space by a filigree-like frame.

There are a number of ways in which the frame can be made. The walls can be formed as with cloisonné, but without a backing. Using thick sheet, the design can be sawn out with a piercing saw. The enamel is loaded as with cloisonné but with the piece supported on a sheet of mica. After firing, the surface is stoned and polished. No gap should be more

than about 3mm ($\frac{1}{8}$in) across for small pieces of jewellery.

The beauty of this form is best seen when light can shine through, as with ear rings.

Painted enamel

If ground very fine and mixed with a suitable binder, enamel can be painted onto a plain enamelled surface with all the precision and delicacy of water-colour. These painting enamels fire at lower temperatures and care must be taken in firing or the design will sink into the base enamel.

Enamelling kiln

Kilns for enamelling, generally electrically heated, are similar in construction to ceramic firing

Fig. 12 *Painting enamel and powdered enamel*

kilns. Smaller in size and frequently of flatter proportions, they need to be capable of firing temperatures of up to 1200°C, although by using lower firing enamels, kilns with a top temperature of 900°C are acceptable.

Enamels

Enamels are essentially finely powdered glass coloured with metal oxides. The basic form of enamel without oxides included is termed flux or frit, and fires clear. The fusing temperature, viscosity and hardness are varied by adjusting the composition of the flux. Small quantities from $1\frac{1}{2}$ to 5 per cent of metal oxides will produce the colours.

Enamel is generally purchased ready ground and may be used as purchased. Alternatively, the enamel may be purchased in lump form and prepared by grinding in a mortar and pestle and washed until the water runs clear.

Enamels are available which fire opaque, which lets no light through; translucent, which will allow some light to pass, and transparent, which allows light to pass through easily. In each of these groups, the colour may be plain or opalescent.

Encapsulation

Small interesting objects can be encapsulated in clear polyester resin and set as stones.

Encrustation

A decorative effect in which a surface is patterned with jewels or other decorative elements.

End mill

A cutting tool used in a milling machine or suitable vertical drill. Similar in construction to a twist drill but with a flat cutting face on the end and cutting edges on the cylindrical part. Its principal use in jewellery is in tool making, but it can be used for machining settings for stones and plaques.

Small size end mills classed as burrs or fraizers in the range 1mm to 4mm diameter are used in the chucks of pendant drills for hand-held work. The removal of excess solder from inside collets is one particularly useful application.

Engraver's block

Used to hold and position a piece being engraved, an engraver's block is essentially a fully adjustable vice.

Spherical in shape with a flat top, the block sits in a ring of rope, leather or felt. This enables it to be rotated and tilted easily. Some models are split horizontally, allowing the top section to rotate freely or lock.

The top part of the top section is a screw-operated vice. The top face has a pattern of holes in which can be set various pegs or jaws for holding the piece. Engraver's blocks are heavy to resist the pressures of engraving.

Engraver's wax

Rubbed over the surface of polished metal, engraver's wax creates a dull surface on which a design can be drawn with a sharp pointed stick. The design can be easily adjusted prior to making a more permanent mark with a scriber.

Engraving

The process of removing metal from a surface to create decoration or lettering with a sharp-edged tool.

Traditionally, engraving is carried out by hand with various types of graver. Commercial engraving is primarily carried out using pantograph machines. Crude identification engraving can be carried out with a vibrating tool for medium hardness materials or with a spark etching tool on hard metals.

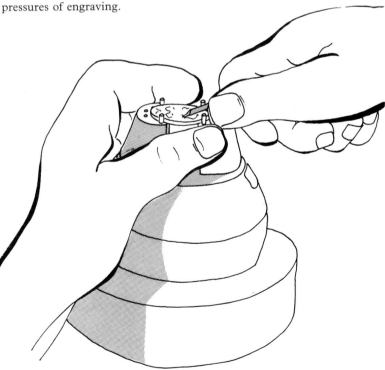

Diag. 117 *Using an engraver's block*

Hand engraving is the process more commonly employed by jewellers. The process is essentially simple but requires considerable practice to achieve acceptable effects, particularly lettering.

The surface of the piece is degreased and finished to a uniform quality very near to the final finish. The design is transferred to the surface and fixed by a fine scribed line.

The piece to be engraved must be supported. There are several ways of doing this. The piece can be set on the surface of a pitch bowl or set on a wood block which has a surface of pitch, or double-sided tape. An engraver's block offers great freedom of movement and clamping without the inconvenience of heating and cooling pitch.

Diag. 118 *Graver*

To engrave a line, a correctly sharpened *graver*, typically of lozenge section, is held in the right hand with the handle well set in the palm of the hand and the tip projecting past the end of the thumb and first finger and supported underneath by the other fingers. The piece and its support are held with the other hand firmly down onto the bench with the thumb on the top. The thumb of this hand acts as a stop against which the thumb of the other hand rests. This arrangement allows the right hand to guide the cutting tip of the graver, pivoting about the thumbs, reducing the chance of skidding.

Fig. 13 *Pierced and engraved pendant set with Awabi shell backing*

Diag. 119 *Graver, showing sharpening of the cutting edge*

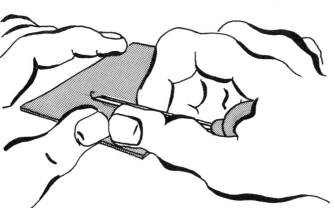

Diag. 120 *Engraving*

To cut a line the graver is angled so that the tip cuts into the surface when it is moved forward. Varying the angle changes the depth of cut.

A twisting action will produce a V groove in which one face is more vertical than the other, creating a changing play of light.

In machine engraving a cutting tool traces a path determined by a pantograph system in which a follower and grooved template determine the path.

The cutter may be either a non-rotating diamond tip or a rotating D section cutter. As a general guide, the diamond tip is suitable for precious metals and the rotating tool for softer materials where a deeper cut is required. A wide selection of lettering styles is available. The pantograph system is adjustable allowing the ratio of template height to engraved character height to be varied.

Engraving machine

A pantographic device which enables the outline of a master shape to be traced and reproduced in a smaller size at the point of a cutter. This cutter may be a non-rotating diamond or a rotating cutter similar to an end mill and powered by an electric motor. A wide variety of master shapes of lettering and numerals is available.

Most machines are adjustable to

Fig. 14 *Engraving machine with diamond point cutter for engraving precious metal*

produce a wide range of reductions in engraved character from the master. Machines vary primarily between powered and non-powered and in the size and shape of piece they can accommodate.

As a general guide but not exclusively so, precious metals are engraved with a non-rotating diamond tip where the depth of cut need not be deep, and a rotating cutting is used on plastics and where the depth of cut needs to be deeper.

Epoxy resin

A two-part resin adhesive of exceptional strength. It is available clear or tinted; colouring dye can be added.

Escapement file

Very fine files, smaller in size than Swiss files, primarily intended for the delicate shaping of clock parts. For jewellery they are ideal for final shaping of delicate pierced work.

Etching (*see also* Resists)

Metal surfaces can be eaten into with selected acids. By protecting part of the surface from the acid, a contrast between the plain and etched surfaces is created. The acids are termed 'mordants' and the protective coatings 'resists'.

Metal	Mordant (acid)
Silver	3 parts nitric acid, 1 part water
Gold	1 part nitric acid, 3 parts hydrochloric acid, 40 parts water
Steel	1 part hydrochloric acid, 1 part water

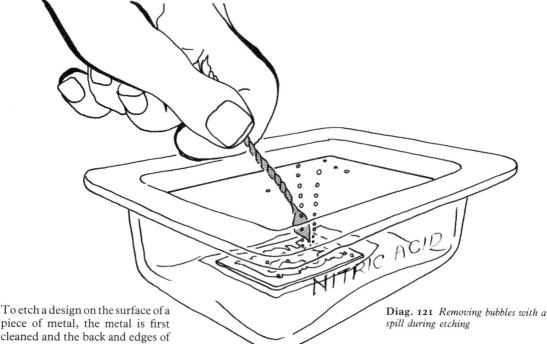

Diag. 121 *Removing bubbles with a spill during etching*

To etch a design on the surface of a piece of metal, the metal is first cleaned and the back and edges of the metal coated with the resist. It is convenient to set the coated piece, even when wet, on a sheet of thick paper to facilitate handling. Those parts of the metal surface which are to remain plain are coated with resist.

When dry, the metal is lowered into the acid bath. A stream of bubbles will rise from the unprotected metal, indicating etching. Those bubbles sticking to the surface should be dislodged with either the tip of a feather or the end of a paper spill.

The depth of etching can be seen and felt with a small wooden splinter or toothpick.

When the etch is of sufficient depth, the piece is lifted out and thoroughly washed in water and dried. The resist can then be removed either with a solvent or by heating the piece, burning off the resist and quenching.

The time taken is primarily dependent on the strength and temperature of the acid. By way of example, nitric acid etching of silver sheet can vary between a few minutes to half an hour.

Expanding mandrel

Rings, particularly wedding rings, can be increased in size with an expanding mandrel.

The outside of the mandrel is tapered as a ring stick and the whole piece is split along its axis into two, three or four arms but held together at the wider end.

A centre rod with a short tapered head can be pulled through the mandrel causing it to splay out and stretch any ring set on it.

Some expanding mandrel arrangements also have the facility for contracting plain rings.

Extruded wax (*see also* Lost wax casting)

Wax for lost wax casting is available in a wide variety of extruded sections for building wax models; round, square, rectangular, half round, bezel and triangular being some of the sections. Large hollow tube, round or with a flat side, is suitable for cutting into ring blanks.

Extrusion (*see also* Draw swage)

Metals and plastic materials can be produced in complex continuous lengths by forcing the material through hard tough dies. One variation of the process uses a centre core smaller than the die and thus produces a tube.

Impact extrusion is used to produce container shapes. In this process, a pellet of material is placed at the bottom of a cavity in the size and shape of the outside of the piece to be produced. A ram the size and shape of the inside of the piece is driven with great force down onto the pellet, causing it to flatten and flow up the gap between the ram and the die.

The machinery to produce extrusions is heavy and expensive. However, small jewellery components in silver and gold can be produced with simple punches and dies driven with a heavy club hammer.

Eyelet

One method of joining components together without heat or adhesive is by riveting. One form of rivet, particularly for softer materials but suitable for most, is the eyelet. Eyelets can also be used to line holes as well as providing a visual contrast.

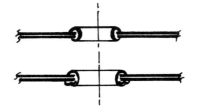

Diag. 122 *Cross section of eyelets without and with a backing washer*

Eyelets are available in many colours and sizes. Simple punches and dies, either free or incorporated in pliers, are used for setting the eyelet.

Eyelets can be one-piece items or may employ a backing washer.

Fabergé

Jewellery designer and manufacturer producing exquisitely executed pieces for the Tzar of Russia and other wealthy patrons. Born in 1846, his work came to prominence in 1900 in Paris. He died in 1920. His work is particularly noted for its use of enamels and carved stone figures. A substantial workforce of highly skilled craftsmen produced the bulk of the pieces.

Fabrication

It is frequently desirable to use different techniques to manufacture the individual parts of a piece which are subsequently joined together to form the complete piece. This is the process of fabrication.

The individual pieces may be assembled by such methods as *welding, fusing, soldering, swaging, riveting* and the use of *adhesives*.

Fabrics

Fabrics can be incorporated in jewellery, although their application has historically been limited.

Using soft toy making techniques, short life matching jewellery, very suitable for young children, can be produced. Bangles, neckpieces and tiny cushion-shaped elements for pendants and ear rings are particularly appropriate.

Narrow lengths of fabric can be twisted and plaited to form cords. Weaving techniques can produce similar items, although the boundary between jewellery and clothing may be less easy to define.

Small pieces of fine fabric, such as lace, can be mounted behind watch glass and set as stones in pendants.

Facet

The individual, angled, flat faces of a cut gemstone. A number of facets make up the surface of the stone.

Diag. 123 *Facetting unit*

Facet cutting

Facets on gemstones are cut on a horizontal rotating lap. The gemstone is set on a dop stick which is held at an angle to the plane of the lap. The two critical angles are this angle to the lap and the angle indexed between facets, as the dop stick is rotated to produce each facet.

The sawn and ground stone is set in the end of the dop stick. Either the crown or the pavilion

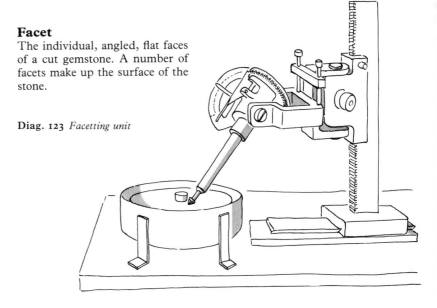

may be cut first. A jig is used when turning the stone around to ensure concentricity.

The most basic equipment consists of a jam peg or board set to one side of the lap. This vertical board has a pattern of shallow holes which accept the end of the dop stick. The combination of length of dop stick and the height, position and hole selected in the jam peg determine the angle of the facet on the stone.

The alternative arrangement is the modern faceting head which holds the dop stick in a head which incorporates an indexing wheel and graduated quadrant. The whole indexing head moves on a vertical rod.

The lap is charged with diamond powder and is made from copper. It sits on the master lap which is the driven rotating part of the equipment.

Polishing laps of tin, plastics material or wood are charged with the finest diamond dust for finishing the stone.

Facetted stones (see also Gemstones)

Stones, generally the more precious and particularly the transparent ones, have the viewed face cut in a pattern of small angled faces. Generally, symmetrical and radiating patterns are used so that the reflection and refraction of light intensifies the light seen in the stone.

Facetted stones are described by defining two essential qualities – the plan or girdle shape and the type of cut. For example, a stone in which the girdle, the largest part of the stone when viewed from above, is circular and is cut in a brilliant cut would be described as a round brilliant. A stone of oval shape so cut would be termed an oval brilliant and so on. The two basic cuts are the brilliant cut and the step cut or emerald cut.

The part of the stone above the girdle is the crown and that part

below the girdle the pavilion. The top face of the crown is the table and the pointed part of the pavilion the culet or apex.

Faience

Developed by Egyptian jewellers as a substitute for the more expensive stones such as lapiz lazuli, faience is a fired ground quartzite plus an oxide to give colour. Initially dark blue, other colours such as black, red, white, yellow and green were added and in some components the pigment was in more than one colour.

Fastenings (see also Findings)

Fastenings are principally used in jewellery for joining together chains, neckpieces and bracelets. Some popular fastenings are illustrated in Diag. 124.

Feather dyeing (see also Dyeing)

Feathers are prepared for dyeing by first tying them into bundles with thread around the quills. They should then be washed by dunking in warm water with detergent and washing soda. This is followed by soaking in fresh solution for about half an hour. The bundles are then rinsed and hung up to dry. They are now ready for dyeing. The natural dyes used for textiles or the modern synthetic dyes may be used. The procedure is as for textiles. To achieve bright colours on dark feathers, the bundles will require bleaching before dyeing.

Feathers

Feathers, dyed or natural, have a long history of incorporation in jewellery. Other than feathers dropped in moulting, the reader is encouraged to consider only feathers from birds bred for consumption and to leave the feathers of wild birds where they

a *Bolt ring*

b *Bar and ring*

c *Hook and ring*

Diag. 124 *Simple fastenings*

Diag. 125 *Feather stripped to use when etching*

are displayed best, on the birds. Feathers may be purchased loose by weight or selected and grouped, strung or bundled.

The two principal methods of incorporation are by setting the quill, singly or grouped, in a tube or by using part of the feather flat. Used flat, the feather is either set in cement or set on a small panel and covered by a watch glass.

Feathers, because of their delicate touch and resistance to acids, are used in etching. The quill is stripped, leaving only a tip, and this is effective in sweeping away the bubbles during etching.

Felt

Felt is formed into mounted and unmounted shapes for polishing. In flat sheets, coloured felt can be cut and assembled into low cost jewellery.

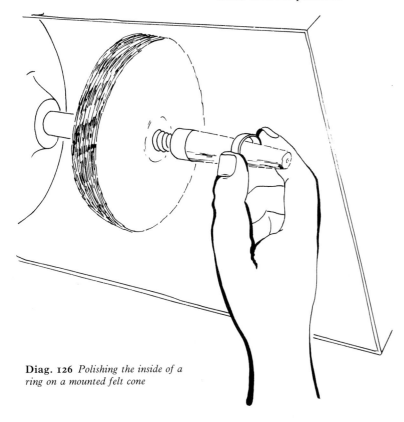

Diag. 126 *Polishing the inside of a ring on a mounted felt cone*

Felt cone

Used to polish the inside of rings, felt cones may be unmounted, that is solid felt with a small central hole, or mounted on a wooden cone. The cones are used on the ends of the pigtails of a polishing machine or on a similar adaptor in a pillar drill. The felt is dressed for polishing in the same way as a polishing wheel.

Felt mop (*see also* Polishing)

Polishing mop used for finishing. Felt mops are harder and less yielding.

Felt pen (*see also* Marking out)

Permanent marking felt pens are most effective in the marking out of metal prior to cutting. Their use is two-fold in that, with a broad stroke, a line can be set down and within that line a fine line can be scribed which contrasts with the pen line.

Ferric chloride (*see also* Etching)

A mordant used for etching copper as an alternative to dilute nitric acid.

Fibreglass

A composite material consisting of strands of glass fibre, generally woven, bonded together with polyester resin. Complex curved shapes may be formed, and the technique is most suited to larger shapes such as bangles and pectorals.

Fibreglass is also suitable for making formers into or over which maleable sheet metal can be formed.

To produce a shell-like shape in fibreglass, a model of the piece is first made in a material which can take a high finish such as metal, plaster or wood. When well finished, the model is coated with a release agent. Resin and hardener are mixed according to the maker's instructions and a thin layer spread over the surface. Into this is stippled a layer of fine woven glass tissue. The process is repeated with coarser glass matt until a sufficient layer is built up.

When hard, the moulding is removed from the model. Replicas of the original model can now be moulded in this mould, repeating the laying-up procedure. Colour can be introduced with dyes and this is sometimes limited to the first coat.

The finished mouldings are trimmed to shape with saws and files, adequate precautions being taken to avoid inhaling the dust.

All work with fibreglass must be carried out in well-ventilated areas and the maker's instructions must be followed.

File card

A flat wire brush, rectangular in plan, with very short bristles, used for cleaning the cut material from files.

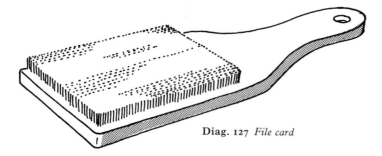

Diag. 127 *File card*

Files

Files of various lengths, cross sections and degrees of coarseness are available for removing material in shaping metal, wood and plastics. Made from hardened steel, the cutting faces are chisel cut to form a pattern of sharp cutting edges across the length of the file.

Files are described by length (excluding the tong), cross sectional shape, the plan shape, which faces cut and which are smooth and the type and coarseness of the cutting faces.

For jewellery work a set of Swiss files is most common. About 150mm (6in) long, they incorporate a handle which is adequate for most applications but can be used to fit a larger size wooden or plastic handle. Swiss files can be purchased singly or in sets. The coarsest cuts have about 30 teeth per inch and the smoothest over 200 cuts per inch. The majority of filing in jewellery making can be achieved with a half round Swiss file.

For removing material more quickly, a 150mm (6in) second cut file is suitable.

For filing plastic, special files are available which do not clog.

Filigree

Filigree is the lace-making of jewellery, where the space between pieces is as important as the pieces themselves.

True filigree is the assembly of a number of small shaped pieces within a frame. This style can be produced by lost wax casting, with the wax model either built up or formed in a mould. The finish is generally white, with only the frame polished.

The outer frame is shaped and soldered with a hard solder, then pickled, washed and dried. This can be used to produce an outline on paper, in which the design is

Diag. 128 *Types of file*

developed. All the small individual pieces can be matched to this layout and finely adjusted to fit the actual frame.

The filigree can be made from thin flat strips, plain or twisted, square section, plain or twisted, braids, plaits and twists. Flattened twist and flattened coil are used for delineation, and beads and granules singly or in clusters for features.

If soldering is to be done in a kiln, then the pieces can be assembled on a sheet of mica. If with a torch, then on a piece of thin iron sheet or charcoal.

Scrolls, rings, S shapes and spiral shapes can be formed with pliers. All the pieces must fit well and touch where they are to be joined.

Filigree work can be soldered

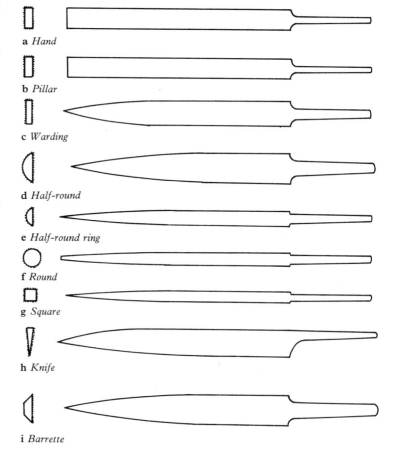

a *Hand*

b *Pillar*

c *Warding*

d *Half-round*

e *Half-round ring*

f *Round*

g *Square*

h *Knife*

i *Barrette*

directly with a torch, but the thin section risks melting. As an alternative, it can be heated gently in a carefully controlled kiln, or indirectly, resting a sheet of iron on a tripod, and heating from underneath.

Even small cut paillons of solder would tend to swamp the delicate shapes, and powdered solder must be used. This can be purchased, but is fresher (more oxide-free) if made when required. A strip of easy solder rubbed on a coarse file will produce fine grains of solder. It can then be used with a dry powder flux, such as borax, or sprinkled onto the piece when it has been wetted with a thin coating of liquid flux.

After soldering, the piece must be inspected and any missed joints resoldered. If a three-dimensional, rather than flat,

piece is required, then it can either be built up from a number of smaller completed frames or the basic frame can be fitted with a piece of fine silver mesh, shaped up as required. Some stretching is possible by doming.

Filing

Filing small jewellery components is best carried out on the bench peg, holding the piece with one hand and using the file with the other. Large pieces can be held in a vice but care must be taken not to mark the piece.

Before filing, ensure that the bench peg is clean and free from any inclusion which could cause marking. The piece to be shaped is held down firmly with the edge just overlapping the edge of the peg. The file is held handle down and against the edge of the piece.

Vertical up and down strokes of the file will remove material.

Filing block

A small block of rubber, wood or plastics material on which pieces are held when being filed. A bench peg used primarily for sawing can serve the same purpose.

Fillet

The infilling of an inside corner, such as occurs with *soldering* or when using an adhesive. Substantial fillets may be incorporated for strength or decoration.

Solder and adhesive fillets can detract from the crisp shape of a corner and can be minimised by chamfering the corner of one of the pieces.

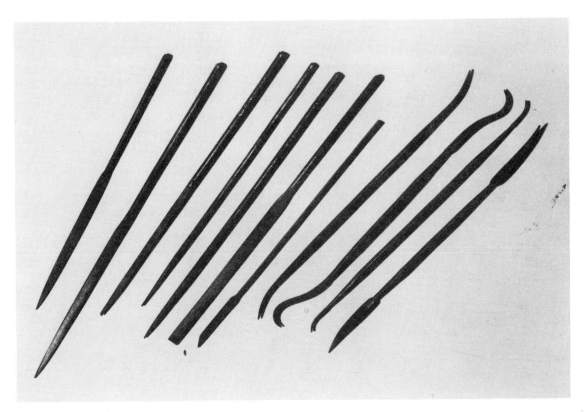

Fig. 15 *Selection of riffler and Swiss files*

Diag. 129 *Normal solder fillet*

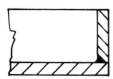

Diag. 130 *Hidden solder fillet*

Diag. 131 *Scroll for ear wires*

Diag. 132 *Bell cap*

Diag. 133 *Barrel screw clasp*

Diag. 134 *Split ring*

Diag. 135 *Safety chain*

Findings

Findings are those small components which are common to many otherwise different pieces of jewellery. Because of their wide application, they can be mass produced and are therefore available at very competitive prices.

The list is extensive and includes bolt rings, jump rings, ear wires, ear screws, brooch pins, brooch pivots, ear butterflies (scrolls), bell caps, screw fasteners, lock fasteners, claws, collets, ring shanks, beads, hinges, catches, swivels, pendant stars and hearts and crosses, sleepers, charms, zodiacs, ear studs, cuff links and tie clips.

It is quite possible to create quite a range of jewellery from commercially available findings. Pieces created in this way will, however, lack the identity of the craftsman. Used carefully, they can reduce the time taken to create a piece without detracting from that piece's individuality.

Fine silver

A nearly pure form of silver containing 999 parts per 1000 of silver.

Finishing metal pieces (*see also* Barrelling, Polishing *and* Water of Ayr)

However good the design and construction, all that is seen of a piece is the finished surface; it therefore warrants much attention.

Finishing is taken to mean all those processes after final shaping excluding stone setting, bead threading and the like. It includes the removal of saw, file and hammer marks.

There are essentially two types of finishing: those processes which remove metal, such as the use of compounds on polishing wheels, and those processes such as burnishing which do not remove metal but change the character of the surface.

To finish a plain piece with polishing and cutting media, the process would be as follows.

1 Removal of saw and file marks by water of Ayr stone creating an overall fine matt finish.

2 Wash with clean water and dry.

3 Polish with lustre on a calico buffing wheel to create a finer dull finish.

Diag. 136 *Water of Ayr stone being used to smooth the edge of a piece*

4 Wash with detergent and dry.

5 Polish with rouge on a soft calico or cotton buffing wheel to create a polished finish.

6 Wash with detergent and dry.

7 Hand polish with a polishing cloth.

When the piece is more intricate, coarse and fine buffing is carried out with small mops in flexible drive chucks from a pendant drill or bench motor. Deep recesses are polished with dressed polishing threads or by dressing thin wooden sticks.

During the polishing of silver pieces, fire stain may show through and must be removed before finishing can be completed. Water of Ayr stone is most suitable.

Finishing metal pieces without significant removal of the metal is carried out by burnishing. This process uses the pressure of a harder smooth surface with a lubricant to flow the microscopic peaks down, producing a smooth, highly polished finish.

Burnishing can be carried out by hand or machine. Machine burnishing is also termed barrelling.

Fion

A raised hemispherical bead. Made of hardened steel, the beads are set on a base plate in graded sizes. The fion is used to polish the inside hemispherical shape of a graining tool.

Fire bricks (see also Brazing hearth)

Bricks formulated to withstand high temperature, they can be used for building brazing hearths and areas for melting metals.

Firescale

When silver is heated during *soldering* or *annealing*, areas will become marked with firescale.

Dull grey in colour, these areas must be removed by stoning with water of Ayr stone or abrasive cloth before an acceptable finish can be obtained. Where this is not practical, repeated heating and quenching in pickle will hide light firescale. For the removal of deeper firescale, the piece is dipped in Bright dip and washed.

Firescale is caused by the surfacing of copper and other oxides. It can be minimised by fully covering the piece with flux before heating.

Where none of the above methods is suitable, silver plating the piece may be appropriate.

Firing

The process in which the form of a material is changed by subjecting it to high temperatures. Ceramic materials require to be fired on a carefully timed progressive cycle with a similarly controlled cooling cycle. In contrast, enamels can be fired quickly but are preferably cooled more slowly. The table below indicates some typical firing temperatures.

Ceramics
  Biscuit fired clay   980°C
  Stoneware   1200°C–1260°C
  Earthenware   1040°C–1150°C
  Porcelain   1300°C
  Ceramic glaze   As stoneware or earthenware

Enamels   700°C to 800°C

Niello   550°C approximately

Diag. 137 *Flap wheel*

Fish glue

A natural glue now generally superseded by modern adhesives, it is used in the process of *granulation*.

Flame types

The three principle types of flame are reducing, oxidising and neutral. The differences lie in the ratios of fuel to air or oxygen.

A reducing flame is low in oxygen and yellow zinc in colour. Because of the low oxygen content, it tends not to oxidise the surface of the metal on which it plays. An oxidising flame has a surplus of oxygen for the fuel and burns blue. Excess oxygen encourages metal oxidation and firescale on silver. A neutral flame has just sufficient air for combustion and has just a hint of blue colour. A neutral flame is generally the best compromise for jewellery work.

Flap wheel

An abrasive wheel composed of flaps of abrasive cloth and used for coarse finishing.

Flat nose pliers (see also Pliers)

Effective in holding and forming, flat nose pliers should have smooth jaws and a full box joint for maximum rigidity.

Flattening

Flattening sheet which has been distorted, as when it has been cut with snips, can be carried out by hammering it on a flat steel plate or stake. A soft-faced hammer should be used or the piece should be protected by a sheet of soft material such as leather or newspaper.

Hand-flattening presses are available for repetition use.

Flattening stake

A heavy, rigidly mounted stake

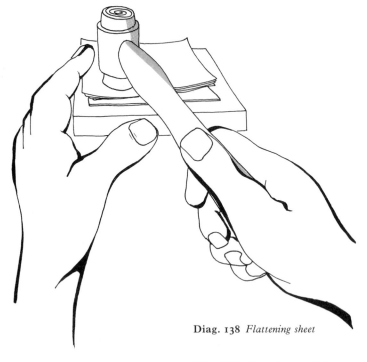

Diag. 138 *Flattening sheet*

Flexible band machine

Metals, plastics and wood can be sanded and shaped on a flexible band machine. The belt can be either horizontal or vertical. Horizontal bands are best suited to sanding the face of a piece, and vertical bands for edge sanding. Bands in a range of abrasive finishes are available. One disadvantage of such machines is the scarfed joint which can be felt as the band moves.

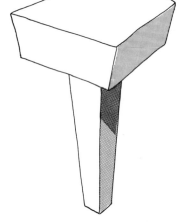

Diag. 139 *Flattening stake*

with a flat face for flattening sheet metal pieces.

Fletcher (*see also* Melting)
A shallow dish of refractory material used for melting metal with a torch.

Flexible drive shaft (*see also* Pendant drill)
A drive unit attached to an electric motor and fitted with a chuck which accepts small drills and burrs. Flexible drive shafts may be integral with an electric motor in the form of a pendant or bench-mounted drill. Alternatively, the drive may be an attachment for a bench drill, polishing or grinding motor.

Flinking (*see also* Engraving)
A decorative effect made in recesses with a *graver* prior to transparent enamelling.

Flour paper
Very fine abrasive paper.

Flowers, dried
Flowers are probably one of the earliest forms of body decoration,

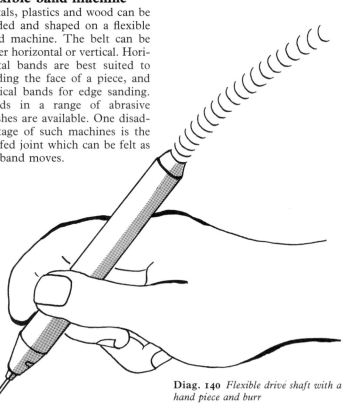

Diag. 140 *Flexible drive shaft with a hand piece and burr*

offering colour and form as well as the ritual association of spring. Daisy chains and flowers worn in the hair still survive.

Dried flowers can be set as brooches and hair pieces in short-life pieces, although, as such, they fall between clothing decoration and jewellery.

Flux

Flux is an aid to *soldering*; without it, soldering would be almost impossible. Its principal action is to create a thin covering to the metal being soldered, resistant to soldering temperatures, preventing oxidisation of the metal yet allowing the solder to flow freely.

The two broad groups are fluxes for soft soldering and those for hard soldering and brazing. Soft solder fluxes are frequently incorporated in the core of the solder but are also available in paste form. Hard solder fluxes may be powder or liquid. Modern fluxes are preferred to borax in that, although only marginally better during soldering, they are much easier to remove afterwards.

Fluxing

Hard soldering requires the metal to be fluxed prior to the application of heat. Powdered flux and the basic borax are made into a paste with water or methylated spirit. Liquid fluxes are used direct. Both can be applied with a splinter of wood, feather tip or a small quill brush.

Foil

Aluminium and pewter foil can be burnished into relief designs using minimal tools. The process is similar to the childhood practice of forming a milk bottle top over a coin. This same technique may be employed if the reproduction of a solid model is required.

Free designs are produced by laying a sheet of foil onto a resilient surface such as a pile of

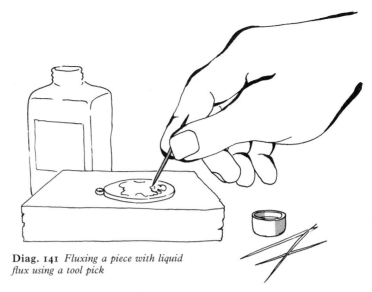

Diag. 141 *Fluxing a piece with liquid flux using a tool pick*

Diag. 142 *Borax cone and dish with brush to produce flux*

newspaper. Using a rounded burnishing tool, the relieved part of the design is formed into the sheet. The remaining raised part can be sharpened by turning the sheet over and working the inside edges with a rounded blade.

With pewter foil, collets for stones and other applied pieces can be soft soldered onto the surface.

The hollow back can now be filled with epoxy resin, plaster, pitch or other appropriate filler and attachment pieces fixed in this filler or to a backing piece.

Folded paper

Simple short-life jewellery can be produced using origami techniques with folded paper. Pendant ear rings are a suitable application for this technique.

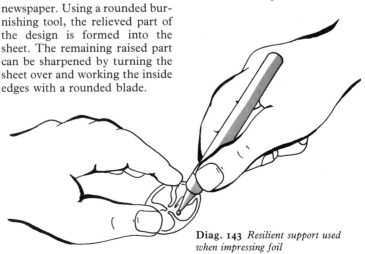

Diag. 143 *Resilient support used when impressing foil*

Diag. 144 *Simple folded paper jewellery*

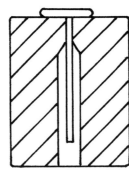

Diag. 147 *Beaded wire hammered flat and the finished product*

Diag. 145 *Beaded wire*

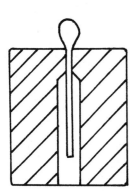

Diag. 146 *Beaded wire set in forming die*

More permanent pieces can be produced by substituting thin acetate film for the paper.

Forging

Metal wire, rod and section can be changed in cross sectional shape by forging. The processes are essentially those employed by blacksmiths but on a very much smaller scale, and the process is performed with cold rather than hot metal in most situations.

The work is done with hammer blows onto a hard polished face such as an anvil, bick iron or swage block.

Blows with a flat-faced hammer made evenly on a bar will reduce its thickness and increase both the length and width. If directed to one side of the bar along its length, its thickness will be reduced more on one side than the other, the length will increase and the section will curve around with the thicker side inside the curve.

Using a rounded-edge, cross

Diag. 148 *Simple forging*

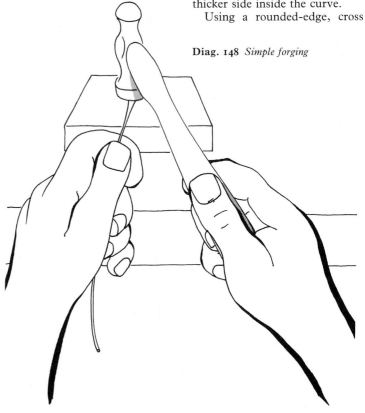

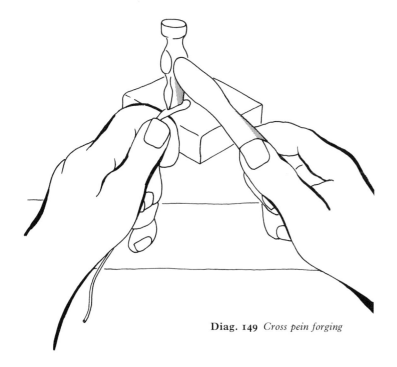

Diag. 149 *Cross pein forging*

pein hammer, the metal will be stretched primarily in one direction at right angles to the line of the hammer head. Using this method enables very specific sections to be formed both straight, curved and tapered.

To taper a piece of bar of moderate section, say between 3mm ($\frac{1}{8}$in) and 6mm ($\frac{1}{4}$in) diameter silver, a cross pein hammer is used with the piece resting on a polished anvil. Blows are struck with the handle in line with the bar, working from the start of the taper towards the end and turning the bar either in discreet steps to produce a hexagon or octagon section, or continuously to produce a roughly circular taper. The piece will work harden during the process and will require frequent annealing.

For smaller sections, a quicker way is to forge the taper in one plane only using a flat-faced hammer. The width of the taper is

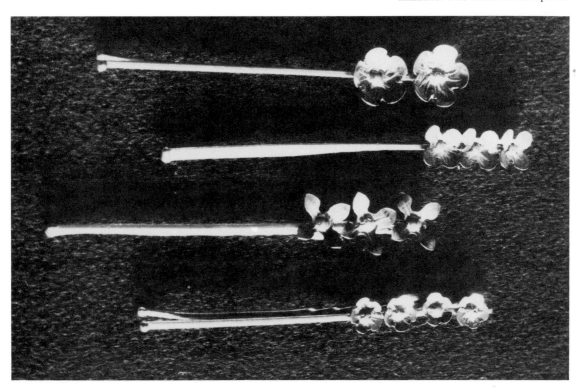

Fig. 16 *Hair pins, forged pin and pressed flowers – silver*

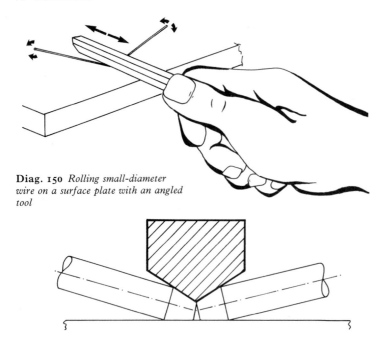

Diag. 150 *Rolling small-diameter wire on a surface plate with an angled tool*

Diag. 151 *Forming on a lead block*

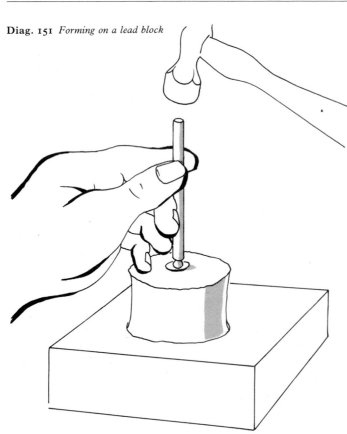

then reduced with tin snips and the piece finished by filing and polishing.

The decorative effect of forging may be left or removed by polishing. A wide variety of decorative effects can be obtained with flat, domed, cross pein or special shaped heads.

Forming

Malleable materials, or materials such as steel or plastics which can be made malleable with heat, can be formed in more than one dimension.

A simple example of the process is doming. More complex shapes can be made by repoussé and chasing.

Simple tooling can produce complex shapes which would otherwise be difficult to fabricate and also allows repetition work. Steel tooling will give long life, but, where limited life is adequate, then brass and tough plastics are adequate.

Diag. 152 shows a simple forming tool made from brass sheet soldered together. Thin annealed silver sheet (0.4mm) is laid over the forming tool. Over the silver is laid a pad of yielding material such as a wad of newspaper or sheet of lead. Hammering this onto the silver forms it over the tool.

Found materials

Historically, nuts, seeds, husks, pebbles, shells, claws, teeth, tusks, horns, bones, feathers, bark and beetle-wing covers have all

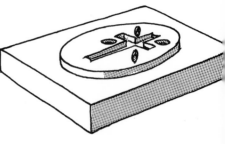

Diag. 152 *Simple fabricated tool for forming thin sheet metal*

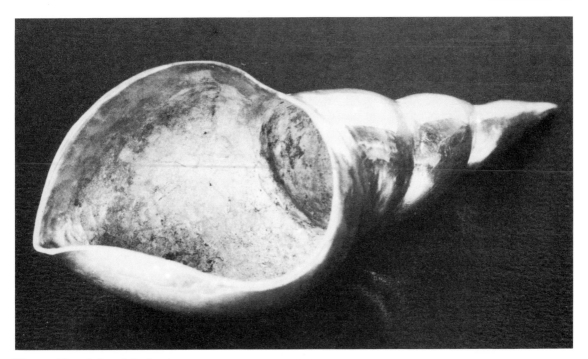

Fig. 17 *Silver shell made by forming up a cone and hammering it up to shape over a mandrel*

been made into jewellery. In more recent times, bottle tops, tickets, beer-can pulls, old forks, corks, polythene bags, drinking straws, tacks, screws, nuts, flexible ducting and plastic stoppers have been employed.

Fraizers (*see also* Burrs)

Fraizers or burrs are small cutting tools used to shape metal. They are used in a pendant drill chuck at high speed and are available in a wide range of shapes and sizes.

In particular, fraizers are available for cutting stone settings.

Frame saw (Jeweller's saw) (*see also* Sawing)

The essential tool of the jeweller working in metal made to accept the range of jeweller's saw blades. Designs differ slightly, although the principal features are the depth of the frame, which limits

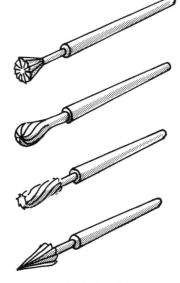

Diag. 153 *A selection of fraizers or burrs*

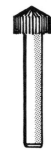

Diag. 154 *Stone seating burr or fraizer*

Fretsaw

A deeper version of a jeweller's saw, primarily used for cutting plywood.

Frit (*see also* Enamelling)

The basic component of enamel is termed frit or flux.

Frosting

A frosted finish can be achieved in a variety of ways on metal. The most straightforward method is by hand with a glass brush on an

how far into a sheet the saw can cut, and whether the length is fixed or adjustable.

already polished surface. This produces a very fine frosted finish. Hand brushing with a steel brush gives a coarser finish. Rotating steel brushes with flaying wires are available for producing a range of graded finishes. Brass brushes run wet are used commercially.

Sand blasting has the advantage of enabling selected areas to be easily masked.

Round-ended burrs used in a pendant drill can work a variety of frosted finishes, depending on the pattern in which they are marked on the surface.

Functional design (see also Measuring)

Jewellery design may be divided into the three principal requirements of aesthetic quality, production and function.

Functional requirements cover such basic demands that rings fit on fingers, chains fit around necks, and ear rings fit through or clip on ears. Bodies come in many different sizes and shapes and any dimensions can only be a general guide.

Some anatomical features are not always fully appreciated. For

example, necks are essentially five-sided, being roughly pointed at the front with parallel sides and a curved back. Wrists are almost parallel with rounded ends, and ankles are egg-shape in section. The size, weight, shape and tactile qualities must be sympathetic with the body or clothing on which it is fitted.

Fur

Small pieces of fur offcuts can be incorporated in jewellery in a similar way to feathers. It is effective when used in tufts and set in a light metal collet.

Furnace (see also Melting)

Gas or electrically heated furnaces are used to melt metal prior to casting. They are designed to accept crucibles and must be capable of achieving in excess of the melting temperature of the metal to be melted. Simple furnaces can be built from fire bricks for gas torch melting.

Fusing glass

Multi-coloured glass plaques can be produced in a kiln by fusing pieces of coloured glass to a single piece.

A base piece of glass is laid on a ceramic tile which is coated with a layer of whiting or powdered used investment material. On the base piece are laid the pattern of coloured pieces, just touching, although an exact fit is not critical.

The tile is placed in a kiln and raised to a temperature at which the glass melts together as a single piece. The kiln temperature is reduced and the piece allowed to cool very slowly. The resultant multi-coloured slab will have a

Diag. 155 *Glass pieces stacked*

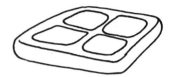

Diag. 156 *Glass panel after firing*

rounded shape and approximate uniform thickness and will have grown in area but reduced in thickness.

Fusing metal

Metal components may be joined without *solder* or welding rod by fusing.

Silver is a particularly suitable material for this process. The final piece will exhibit a variety of surface textures from smooth to orange peel in natural, water-worn, rock-like forms. During the process, any geometrically formed piece will lose some degree of definition as it blends with adjoining pieces.

Components for fusing may themselves be formed by heating, and dropping molten beads into water is one process.

As with any hot joining process, the pieces should be clean, which is best achieved by heating and quenching in pickle followed by washing and drying.

Pieces may simply be laid end to end or side by side, or smaller components may be laid on a piece of sheet. Any very small components, such as beads, are best applied during the process to avoid excess heating.

Heating is best carried out with a very hot small flame such as is produced by an oxygen hydrogen

Dimensional guide lines

Chains

Choker	350mm to 380mm (14in to 15in)
Short chain	406mm (16in)
Medium chain	460mm (18in)
Long chain	560mm (22in)
Opening bracelets	165mm inside circumference (6½in)
Bangles	66mm inside diameter (2$\frac{9}{16}$in) 208mm inside circumference (8$\frac{3}{16}$in)
Ear wires – straight	9½mm to 12½mm (⅜in to ½in) long

Most popular ring sizes

	J	K	L	M	N	O	P
English sizes							
Inside diameter (in)	0.6145	0.63	0.646	0.661	0.677	0.692	0.708
(mm)	15.6	16	16.4	16.8	17.2	17.6	18
USA sizes	5	5½	6	6½	7	7½	8
Inside diameter (in)	0.618	0.634	0.650	0.666	0.682	0.698	0.714

Fig. 18 *Jump rings fused to a sheet backing cut to shape and set with ruby stones – clip ear rings*

generator. Touching pieces are heated until the surface becomes moulten yet still retaining their shape. The time between this stage and full melting is short and the torch must be removed quickly after the surfaces have fused but before the pieces fully melt. Surface texture will change to an orange peel texture and this is one indication of the fusing point. A very small amount of liquid flux will assist fusing.

Small components can be placed prior to heating but may overheat and lose shape. They are best placed in position when the base piece reaches fusing temperature. They will very quickly fuse in place and the flame must be removed immediately.

The surface may be textured by sifting silver filings and small granules onto it when at fusing temperature.

If the fusing does not go according to plan, then remove the flame, pickle the piece and start again.

Fig. 19 *Fused silver backing set with engraved, forged, stamped and beaded decoration – pendant*

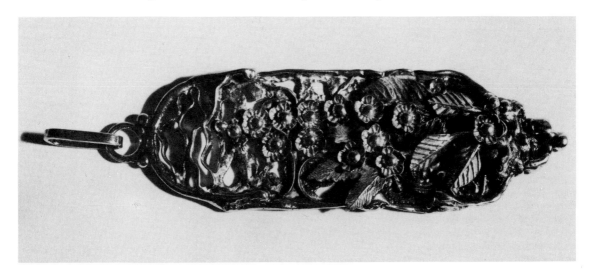

Gallery strip (*see also* Bezel)

A decorated strip generally punched from precious metal. It is used to edge pieces and can be adapted to set stones.

Garnet paper

An abrasive paper used for light shaping and finishing metals.

Gemstone settings (*see also* Collet *and* Bezel)

Gemstones may conveniently be divided between those cut as a cabochon and set in a full bezel, and facetted stones set in claws. This is the popular division, but facetted stones can be set in a bezel and cabochon cut stones in claw settings. In both forms of setting, the essential features are a face or faces on which the stone sits and a face or faces which is formed over to grip the stone.

Baroque and native cut gemstones may be set, particularly as pendants with a bail either fixed with adhesive, by a peg in a hole or with a through hole. Cages of wire can also be used to hold baroque and tumbled stones.

Gemstones

The term generally used to define those translucent or transparent stones which are facet cut.

German silver

Containing no silver at all, German silver is a white metal alloy consisting of copper (65 per cent), zinc (23 per cent) and nickel (12 per cent). It can be forged, drawn and soldered. It has a yellow silver soft colour.

Diag. 157 *Gallery strip*

Gilding

Non-metallic materials are gilded with gold leaf set with gold size. Metals are gilded by coating the surface of the piece with an amalgam of gold and mercury. The mercury is then vaporised, leaving a layer of gold. Mercury, and particularly mercury vapour, is highly toxic and the process should not be attempted without comprehensive precautions being taken against contact and inhalation. A process alternative is electroplating.

Girdle

The outermost edge of a gemstone which rests in the setting.

Diag. 158 *Shapes of calibrated gemstones*

a *Oval*   b *Marquis*   c *Baquette*   d *Round*   e *Square*

Diag. 159 *Standard cabochon stones*

    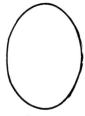

a *8 ×6*   b *10 ×8*   c *14 ×10*   d *18 ×13*   e *25 ×18*   f *40 ×30*

g *5 dia.*   h *6 dia.*   i *8 dia.*   j *10 dia.*

Glass beads

Glass beads in the size range of 1 to 1½mm diameter are available in a vast range of solid, translucent and transparent colours. They can be simply strung, woven or threaded on wire.

Small beads can be made by firing a small mound of enamel on a charcoal- or whiting-coated ceramic block. While moulten they can be pierced with a wire. Alternatively, glass tube can be cut to length and the ends softened with a flame. Larger beads can be formed by first drawing a glass thread from a heated heap of enamel. The thread, while hot, can be wound around a former of wood which can subsequently be burnt out. Beads made in this way will be fragile and require annealing after forming.

Glass brush

Used for finishing metal pieces with a satin finish, glass brushes

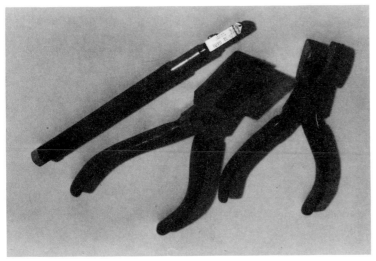

Fig. 20 *Glass cutting tools*

Grain setting

Stones can be set with grains formed up from the piece. The process consists of first cutting a recess in which the girdle of the stone sits. From three, four or more radial points, a graver forms up a shaving of the material without removing it from the piece. This shaving is subsequently formed into a small grain or bead with a beading tool. Care and practice is required before attempting this type of setting.

Graining tool (*see also* Fion)

A small hand-held tool similar to a graver. The shank is round and tapers towards the tip which is in the form of a hollow hemisphere. It is generally a handle with a range of interchangeable shanks in a variety of hemispherical sizes. The graining tool is used to form raised beads from attached shavings of metal raised with a graver.

Diag. 160 *Glass brush used for cleaning*

about 5mm ($\frac{3}{16}$in) in diameter consist of densely packed strands of glass. The finish produced is satin-like and may be the final finish or as preparation for a finer finish. Glass brushes are useful for cleaning otherwise difficult to reach areas.

Glaze (*see also* Firing)

The material used to finish ceramic pieces. Glaze is supplied in powder form and is mixed with water to produce a slurry. The piece to be glazed is immersed in the liquid and, after drying, is fired at high temperature.

Gold leaf

Used for gilding non-metallic materials, gold leaf is supplied in books 80mm ($3\frac{1}{8}$in) × 80mm ($3\frac{1}{8}$in) or 85mm ($3\frac{1}{2}$in) × 85mm ($3\frac{1}{2}$in) and from about .008mm to .0001 mm thick.

Granulation (*see also* Chemical bonding)

Granulation is the process in which a pattern of granules is fusion-welded to a backing piece. Large granules can be soldered in position but problems can be encountered with movement due to the flux and flooding of the gaps between the granules with solder.

The process was widely practised by the ancient civilisations of Egypt, India and the Far East.

The theory behind fusion-welding is variously interpreted, but in essence relies on the creation of a copper interface created by the combination of a copper-rich salt and an organic binder. The organic binder is conveniently in the form of a natural glue which is also used to position the granules. A number of formulas have been published, and the one used by Mr Littledale, who is credited with rediscovering the process in 1936, is given.

Equal parts of copper hydroxide and natural glue such as gum tragacanth, gum acacia or seccotine glue are mixed to a paste with a little water. The gold granules are glued to the backing sheet with this mix and allowed to dry. The whole piece is raised to a temperature of between 900°C and 1000°C, at which point the carbonised glue and copper salts have combined to produce a copper interface between the granules and the base. The process is curious in that copper in isolation would only melt at 1084°C, yet in combination with the gold combines at 890°C, which is below the melting point of gold – 1062°C. Silver and copper combine at 890°C, which is near the 960°C melting point for silver requiring more careful temperature control. A reducing flame can be used in place of a furnace, but very careful observation of temperature is required. As with all hot joining processes, cleanliness of the parts is essential for success.

Granule

A small sphere of metal. Granules are set in patterns and joined to the surface by fusion welding. Gold is most commonly used, but the process is also suitable for silver.

Granules are made by melting small pieces of the precious metal on a charcoal block and quenching in pickle. Uniformity of size can be made by snipping the material to be formed in equal lengths from wire or strip. Very small granules will be blown away by a torch. To make tiny granules, the strip or wire pieces are sifted onto a layer of powdered charcoal in a stainless steel box or tray. Successive layers of charcoal and snippets fill the tray which is kiln heated to melting temperature. The snippets will melt and form into spheres which can be sifted out, washed and barrelled.

Prior to setting, the granules are

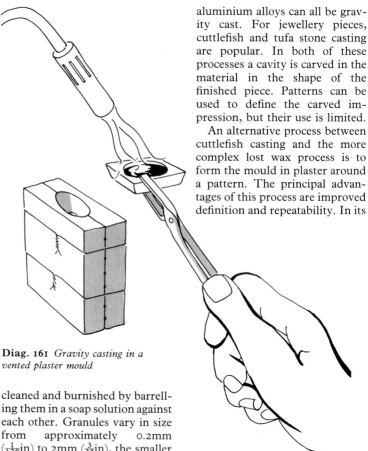

Diag. 161 *Gravity casting in a vented plaster mould*

cleaned and burnished by barrelling them in a soap solution against each other. Granules vary in size from approximately 0.2mm ($\frac{1}{128}$in) to 2mm ($\frac{3}{32}$in), the smaller ones being sorted by passing them through progressively graded sieves.

Graphite (*see also* Melting)

A grey black mineral, a form of carbon graphite, used for refractory components such as crucibles and stirring rods. Because of its electrical conductive properties, it is also used in electroforming processes. Graphite is also a natural lubricant.

Graver

A hand-held cutting tool used for engraving. Also called a burin.

Gravity casting (*see also* Casting *and* Casting plaster)

Gold, silver, pewter, tin and aluminium alloys can all be gravity cast. For jewellery pieces, cuttlefish and tufa stone casting are popular. In both of these processes a cavity is carved in the material in the shape of the finished piece. Patterns can be used to define the carved impression, but their use is limited.

An alternative process between cuttlefish casting and the more complex lost wax process is to form the mould in plaster around a pattern. The principal advantages of this process are improved definition and repeatability. In its most simple form the item is flat-backed. Fully round pieces are possible but mould production is more complex.

To cast a simple flat-backed piece the process is as follows.

The design is drawn actual size in plan view on a piece of paper and laid on the bench. Over this is laid a small sheet of glass. A model of the piece to be made is formed in plasticine, modelling wax or similar material over the design seen through the glass with the heights and fine detail required. A wall of similar modelling material is built around the model some 30mm (1⅛in) from it on three sides and at least 50mm (2in) on the fourth side, from which the hot metal will eventually be poured.

The wall should extend at least 10mm ($\frac{3}{8}$in) above the height of the highest point of the model. A funnel is formed in modelling material on the widest side, tapering from about 40mm ($1\frac{1}{2}$in) wide at the edge to 10mm ($\frac{3}{8}$in) wide where it joins the model, with a depth equal to the height of the model.

The space inside the wall is now filled with dental plaster mixed with water to the consistency of smooth cream. Care should be taken in pouring the mix over the model, avoiding bubbles. A water-colour brush can be used for this purpose, painting the model before general pouring.

When set, all modelling material can be removed and the cast mould set aside to dry thoroughly. This is essential to avoid bursting when in contact with hot metal. Vents are now radially scored in the face of the mould which will allow the air to escape during casting.

A backing mould of the same size but without any patterns is cast in a similar way and dried.

The two pieces are bound together with iron binding wire and the casting process carried out as for cuttlefish casting. It is convenient to set the mould in a tray of dry sand, taking care not to block the venting holes.

Grinding

Hard materials such as stones, ceramic and steel can be shaped and finished by grinding. In jewellery work the piece is generally hand-held against the rotating grinding wheel in a similar way to polishing. Grinding wheels in degrees of coarseness and composition are available for different materials. The wheels are composed of a bonded abrasive. As a general guide, stones and ceramic are ground wet on a green wheel and steel ground dry on a black wheel.

Grisaille enamelling (see also Enamelling)

Over a black enamel base the design is set in thin white enamel. Toning is done with a sharp pointed tool in a similar way to an etching. When the piece of fixed, the fine white lines sink into the black, giving tones of grey.

Grit blasting

A finishing process producing a textured finish and used to clean castings. The equipment consists of a cabinet with inset rubber gloves allowing pieces to be held and manipulated inside it. Compressed air directs a stream of grit into the cabinet in which the piece is held. The grit is recycled and cleaned.

Other materials can be used in place of grit, offering a variety of finishes.

Grits

A term used to describe loose abrasive cutting materials used for cutting and polishing stones.

Gum arabic

A natural gum used to bind wet enamels and in *granulation* work.

Gum tragacanth

A natural gum used in *enamelling* and other processes.

Gypsy setting

A form of setting frequently used in signet rings. It enables the stone to be set flush or nearly flush with the piece without any projections.

A hole is first drilled right through the piece, smaller than the outside size of the stone by about 1mm. A setting burr is then used to cut a seat for the stone with the edge of the stone below the surface by about 0.5mm. Outside this rim the material of the piece is relieved by filing to form a raised ridge around the stone, with a smooth transition to the rest of the piece. The stone is set and the rim is burnished in place.

Hacksaw

A frame saw capable of holding various lengths of blade suitable for cutting steel and many other materials.

Hair

Hair both human and animal has been incorporated in jewellery since ancient times. It was particularly popular in Victorian times. Pieces are principally formed by plaiting and braiding with precious metal findings.

Hair pin

Both practical and decorative, hair pins are either straight or bent double. They are an ancient form of jewellery.

Diag. 162 *Hallmarking tab*

Fig. 21 *Hallmark*

Hallmark tabs (*see also* Assay)

Fine pieces of precious metal jewellery such as neck chains may not have sufficient space for a hallmark. When this is so, then a link-shaped flat tab can be included in the piece to provide a small flat area for hallmarking.

Hammers

Hammers may be divided between those used to strike tools such as punches and those used to strike the material directly. Many of the wide variety of hammers available in jewellers' suppliers are used primarily for silver smithing rather than jewellery.

Riveting hammer: the lightest weight hammer used for riveting and very light forming operations. 1oz or 1½oz head.

Repoussé hammer: used for repoussé chasing and light punching. 4oz and 6oz head.

Planishing: used for smoothing by hammering the surface. Flat and round-ended head. 4oz, 5oz, 8oz, 10oz.

Creasing: used to form creases as part of the process of raising, but also useful for forming sheet into a swage block. 4oz.

Setting: a heavy hammer for flattening sheet. 2½lb.

Ball pein and warrington: general-purpose hammers. 4oz, 8oz, 12oz.

Soft-faced hammers with striking faces of plastic or hide used for shaping without imparting a planished surface.

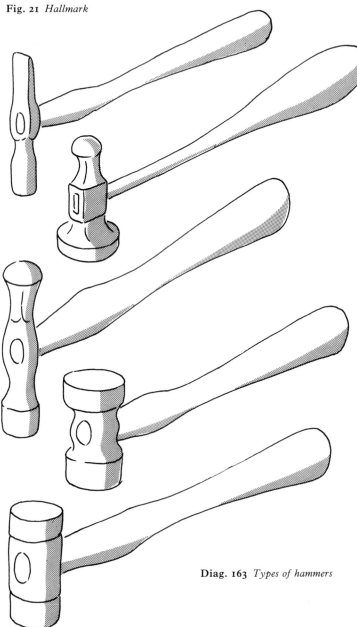

Diag. 163 *Types of hammers*

Hand vice

A holding device for clamping components being shaped or finished. Designs vary from heavy screw clamps and miniature vices on handles to light-weight spring and screw types.

Hard solder (*see also* Soldering)

A range of solder with melting temperatures in the range 667°C to 800°C. Solders are available for base metals such as brass and copper. Solders for silver and gold can be purchased in various qualities, making them suitable for work to be assayed. Gold solders are also available in different gold colours.

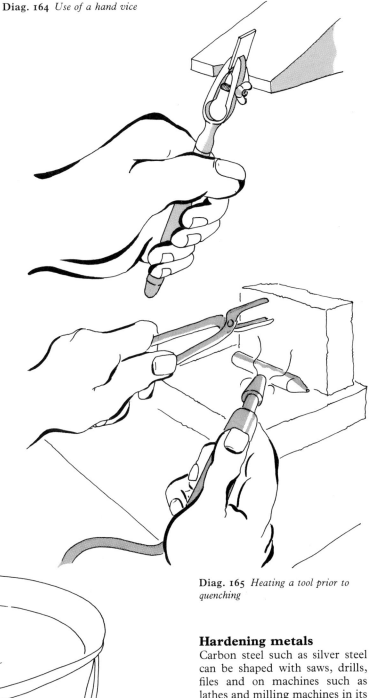

Diag. 164 *Use of a hand vice*

Diag. 165 *Heating a tool prior to quenching*

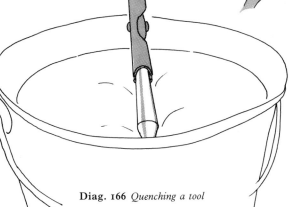

Diag. 166 *Quenching a tool*

Hardening metals

Carbon steel such as silver steel can be shaped with saws, drills, files and on machines such as lathes and milling machines in its purchased 'soft' condition. After shaping, it can be hardened by heating to a cherry red heat, about 780°C and quenching it quickly in water. This will create a dead hard

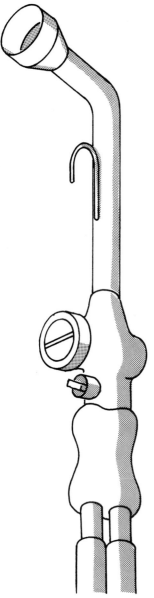

Diag. 167 *Air-gas torch*

condition in the metal but one which is likely to fracture if subjected to stress. A hard condition can be retained but with a resistance to stress by tempering.

Hardness table (*see also* Moh's scale)
Stones are graded on a scale of

relative hardness in which a higher number is harder than the lower number.

Hardwood
Hardwood, particularly the darker coloured types, can be incorporated in jewellery either cut and set like stones and cameos or carved like bone or ivory.

Hearth
Where more heat is used than is comfortable or safe to proceed on a charcoal block, the work is carried out on a hearth.

Hearths vary in design from large trays of small pieces of ceramic to simple assemblies of fire bricks. This latter arrangement is suitable for most processes associated with jewellery making and has the advantage of flexibility.

Heating methods
Heat is required in a number of jewellery making techniques. The techniques and appropriate heating methods are as follows.

Hide mallet
The head of a hide mallet is formed from a piece of tightly rolled hide through which the wooden handle passes. Other models have metal heads allowing more impact, with interchangeable or fixed hide inserts.

Hide mallets are used for forming and bending metal without the surface indentation associated with hammers.

Hinge making
A hinge, as used on items of jewellery such as lockets, is formed from a small tube through which runs a coaxial hinge pin. The *tube* is cut into any number of lengths, but more than three. These lengths of tube are joined alternately to each of the parts being hinged.

The position of the hinge on the piece must be chosen to allow the lid or moving part to open. It is also generally preferable to recess the hinge to minimise it visually.

Although it is possible to arrange the short lengths of tube on each part correctly and solder them in position, difficulty will be

Technique	Heating methods
Soft soldering	Soldering iron, preferably electrically heated. Those used for electronic component assembly are appropriate for most jewellery work.
Hard soldering	Gas flame torches from fine to large, using either self induced air or compressed air. Electric hard soldering machines for specific operations.
Melting	Gas and compressed air torches for small amounts of metal. Larger amounts are melted in gas or electrically heated crucibles.
Enamelling	Electric and occasionally gas fired enamelling kilns.
Manipulating hot glass	Gas torch with variable nozzles.
Ceramic	High temperature kiln.
Plastic sheet forming	Electric hot plate.
Drying wet components	Warm air fan.
Heating pickle	Electric hot plate or immersion heater, heated water jacket.

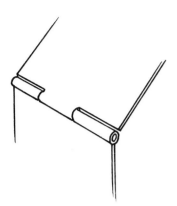

Diag. 168 *Simple hinge made from tube*

Diag. 169 *Stone holder*

Holding tools

A range of holding tools has been developed over the centuries to suit the needs of the jeweller, some for hot processes, others for cold.

They all aim to allow processes to be performed better than if the piece were held with fingers. It must not be forgotten, though, that fingers are still the most adaptable and sensitive holding device.

Ring clamps for holding rings and similar small items for cold operations such as sawing, filing, engraving and polishing.

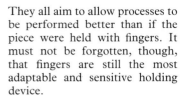

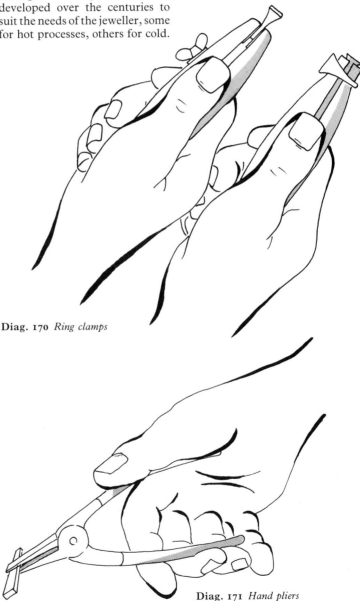

Diag. 170 *Ring clamps*

Diag. 171 *Hand pliers*

encountered with accuracy and the flow of solder into the tube. A more convenient way is to solder a full length of tube to each part by first wiring the tube to a bevelled edge with iron binding wire. By positioning the centre line of the tube in line with the outside face of the part, the moving part is allowed to open fully. The bevel must continue the full length of the part to allow the hinge pin to be inserted.

With the two lengths of tube soldered in position, the pieces can be placed back to back and the spacing of the joints in the tubes marked. To avoid errors, it is helpful to mark the parts to be removed. The unmarked parts can first be filed out on one piece down to the level of the piece and the original bevel. The end faces must be finished smooth. The unwanted parts of the tube on the other part can now be removed using the first part to check accuracy. This method, although it wastes a small length of tube, does make it easier to create accuracy of fit.

The outermost ends of the hinge are countersunk using a drill the size of the hinge tube. With the two pieces together, a wire pin is drawn to be a slide fit in the hinge and just over the length. Using a rivetting hammer, the pin is very lightly peined over filling the countersunk hinge pieces. A trace of oil will ensure long life.

Fig. 22 *Hand vices*

Pearl holder for holding pearls for drilling.

Pin chuck for holding small tools such as broaches and drills as well as wire components such as ear wires for cold operations. The hand vice is frequently wedged in the V of the bench pin for rigidity.

Engraver's block for holding flat items for engraving and similar operations.

Pliers are used for holding pieces for many cold operations particularly when forming wire and strip.

Tweezers are used for both hot and cold operations such as lifting paillons of solder or handling pivot pins.

Soldering tweezers typically are normally closed and open under pressure. Some method of insulating the handle is incorporated.

They may be mounted on adjustable stands, singly or in pairs.

Tongs are used to hold hot pieces of metal and containers such as crucibles. The ends may be straight or shaped to suit the piece to be held.

As well as commercial tools, simple tools can be made by the craftsman, one example being a tapered length of wood simply shaped with a knife on which rings are wedged for polishing.

Hollow rivets
A form of rivet also referred to as an eyelet and used for joining softer materials where a larger

Diag. 172 *Hollow rivet*

area of contact is required, without the associated heavy forming pressures of a solid rivet.

Hook clasp
A simple yet effective method of joining a necklace or chain. A typical design is shown in Diag. 173.

Diag. 173 *Hook clasp*

Horn mallet
A soft mallet made from a section of horn or antler and used for forming sheet metal, without deforming the surface, as occurs with a metal-headed hammer.

Hot dropping

Manufacturing techniques generally allow the craftsman to create predetermined shapes. In this process, although the craftsman has some control over the result, the shape is essentially randomly produced.

The technique is to drop small amounts of molten silver into water. The resultant shape will be influenced by the size of the piece of silver, its temperature, the height from which it is dropped and the temperature of the water.

Some kind of crucible is needed in which to melt the silver, and probably the most simple and efficient is a block of charcoal wired with iron binding wire to a metal tool with handle. A discarded kitchen tool such as a slice or ladle will serve. The top face of the charcoal must be slightly hollowed out – scraping with a knife blade is effective. Heavy-gauge iron wire should be used to secure it, and the wire must be kept well away from the hollow. A medium-sized soldering torch will provide sufficient heat.

The water should be in a metal container. Glass and plastic are not recommended. A depth of about 100mm to 150mm (4in to 6in) of water is needed.

Different shapes will result depending on the height above the water from which the molten silver falls. As a starting point, try 150mm (6in). The water container will need to be set at a height at which the melting can easily be handled, and a normal bench is too high.

As with any hot process, safety precautions must be taken to protect both the operator and the surroundings. What is appropriate must be left to the reader, but eyes, hands, face and the prevention of fire must be considered.

With the water container set at a convenient height, about 5 to 10 grams of clean, fluxed scrap silver are placed in the hollow of the charcoal block. The torch is then played on the silver until it melts.

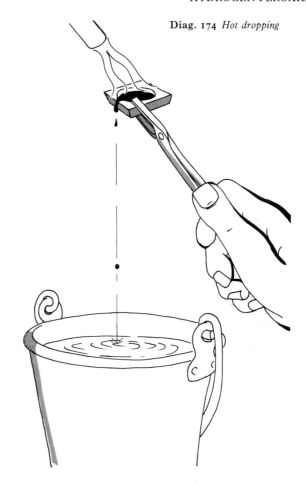

Diag. 174 *Hot dropping*

When it is 'spinning' the block is tipped, and some or all of the silver allowed to fall into the water. The silver will be cooled more quickly if ice blocks are put in the water.

The result will be small irregular shell-shaped pieces caused by the fracturing of hollow spheres. These pieces can be used singly or in combination. They can form an interesting backing to more formal centre pieces.

Similar effects can be obtained by forming wax for wax castings in the same way, but at lower temperatures.

Hotel dip

A deoxidising fluid used for cleaning the oxide from silver pieces. The piece is dipped in or brushed with the fluid and then washed in water.

Hydraulic press (*see also* Deep drawing)

A form of press using hydraulic force to apply pressure to die sets and other forming tools. Models vary from simple hand-pumped bench models to large, motorised, quick acting models. For jewellery work, pressure ranges from 2 ton to 10 ton are employed.

Hydrogen peroxide

A bleaching agent used to remove colour from such items as feathers and fibres.

I

Impressing

Designs can be impressed into soft materials with hard materials: for example simple or complex patterns into wet clay, steel punches into softer metal, wood and leather. A composite material of pewter or annealed copper foil backed by a soft straw board or similar resilient material can be easily impressed with simple burnishing tools. The backing can be permanent or temporary when the piece is subsequently back filled with resin or pitch.

Indenting

Flat metal sheet is made three-dimensional by indenting with punches and hammers. The processes used are described under *repoussé*, *chasing* and *punching*.

Indian ink

A solid black ink, water-resistant when dry, used for drawing. Indian ink may be applied with a pen or brush. It is suitable for lining out designs on paper and on varnished wood.

Ingot (*see also* Casting)

The simple form of slab in which metal is cast prior to being processed into other shapes and sections.

Ingot mould

A simple open mould for casting ingots primarily from recovered scrap. Various shapes are available for bar and sheet.

Injection wax (*see also* Casting)

Wax used to produce models for lost wax casting, where the wax is injected into a prepared mould and used for repetition castings.

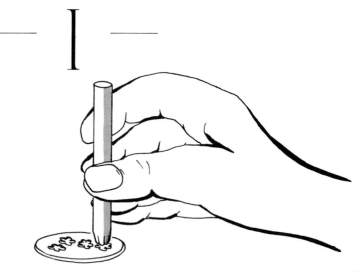

Diag. 175 *Impressing soft clay with a wooden tool*

Inlay

Many different types of materials can be inlaid into each other to produce contrasting patterns. Early examples of inlay are shell, bone and stone shaped wafers being set in pitch on a wooden base in Sumaria around 2500 BC. The ancient Egyptians used similar techniques for inlaying semi-precious stones into sheet gold frames.

The Anglo Saxons had perfected the inlaying of precious stones, particularly garnets, into precious metals by the seventh century.

In Japan the art of inlaying metal sheet and strip into a metal base was well developed in the early nineteenth century. Shell, mother of pearl and metal wire are inlaid directly into wood and bone in much ethnic work. Niello is used to contrast in silver. Marquetry and parquetry are forms of inlay.

Inlaying metal in metal – principal techniques

In its most simple yet effective form, small pieces of interlocking metal shapes, cut and filed to fit each other, are set using an epoxy resin with a backed frame. Individual pieces may be raised and chased and the metal parts can be contrasted with non-metal material. It is preferable to use a consistent gauge of metal to create a uniform surface for subsequent finishing. A further elaboration is to use a coloured resin which shows through pierced parts of some of the inlaid metal pieces, approaching the visual effects of enamel work.

The more traditional method of inlaying metal is the range of techniques so expertly practised in Japan.

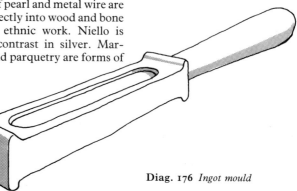

Diag. 176 *Ingot mould*

Wire is inlaid by cutting a groove with shaped chisels, forcing wire into the groove. The Japanese name is *Honzogan*. The groove is cut narrower than the diameter of the wire. The rectangular channel is then undercut outwards at the base of the groove and the top edges swaged up to allow the round wire to be forced in. The wire is then driven into the groove flowing into the undercut. This is done with a round-edged, flat-ended punch which also flattens the top of the wire and forces back the top edges of the base metal. The remaining raised hump is reduced to the background level by filing and eventually polishing, care being taken, if, for example, the inlay is softer than the base metal, not to polish the softer metal into a hollow.

As an alternative, the initial groove can be in an inverted V form made by sharp-ended cutting chisels leaving a raised edge in the centre of the channel which divides the lower part of the wire into the two side undercuts.

Small dots can easily be formed by driving short lengths of wire into plain drilled holes. Any projecting wire is cut off and finished flush. In contrast, small beads of metal can be set in plain holes which have been splayed out near the top with a round punch. After positioning, the bead is set with a hollow punch or graining tool.

Wire can be finished in a similar way by driving it in with a grooved punch leaving a raised ridge.

Sheet metal can be inlaid flush with the base metal in the *Hirazogan* process. An easily carved base metal such as shakudo or copper is preferable. The piece to be inlaid is made and the edges filed back at an angle of 20° to 30°. The position is marked lightly on the base material and, with a sharp flat chisel, a furrow is cut raising a burr wall. The inset is positioned against this burr and the burr checked for accuracy. This pro-

cess is continued until a complete wall is raised into which the piece fits accurately. The edge of the wall is trimmed to be level and clean. All this work is carried out with the base firmly anchored on a pitch bowl or block. If steel is being used then a magnetic chuck as used for engineering grinding operations is effective.

Having raised the wall, the centre area is cut down to a depth from the surface equal to the thickness of the insert. The insert is positioned in the recess and the raised wall of the base metal punched and burnished over to hold it in place. The surface is finished level.

Soft materials, such as the higher carat golds, can be inlaid on harder materials, such as steel, without the need to cut the recess, as in the *Hirazogan* process. The technique, practised in many countries, is called *Nunomezogan* in Japan. The process requires the surface of the base material to be cut with gravers or chisels, to provide a crisp toothed surface. This may be local to the inlay or cover the whole surface. The cutting is done at right angles to produce a field of crisp sharp-textured teeth. Onto this face the softer material is positioned and, with hammer and punch, driven onto the base. The inlay is finished by burnishing. Traditionally, the piece is lacquered black, creating a contrast with the inlay which is subsequently polished free of lacquer.

The author has developed a technique which uses a flat-ended sharp punch to indent a depression into the background material which rests on a substantial hard anvil. The same punch is used to pierce the inlay piece from thin contrasting material laid on a soft bed of paper or card. An exact fit is assured and the pieces may be joined by solder or adhesive depending on the materials being used.

Inlaying non-metals in metal

Inlaying non-metals in metal is achieved by the use of an adhesive and filler, such as when shell and stones are set in pitch on a metal base and frame, or by swaging and burnishing, as when setting stones.

Resins, both clear and coloured, are effective for inlay work. Virtually any item can be inlaid using resin. All that is required is a shallow container which holds the inlaid item and resin. It is important to remember that any attachments to the basic element must be attached before resin is inlaid, as subsequent heating can damage the resin. Clear casting polyester resins are effective and purpose-designed for this type of work. It is important to follow the makers' instructions. The frame itself may be fabricated from thin sheet, or standard stone collets may be used for small items. As with enamelling, sufficient resin must be used to allow the surface to be levelled and polished. More than one application of resin may be necessary.

Metal wire and shapes can be inlaid in other materials. Plastics, bone, horn, ivory, tortoise shell and wood are typical. Pique work, the inlaying of short lengths of wire endwise into predrilled holes, is carried out on all these materials.

Some horn, tortoise shell and plastics may be inlaid by pressing the heated metal inlay into the surface to create the recess, the inlay then being fixed with adhesive.

Intaglio

The creation of designs by *engraving* a surface. The design is cut down into the surface in the reverse of reliefs. The technique is used particularly to create designs on the surface of gemstones. Set as seals or in rings, intaglio designs create a low relief design when impressed into a soft surface.

Investing (*see also* Lost wax casting)

The process of surrounding a wax model with an investment material which, when dry and fired, forms the hollow into which metal is forced when casting.

For lost wax casting the investment is contained in a short tube of stainless steel, open both ends, called a flask. The model is set on a spure shape which may be of wax or shaped rubber. The model is fixed to the sprue base with a short length of wax sprue. A flask is selected which, when placed over the model, gives a clearance of 3mm ($\frac{1}{8}$in) minimum.

The investment can now be mixed. A specially formulated investment powder should be used. Plaster of Paris, although having very similar properties, is not suitable. The suppliers' instructions on ratio of water to investment must be followed, but as a guide, about 170ml to $\frac{1}{2}$kg (6fl.oz to 1lb) is required.

The water is measured into a household plastic mixing bowl, and the investment slowly poured in, all the time being stirred gently with a plastic or wooden spatula. Over-energetic mixing and pouring will induce air bubbles, which, if they eventually attach to the model, will cast as small spheres.

When fully mixed, the investment should have the consistency of thin cream. Bubbles should be encouraged to rise to the surface by lifting one side of the bowl and firmly hitting it on the table. Any bubbles that rise should be skimmed to one side. The investment can now be tipped slowly into a household jug with good pouring qualities and then poured into the flask in a fine even trickle (working around the model right to the top of the flask) and left to set.

Burning out is the next stage, and is carried out once the investment is fully set. Some casters recommend wetting a completely dried out investment before burning out, but I have never found this necessary.

Diag. 177 *Investing a flask*

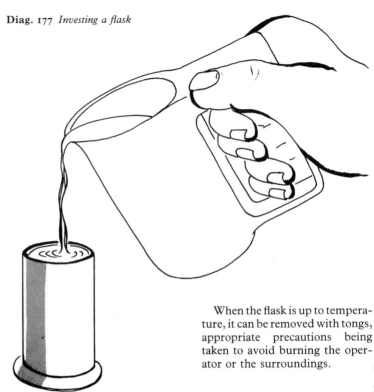

There are two stages to burning out. First the simple melting out of the wax where temperatures of only 120°C are required. This can be done in a domestic oven; a container must be provided into which the wax can drip. The collected wax should be disposed of. It will have lost many of the lighter fractions and thus upset the blend.

The second stage should be commenced when the casting machine is set up ready to take a hot flask.

The flask must be gradually raised to a temperature of about 750°C for from one to three hours, depending on the size of the flask. This process will fire the investment and drive out any wax residue.

Depending on the equipment, the removal of wax and full burn out can be one continuous process. A word of warning: burning out wax produces strong fumes, and it is essential to carry out the process in a well-ventilated place.

When the flask is up to temperature, it can be removed with tongs, appropriate precautions being taken to avoid burning the operator or the surroundings.

Investment

The porous material poured as a liquid around a wax model in the initial stages of lost wax casting. It has unique properties of porosity, fineness of surface, hardening at high temperature and ease of fracturing after casting. It should not be confused with plaster of Paris, which does not have all these properties.

Iron binding wire (*see also* Soldering jigs)

Fine iron wire used for temporary binding together of pieces. It is particularly useful when hard soldering as it does not easily solder. This quality can improve with repeated use. Silver parts held with iron binding wire should not be quenched in pickle with the wire still in place as this causes a copper deposit to form on the silver.

Iron binding wire is also used in binding found materials, such as feathers, in place.

Iron oxide

Results from the corrosion of iron and is used as an abrasive in the form of rouge.

Ivory

A general term applied to the tusks of animals, particularly elephants. Other animals, such as walrus, boar, and sperm whale, have teeth which are also a source of ivory.

J

Jeweller's bench (*see also* Bench)

The principal work place used by jewellers producing hand-made jewellery. Most operations can be performed seated at the bench. When the craftsman is thus seated, the top should be just under chest height. An acceptable bench height is 110cm (43in) with a stool 67cm (25in) high. If only a standard height bench is available, then a stool should be cut down accordingly.

Bench designs vary. In Europe, a jeweller's bench traditionally has a half round cut out providing wings on which to rest the arms, and to act as a support for a skin of leather which hangs underneath. In North America, a flat-fronted bench is more common, with adjustable arms projecting forward to rest on. The skin below the bench is traditionally to collect the filings (lemel) but primarily catches pieces that are accidentally dropped, and provides a convenient place to lay tools. Metal bins are available, half round in shape and with a sieve and cup to collect the lemel. Around the back are tool racks. The metal bin has the advantage over a skin in that it is resistant to hot metal. Straightforward benches are fitted with a shelf or pull-out tray, which serves the same purpose.

In the front is the bench pin. This wooden peg is used to rest the metal on during sawing, filing and most other operations. Much of the work is carried out on the bench pin. The pin, being wood,

Fig. 23 *Jeweller's bench*

eventually wears away and requires replacing. A variety of clamping methods are employed. Some systems incorporate a small anvil in the clamp and others allow triblets for rings and bracelets to be clamped to the bench.

Fig. 24 *Basic selection of tools*

Good lighting at the bench is essential. It should be of high intensity, such as that provided by a 100W reflector bulb, and capable of being accurately positioned. Adjustable lights are available which incorporate a magnifying lens, but their use and selection is a very personal choice by the craftsman.

Jig
Jigs or fixtures are arrangements of pins, pegs, brackets, supports, guides and bases used to position and hold components for operations such as soldering, drilling, machining, riveting and welding. The materials used depend on the operation but the range includes wood, brass, ceramic, carbon and steel.

Jigs are also used to form components from wire, section and sheet. A simple example would be an arrangement of pins used to form ear wires from wire.

Jig saw (*see also* Sawing)
A powered saw creating a similar vertical motion as a jeweller imparts when hand sawing with a jeweller's saw. Useful when sawing intricate shapes in heavy gauge sheet material, but limited to the heavier weight of a jeweller's saw blade and with less sensitivity than hand sawing. Some models with the blade held as part of a mechanical linkage system impart a fore and aft motion to the blade.

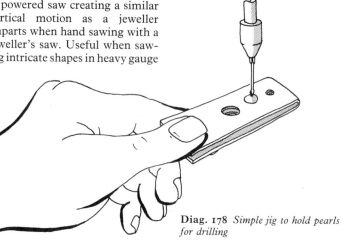

Diag. 178 *Simple jig to hold pearls for drilling*

Forged bracelet

*Jewellery in ceramic, embroidery and shells, and carved
shell cameo*

Found materials—necklace from seeds and nuts

Necklaces from coloured glass beads

Selection of stones, shell, pearls and beads

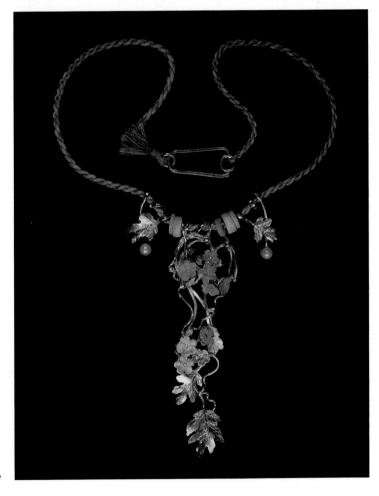

Silk cord, shell and forged silver necklace

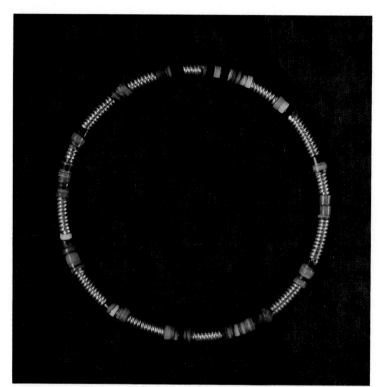

Shell beads and wound silver bangle

Tapered forged neck piece with fabrications

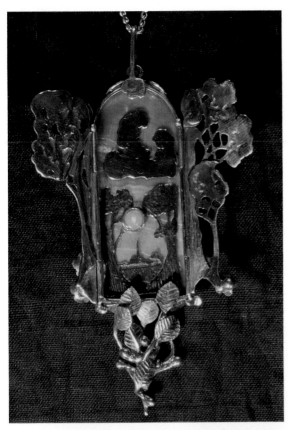

Shell-backed fabricated pendant with opening wings

Die stamped gold elements in soldered unit

Cuttlefish cast silver pendant

Enamelled copper inset in silver

Fabricating a ring

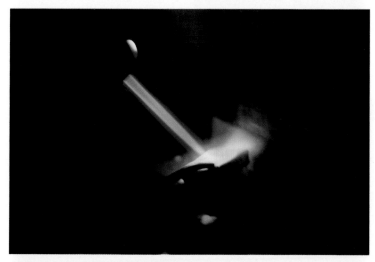

Melting and casting an ingot

Placing solder for making an ear ring

Stakes made from found materials

Fusing silver sheet and pieces of silver under a hot gas flame

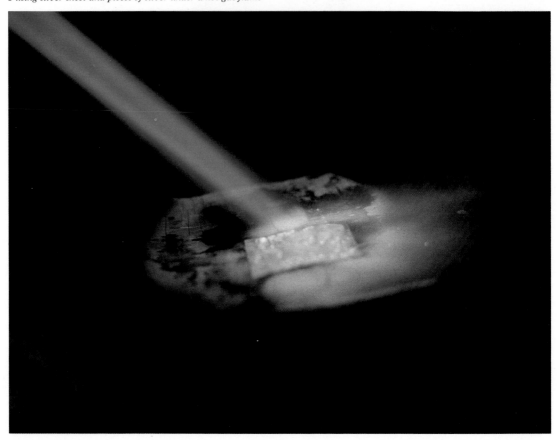

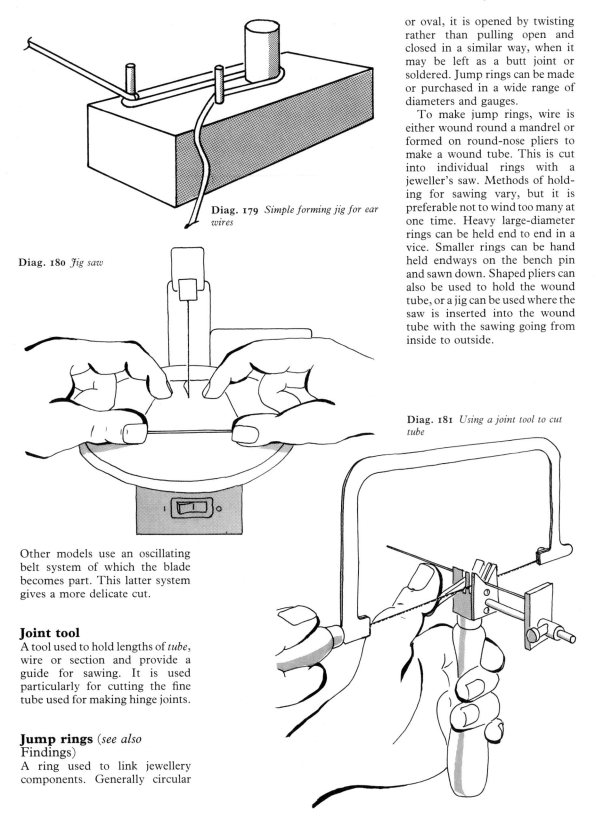

Diag. 179 *Simple forming jig for ear wires*

Diag. 180 *Jig saw*

Diag. 181 *Using a joint tool to cut tube*

or oval, it is opened by twisting rather than pulling open and closed in a similar way, when it may be left as a butt joint or soldered. Jump rings can be made or purchased in a wide range of diameters and gauges.

To make jump rings, wire is either wound round a mandrel or formed on round-nose pliers to make a wound tube. This is cut into individual rings with a jeweller's saw. Methods of holding for sawing vary, but it is preferable not to wind too many at one time. Heavy large-diameter rings can be held end to end in a vice. Smaller rings can be hand held endways on the bench pin and sawn down. Shaped pliers can also be used to hold the wound tube, or a jig can be used where the saw is inserted into the wound tube with the sawing going from inside to outside.

Other models use an oscillating belt system of which the blade becomes part. This latter system gives a more delicate cut.

Joint tool

A tool used to hold lengths of *tube*, wire or section and provide a guide for sawing. It is used particularly for cutting the fine tube used for making hinge joints.

Jump rings (*see also* Findings)

A ring used to link jewellery components. Generally circular

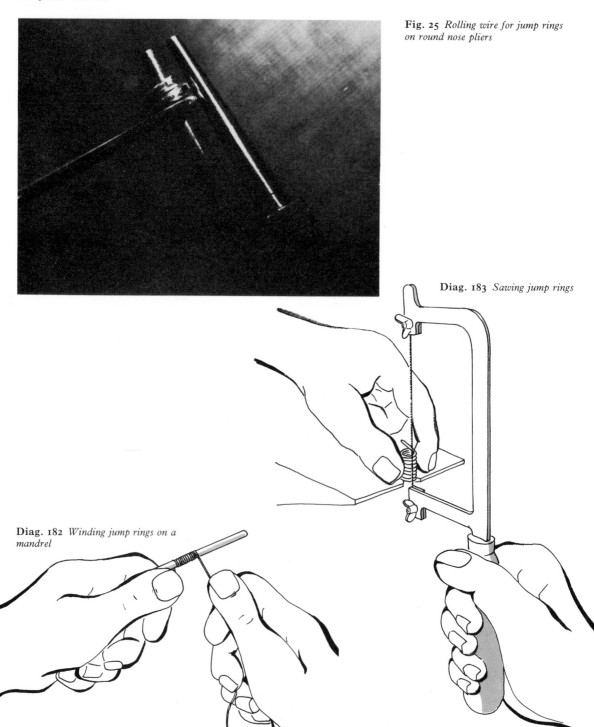

Fig. 25 *Rolling wire for jump rings on round nose pliers*

Diag. 183 *Sawing jump rings*

Diag. 182 *Winding jump rings on a mandrel*

K

Kiln

An enclosure capable of having its interior raised to temperatures between 900°C and 1300°C or above. Kilns are used in jewellery making for melting, enamelling and firing ceramic. Types of insulation and methods of heating vary, although for the jeweller electrical heating is convenient.

Knitting

The techniques of hand knitting can be applied to the construction of jewellery both by making complete pieces used flat or by joining flat pieces and stuffing them to create three-dimensional shapes. The range of materials is wide and includes lurex metal-like threads and nylon. It is possible to knit with fine precious metal wire. This can be made more flexible by using a twisted wire.

Knives

A general-purpose penknife for minor activities associated with jewellery making, and craft knives with replaceable blades for cutting work requiring a crisp sharp edge, are essential tools for the jeweller.

Knock-over plate

A simple type of forming tool used to raise an edge on sheet metal.

Making collets and generally raising edges on sheet can be done by repoussé and chasing or on forming stakes.

Where repeated shapes are needed, then a knock-over plate simplifies the process. In its most simple form it is a short length of round steel or brass bar, the diameter of which is the inside diameter of the collet, and a disc of metal cut to the diameter plus twice the required depth.

This is placed centrally over the end of the bar, and the pair clamped low down in a vice. It is preferable even with soft jaws to protect the piece with layers of self-adhesive tape on the vice jaws. This can be replaced as it wears.

With a well-polished hammer, the protruding sheet is tapped over, working opposite sides and planishing the smooth surface. The resulting edge will be a little uneven, but this is easily filed to shape. By filing, a round bar can be made oval for oval collets.

More elaborate shapes can be cut from thick plate and, provided any internal corner is not too sharp, it is possible to raise edges on quite complex shapes.

This technique is very advantageous for making shallow boxes and lockets, where the box and lid must be a perfect match.

A development of this technique is to produce an engraved design on the flat end of the knock-over plate. After the edge is raised, the box can be patterned. With the plate on a heavy anvil, hammering on the back, with a strip of lead or wad of paper between the hammer and the silver, will force the silver into the engraved design.

If this design is subsequently enamelled with transparent enamels, the raised design can be particularly effective. Alternatively, with deep engraving and raising, a psuedo-cloisonné effect can be achieved. There is much potential for the craftsman jeweller using this technique.

Returning to collets, an alternative technique is to drive the silver into a lead block with a shaped dopping punch. There are alternative materials to lead available, such as kirksite. These low melting point alloys can be poured into a shallow container and the punch set in while the alloy is still molten. Removing when the alloy has solidified produces a matching punch and die. Deep collets will tend to wrinkle and are best produced with a knock-over plate or with a simple punch and die.

L

Lace

Not generally suitable for jewellery, lace is frequently attached more permanently to clothing. Small pieces of lace can be incorporated behind glass in pendants and lockets.

Lacquering

Metals which are prone to oxidisation such as brass and copper can be protected. In Japan a technique is practised where a surface built up with many layers of lacquer is carved in fine detail. Lacquer can also be used as a resist in etching and to mask areas in selective plating.

Lacquers, generally cellulose-based, need a chemically clean base to ensure good adhesion. Application may be by dipping the whole piece and allowing it to drip dry or applying the lacquer with a wide soft brush. The piece is frequently heated before applying the lacquer or dried in a warm oven.

Dust-free, dry and well-ventilated conditions are essential to retain a smooth bloom-free surface. Lacquer can be reduced by the use of thinners.

Coloured lacquers conveniently sold as nail varnish can be used as a low cost alternative to enamel. Pearl finishes offer interesting possibilities and the application of a drop of acetone can cause dramatic surface changes creating swirls and stars. Simple cloisonné effects can be used by simply fixing round wires in place with clear lacquer.

Laminating

A number of effects can be obtained by laminating flat materials. In its most simple form, contrasting layers are built up and viewed edge on. Beads, made from coloured wooden discs of contrasting colour and tone, are one example.

The same techniques can be applied to metals, for example brass, copper and steel. Different materials can be laminated using epoxy adhesives. The effect of laminated metals can be exploited by cutting through the laminations. The Japanese mokume cane process consists in one form of building up a laminate of thin contrasting sheet. The sheets are soldered together ensuring that no air bubbles are trapped. The laminate is rolled to reduce the thickness to about 1mm, with appropriate annealing between rollings and after the final rolling. This laminate is then set on a lead or pitch base and a pattern of shallow, ½mm deep, indentations is made over the whole surface. The piece is removed from the base and the high spots filed level with the surface cutting through the contrasting layers. Finishing should be carried out with great care, as the softer materials will polish away more quickly than the harder ones.

A more geometrical pattern can be achieved using twisted wires. Contrasting metals are twisted in pairs and rolled to a square section and soldered. The resultant stick can be simply cut into short lengths and laid side by side, or coiled and bent into shapes which fit together in pattern. The pieces are soldered to a backing sheet or just simply to each other, and finally rolled and finished.

Laminating can also be used to create three-dimensional effects from sheet material. A scene can be built up as on a stage set with, say, three pieces of sheet pierced to form the foreground, middle distance and background. Designs like the contours on a map can be created in the same way. Interesting designs can be created by cutting a piece in two with an irregular cut and assembling them back together with a different alignment.

Lamp

The most elementary form of heating for soldering and melting is the spirit or oil lamp. The flame from a wick does not have sufficient heat, but if it is blown with a jet of air then soldering, annealing and limited melting is possible. The blowing pipe can be metal or, as in ancient Egypt, a straw or reed tipped with clay to prevent burning. Such lamps are still in use in India today.

Lap joints

A joint where one piece of material overlaps the piece to which it is fitted. The fixing of the two pieces may be by solder, welding, adhesive, rivets, screws or by driving the parts together in an interference fit as a pin in the hole.

The term is generally applied to flat sheets but is equally applicable to sections such as rods and tubes.

Diag. 184 *Simple lap joint*

Lapidary

The art of selecting, cutting, shaping and polishing stones.

Lapping

Lapping is the process of creating a flat polished surface on hard materials where sharp edges must be retained. Lapping differs from polishing in that lapping wheels have virtually no resilience compared with polishing wheels, which form around the shape being polished.

Lapping wheels are made from wood, copper, tin or perspex (plexiglass). The cutting or polishing compound is set into the surface of the lap and the cutting is carried out with a gentle supply of water to take away heat and waste material.

Lapping can also be carried out by hand although the process is slower and the equipment is minimal. A sheet of plate glass is dampened and sprinkled with the selected cutting compound. The face to be finished is moved by hand in a figure of eight over the surface. Initial cutting of a sawn face could be done with a coarse grit of, say, 220 size. When a uniform finish is obtained, the piece and the plate are thoroughly washed and a finer grit, say 400 size, is used followed by 600 grit, washing between the stages. The final polishing is done on a thick felt pad with dampened tin oxide or cerium oxide. Such a process is suitable for materials such as agates.

Lapping machine

A machine used to cut precise faces on preformed pieces of precious or semi-precious stone.

The essential part of a lapping machine is the rotating master lap. Size 200mm (7¾in) to 250mm (9¾in) in diameter, the master lap rotates in a horizontal plane in robust bearings. On top of the master lap sits the cutting lap which is charged with the cutting compound.

The preformed stone is set in a drop arm. This is held at predetermined angles either in the traditional jamb peg, a set of holes in a block or board assembly, or in a mechanical head equipped with scaled adjustable bearings. A water drip-feed cools and clears the waste material.

Lathework

Lathework or turning involves the use of a lathe, primarily to produce cylindrical parts, both solid and hollow.

Small lathes with working centres of around 20cm (8in) as used for general model making are suitable for turning jewellery components. Larger lathes are equally suitable and have the added advantage of enabling better tools to be manufactured.

For most operations, a self-centering three jaw chuck is convenient. Where regular use is made of ground stock, such as silver steel or other specific size round bar, then precision collets are preferable.

The principal operations are turning, facing, drilling, boring and parting off. The tools used for these operations are shown in the diagrams. The speed selected depends on the diameter of the piece and the material from which it is made. The instruction book provided with the lathe should give specific guidance. The following table will give a broad indication.

Diameter range	Steel (rpm)	Alloys (rpm)
Up to 10mm	1200	1500
19mm to 15mm	800	1500
15mm to 30mm	300	800

Tapered pieces can be turned using an angled cross slide or, on some lathes, with the piece held in a collet or chuck, by swivelling the complete headstock.

Small-diameter long pieces require supporting with a fixed or travelling steady.

When precision bores are required, these are most easily achieved by drilling and reaming. Cutting operations are improved by using a coolant on the tool.

Lead

A soft metal with a low melting temperature and high relative density, lead is very suitable as a yielding body on which to form sheet metal.

Fig. 26 *Metal turning lathe set up for drilling and turning a piece mounted in a three-jaw chuck*

Lead block

Lead, cast in the form of a block, is used as a resilient support for forming sheet metal items with punches and hammers.

Leather

Leather, with its strength, ability to be carved, stamped, braided, dyed and stitched, lends itself to use in jewellery.

Leather collar

Pitch bowls and engraving blocks are manufactured with a hemispherical base. This allows it to sit in a circular collar allowing the bowl or block to be set at any angle. Frequently made from leather but also from rope and felt.

Leg vice

A substantial vice with a rear leg which reaches to the floor, thus taking the force of any blows to pieces or supports in the vice.

Lemel

The waste material produced from such operations as *sawing*, *filing* and *drilling*. The term is primarily used to describe precious metal waste.

Lemel collecting

Lemel is the waste created by sawing, filing, scraping and other similar operations from precious metal working. Because of the cost of precious metals, the effort in recovering scraps is deemed economic.

All places where lemel can accumulate are searched, the most obvious being the bench tray. Some of these are equipped with a small container beneath a sieved entrance in the base of the tray. All sweepings from the floor after removal of obvious rubbish are bagged. Water systems are fitted with settlement tanks from which the heavier metals can be re-covered. Acids and plating solutions require treatment by experienced personnel. Buffing wheels can be burnt when the precious metal content will be collected from the ashes.

Bullion dealers will charge for melting and assay and will pay a percentage of daily fix for the recovered material.

Limoges (*see also* Enamelling)

A form of painted enamelling, particularly at Limoges in France from the twelfth century onwards. The area was also well known for champleve and other forms of enamelling. Enamels very finely ground, set with a binding agent and presented like water-colour pans, are available commercially.

Linishing

The process of removing burrs or finishing a surface with a moving surface of abrasive cloth such as emery or silicone carbide.

Linishing machines employ either a rotating disc of abrasive or an endless belt. Flat faces are shaped by setting the piece against the surface of the belt. The belt may hang free between the rollers, in which case the piece will be shaped with rounded edges and convex face. Alternatively, the belt is fitted with a metal backing plate over which the belt travels, presenting a non-resilient cutting face and creating a flat surface on the piece. For finishing edges the belt is set to run vertically and the piece rests on a machined metal face at right angles to the belt.

Belt widths range from 25mm to 150mm (1in to 6in) or greater.

Link (*see also* Chain making)

A chain is composed of links, each freely fitted to the next in a continuous length. The essential feature of a link is its ability to form a chain. This can most easily be achieved with a circular or oval loop of wire, joined or touching at the ends.

Liquid silver

Term used to describe very fine tubular beads used to make necklaces.

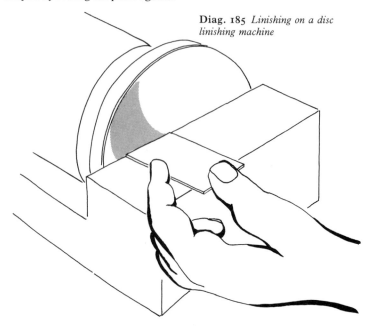

Diag. 185 *Linishing on a disc linishing machine*

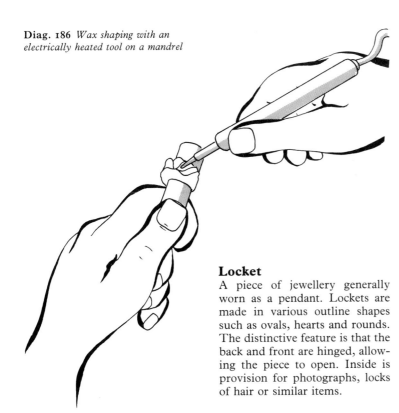

Diag. 186 *Wax shaping with an electrically heated tool on a mandrel*

Locket

A piece of jewellery generally worn as a pendant. Lockets are made in various outline shapes such as ovals, hearts and rounds. The distinctive feature is that the back and front are hinged, allowing the piece to open. Inside is provision for photographs, locks of hair or similar items.

Lost wax casting (*see also* Casting)

A casting process in which a wax model of the piece, having been surrounded by investment, is melted out, wasted, leaving a cavity in which the molten metal is forced.

Loupe

Eye-glass used for close inspection of small areas.

Low temperature solder
(*see also* Soft soldering)

This is most conveniently available already cored with a flux in wire form. Much heavier sticks can also be purchased which have no flux core and require a separate application of flux.

Lustre

An abrasive in block form used for dressing wheels.

Machine vice (*see also* Drilling)

Designs of machine vice vary, but in essence they have a low profile with precision jaws. They are used to hold material which is being machined.

The most general use for the jeweller is in drilling. A machine vice for use on a drilling machine will have both horizontal and vertical grooves to hold round pieces. As well as holding a piece true to the machine face, the use of a machine vice is an essential contribution to safety. It helps to protect the operator in instances such as when a drill seizes on a piece and the two try to rotate.

Other designs of machine vice are produced for milling and grinding operations in various weights.

Macramé

The art of knotting yarn to produce braids and decorative areas of material. Bracelets, thongs and neckpieces can be produced by macramé.

The flat knot is the basis of a simple braid. It consists of a series of left right, right left, knots across two central core threads, formed from the inside cords of a pair, each knotted over a holding cord or terminal ring.

It is possible to form the two core elements from metal wire encased in contrasting threads, giving both rigidity and contrast of colour and texture. Between the flat knots, beads can be threaded over the central core wires individually or as a pair.

Another simple knot is the double chain knot.

Solid areas of yarn can be produced by cording. This is achieved by using more pairs of threads and weaving them into a wide ribbon.

steel face. Box wood, hide, rubber and composition are some of the materials used in the construction of mallet heads.

Mandrel

A precision metal bar used to hold cutting and polishing tools and heads. Small mandrels are used to hold slitting saws in hand-held pendant drills. Larger versions will hold abrasive discs for use in large electric drills.

Diag. 188 *Marking out on a surface plate with a scribing block*

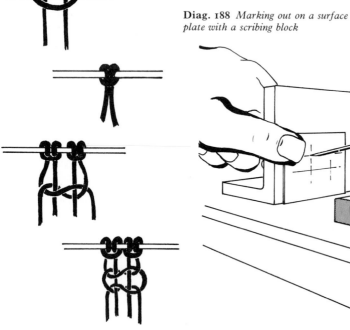

Diag. 187 *Basic macramé*

Maker's mark (*see also* Assay)

The part of a hallmark which identifies the maker. Marks generally comprise the initials of the maker within a frame. Maker's marks are defined and issued by an assay office.

Mallet

Of a similar form to hammers, mallets have the essential quality of a soft face rather than a hard

Marking out (*see also* Carbon transfer)

The process of putting lines and centres on material, principally metal, prior to cutting and drilling.

The work is carried out on a surface plate. An angle plate is used to hold the sheet metal piece vertical and to which the piece is held or clamped. Measurements are made from the surface of the plate. A calibrated height gauge or scribing block is used in conjunction with a steel rule or slip gauges. Using two datum edges by

MATERIALS FOR JEWELLERY

Metals		Minerals		Organic	Man-made
Precious	*Non-precious*	*Precious*	*Non-precious*		
Platinum	Copper	Diamond	Agates	Pearl	Plastics
Gold	Steel	Beryls	Amythest	Ivory	Resins
Silver	Aluminium	Corundeum	Carnelian	Bone	
	Aluminium alloys	Crysoberyl	Garnet	Feathers	
	Copper alloys	Alexandnite	Jade	Horn	
			Malachite	Coral	
			Onyx	Amber	
			Quartz	Wood	
			Obsidian		
			Sand		
			Soapstone		

rotating the plate, any complex shape can be marked out with precision. The lines can be scribed direct onto the metal surface or, to aid contrast, the metal can be coloured with engineer's blue or felt-pen giving greater contrast to the scribed line.

Materials for jewellery
Virtually any material can be formed into a piece of jewellery. The lists on p. 100 and below show the more popular types.

Found materials
Screws, nuts, nails and other fastenings
Used containers, tins and plastic
Bark
Modelling materials
Nuts, seeds, dried flowers

Matting punch
A hand-held punch with a textured face. It is used in *repoussé* work and stone setting.

Measuring
Free form jewellery and jewellery constructed from uniform elements such as beads require little or no measuring. All other pieces of jewellery require some element of measurement for both making and fitting.

Jewellery decorates the human form and dress. All such forms are different and require measuring to achieve acceptable fits between the piece and the person. The most well known and used measurement is that of finger size. In its most simple form it can be a selection of holes punched into a card. This method is particularly employed in catalogue selling, due to the low cost and ease of posting. More common is a set of rings in metal or plastic material in full or full and half sizes. These are available in two patterns: a narrow shank for normal rings and a wide shank, used particularly for wedding rings. Rings themselves are

Fig. 27 *Marking out equipment on a surface plate*

Fig. 28 *Ring gauges*

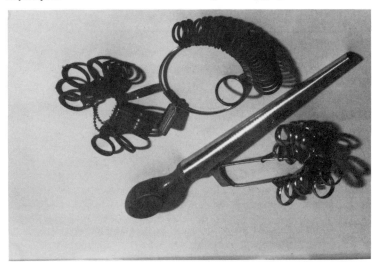

checked by sliding them on to a calibrated tapered mandrel, generally called a ring stick.

Rings are made round primarily for convenience of manufacture, although fingers can be nearer square than round. Ring gauges are made for square-shaped rings.

Wrists and hands, like fingers, vary in size and need to be measured for bangles and bracelets. Calibrated and adjustable flexible steel measuring bracelet gauges will indicate the length of material used. A narrow tailor's tape-measure will effectively measure the lengths of chains for neck and wrist, although using an actual chain can be more effective.

The precision measurement of stones, wire and sheet material is carried out by using both measuring instruments, such as micrometers and vernier gauges and by comparative methods using sheet metal gauges and stone gauges.

Melting (*see also* Casting)
Small amounts of precious metal can be melted with a torch in a square shallow fletcher, sited in a

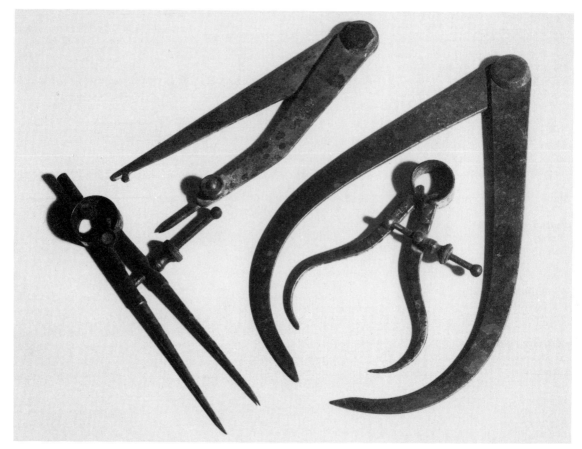

Fig. 29 *Dividers and callipers for marking out and comparing*

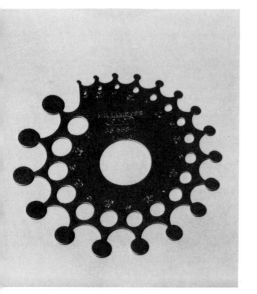

Fig. 30 *Gauge for stones and settings*

The Moe
Diamond
Weight
Calculator

Fig. 31 *Pocket diamond gauge set*

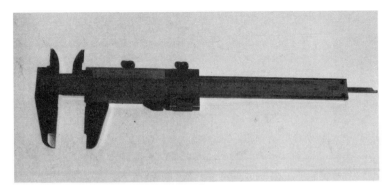

Fig. 32 *Vernier gauge*

Fig. 33 *Loupe and magnifying glass*

Metal oxides

Metal oxides are the principle source of colour in the making of enamels.

In the heating of metals, metal oxides produce colours and are the cause of fine stains in silver.

Methylated spirit (*see also* Spirit lamp)

Denatured ethyl alcohol with the addition of methyl alcohol and supplied dyed violet is sold in retail outlets. It is used as a fuel in spirit lamps, as a cleaning fluid and for making powdered *flux* into a slurry. It evaporates quickly.

Mica

A naturally occurring silicate. Mica has perfect cleavage, easily splitting into thin sheets. It will withstand high temperatures and is used for windows in kilns, insulation in heating elements and as a base for enamelling pierced work.

Micrometer (*see also* Measuring)

A measuring instrument comprising a precision calibrated screw

surround of fire bricks to conserve the heat. Larger amounts can be contained in a salamander-type crucible, using a more powerful torch and set on a more substantial brazing hearth. Alternatively, the crucible can be set in a kiln.

For regular melting of larger amounts of metal, a purpose-built heated crucible is employed.

During melting it is desirable to use a flux on the surface of the melt and to stir the material with a carbon or graphite stirring rod to ensure complete melting. It is necessary to raise the metal above the melting point to ensure there is a complete melting and enough heat to keep the metal fluid during the pouring. All heating should be carried out as quickly as possible.

The *dross* which forms on the surface is prevented from entering the mould when pouring with a graphite rod.

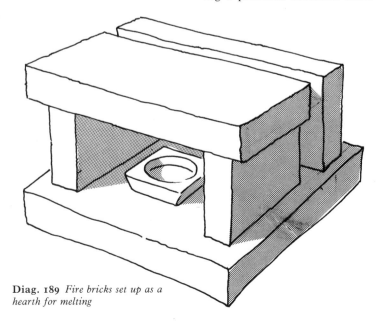

Diag. 189 *Fire bricks set up as a hearth for melting*

Fig. 34 *Fletchers and crucible*

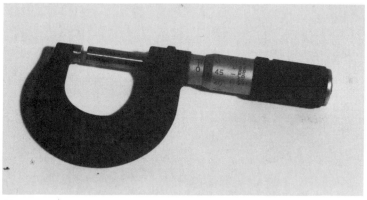

Fig. 35 *Micrometer*

Fig. 36 *Mill grain tools*

and barrel which moves in relation to an anvil. Micrometers allow accurate measurements of sheet, bar and stones. A suitable range for jewellery is 0 to 25mm (0–1in).

Microwelding

The formation of oxygen and hydrogen from water is used to produce a very high temperature yet very small flame. The addition of intermediary fluids conditions the flame.

The very high temperature enables fusion of metal in localised areas. Repairs of gem rings is also possible with minimal potential damage to the gem.

Mill grain tool

Available in various sizes, mill grain tools consist of a tiny rotating wheel set at the end of a rod which is fitted in a handle or hand chuck. The rotating wheel has a continuous pattern of indents around the edge. When the wheel is forced along the edge of a piece of sheet material, a series of small raised pips is formed. This is frequently carried out on the top edge of a collet for stone setting.

Millefiori

'A thousand flowers' is the literal translation of the Italian term used to describe the glass rods whose geometric coloured cross section, broken into very short lengths, is used in enamelling and glass work.

Milling

In milling, the rigidly held piece is passed into the cutting edges of a rotating milling cutter. Machines may have vertical, horizontal or universal arbours. Conventional engineering milling, primarily used in jewellery manufacture for the production of tools, is achieved using tool steel cutters. Diamond milling using diamond tools is carried out on specialised machinery capable of producing intricate patterns. The use of a diamond tool produces sharp, highly reflective cuts requiring no further finishing.

Mock up (*see also* Designing)

A model of a piece created from any easy to work material and used to create a three-dimensional construction to test visual or functional qualities.

Moh's scale

A scale of relative hardness of stones.

Moh's scale	Mineral type	Scratch test
1	Talc	
2	Gypsum	Finger nail
3	Calcite	Copper coin
4	Fluorite	Copper coin
5	Apatite	Penknife blade
6	Orthoclase	
7	Quartz	
8	Topaz	
9	Corundum	
10	Diamond	

Mokume gane

A Japanese term, literally translated as wood grain metal. The technique is used to produce a wide variety of colour contrasting surfaces similar to the effects of grain and burns in wood. For jewellery work, coloured golds, copper, silver, gilding metal and the specialised Japanese alloys shakudo and shibuichi are used.

A laminate is built up with contrasting sheets of metal. These are joined by soldering or heat bonding in which one of the metals is taken to its melting point. It is essential to ensure that no air bubbles are trapped between the layers. The laminate, which can contain up to 20 thin sheets, is reduced in thickness by rolling or forging. Very frequent annealing is essential to avoid cracking from work hardening. The pattern can be developed by various means, the most simple being to cut the laminate so that the piece is viewed on edge. The laminate can be sliced up and a larger area formed. Strips can be cut rolled and twisted then re-rolled. Such strips can be combined with other sections.

By indenting the surface and filing away the projections the multiple layers are revealed.

More geometrical patterns can be formed by placing identical pieces on a backing plate in arrangements similar to those used in wood inlay.

Mop

A rotating *polishing* pad made from cotton and other materials.

Mortar and pestle

The traditional equipment used to grind enamel. A rocking circular motion will effectively reduce *enamel* chips to powder.

Mosaic

Mosaic jewellery can be produced using a variety of material. Shell, glass, ceramic and seeds have all been used.

As the material thickness of the individual elements can vary, it is convenient to build the piece face down. A design is drawn in reverse and laid flat on the work top. The pieces are either positioned freely or constrained by a bezel. When the frame is filled, a bonding adhesive is poured over the back and levelled. When this is dry, the piece is removed and cleaned. A fine grouting is then rubbed into the joints and the face finished.

Moulding (*see also* Craft materials)

Plaster, clay, papier mâché, resins and other modelling materials can be shaped by moulding.

Diag. 190 *Mortar and pestle*

The essential qualities of a mould are that the cavity can be easily produced and that it will not adhere to the dry and set moulded component.

Plaster of Paris is a convenient material from which to make simple open top moulds. Plasticine is convenient for making the master.

Clay is best moulded by pressing it into the cavity and allowing the dry plaster to take out the water, thus drying the clay. Other moulding materials require the surface of the mould to be treated with a release agent. Wax polish with a silicone content applied to a warm mould and polished with a soft cloth is effective.

Moulding glass

Thin sheet glass can be moulded by allowing it to drape over or into a former when raised to its softening temperature in a kiln. The former in a refractory material is produced by making a master and creating a plaster mould in which the former is made. The process is most suitable for producing pieces of shaped glass with gentle curves.

Mouth blow pipes (see also Birmingham side light)

A high-intensity flame can be obtained from a simple wick or unvented gas flame by blowing a jet of air across it. This technique has been used since ancient times and is still in use in some countries today.

The short mouth piece is fitted into the end of a length of flexible rubber tube, which is attached to the blow pipe. Generally made of brass, the blow pipe is a tapered tube, bent at the narrow end, which terminates in a fine hole producing the air jet.

—N—

Nacre

The pearl surface in some *shells* and on *pearls*.

Native cut stones

Stones cut by hand, generally of the semi-precious type, where the size is variable, unlike the precision machine-cut stones.

Needle file (see also Files)

Also called Swiss files, they incorporate a handle and are available in various shapes and cuts.

Niello

The surface of silver can be decorated with a contrasting dark metallic finish, Niello. The process is similar to enamelling, and requires the design to be cut into the surface of the metal. A depth of about 0.5mm is satisfactory, but the metal should be sufficiently rigid not to bend easily, and not less than 1.5mm thick if small or well supported, or 2mm or more if self-supporting. The design can be engraved, etched or punched into the silver. It should be crisply executed with well-defined edges. As with enamelling, the silver must be cleaned by pickling, then washed and dried.

There are a number of formulae for Niello, all similar and based on silver, copper, lead and sulphur. Two parts silver, one part copper, half a part lead and six parts sulphur is typical, though the amount of sulphur is variable.

The preparation of Niello produces strong fumes from molten lead, copper and sulphur, and the need for adequate ventilation cannot be over-emphasised.

To prepare the Niello, melt the silver in a clean crucible and add the copper. When the two are molten, stir well with a graphite rod and add the lead. The sulphur should be stirred in and any dross forming on the surface removed. When all the ingredients are well mixed, the contents can be poured out on to an oiled sheet of steel or into a large ingot mould or dross box.

The lump of Niello is now prepared for application in the same way as enamel. Initially it is broken up into small pieces which can be prevented from flying about by wrapping the lump in a sheet of soft leather or heavy material. The resulting lumps can be further crushed by using a heavy hammer with a rocking motion on a steel slab. Final grinding is done with a ceramic mortar and pestle, followed by sieving through an 80-gauge sieve.

The ground material should be washed under running water by being placed in the bottom of a tall container with the water overflowing, carrying away the impurities. The material should be stirred during this washing. It is best stored in a bottle containing distilled or deionised water.

When needed, sufficient Niello should be dried and applied to the lightly fluxed depression with a spatula. As with enamel, it should be pressed well down into the depression and, if the area is large, slightly heaped up to compensate for sinking. Any Niello which is allowed to settle on the surface will adhere during firing and cause a blemish.

Firing can be done in an enamelling kiln or with a flame, provided the surface of Niello can be protected from the direct flame, either by the piece itself or with a thin sheet of iron. Firing with a flame has the advantage of access and vision. When the Niello starts to melt, it can be manipulated with a thin pointed poker bent over at the end, fitted with a wooden handle. When the cavity is filled evenly, the piece should be allowed to cool. The surface of the Niello is filed down, and then polished with the silver. Since it is a soft material, care must be taken if a polishing mop is used not to polish the Niello out of its cavity. Hand polishing is preferable.

Nippers
Cutting pliers.

Niter blueing (see also Blued metal)
Steel can be given a brilliant blue finish by first coating the surface in oil and then immersing it in a bath of molten potassium nitrate which is raised to a temperature of over 320°C. On achieving the desired colour, the piece is removed and quenched in water, dried and finally dipped in hot oil to preserve the finish.

An alternative method, but with less predictable results, is to heat the steel piece and quench it in thick oil.

Another alternative is simply to use a blueing chemical such as is sold for refurbishing shotgun barrels.

Nut – machine
The short length of hexagon bar with an axial female thread. Used with screws and bolts to hold pieces together, nuts can also be used for decorative elements as beads.

Nut – natural
Dried nuts can be threaded and used as beads. Some larger nuts have a hard white inner shell which can be carved like ivory.

Nylon mesh – net
In soft jewellery produced primarily with textiles and threads, nylon mesh can be incorporated to contain decorative elements to form part of the structure.

Ochre
A natural earth used wet and applied as a fine slurry to metal parts being soldered to keep selected areas, not required to be soldered, free from *solder*.

Oilstone (see also Sharpening tools)
Hard man-made or natural stone used, lubricated with oil, to sharpen cutting tools. The finest sharpening stone is Arkansas stone. Pale grey white in colour, it will produce a sharp keen edge. More coarse stones sometimes called India stones are based on carborundum.

Open mould casting (see also Casting)
Simple ingots and other basic shapes can be gravity cast in open moulds. Metal moulds are available for casting sheet and bars. For small amounts of metal, ingots can be cast in moulds carved into charcoal blocks.

Optician's screwdrivers
Graded screwdrivers of the flat blade type and covering the range of small screws used in the construction of spectacles and other instruments.

Oxide (see also Antique finish)
The combination of a chemical element with oxygen; rust on iron is one example. Oxides are used to create colour in enamels and glazes.

Oxidising (see also Antique finish)
The formation of oxides on the surface of metal.

Oxidising flame (see also Flame types)
A gas flame with an excess of oxygen. The flame is bright blue in colour. An excessive amount of oxygen will cause unwelcome oxidising of the surface of metal. The excess of oxygen is generally due to the use of compressed air giving a hotter and better-shaped flame.

P

Paillon (*see also* Soldering)
A small snippet of metal, generally solder.

Painted enamel (*see also* Enamel)
Enamel work using very finely ground enamel with a water miscible binder. The compound is applied with a brush, as in water-colour painting, and fired at a low temperature.

Painted paper
Paper stuck to shaped plywood, the surface of papier mâché, or simple folded or moulded paper, can be given colour with paint. Water-colour with a spray varnish finish is effective.

Painting
Paint is primarily used on low cost fashion jewellery as a substitute for enamel. It is also used with great effect on wooden jewellery. This can be particularly effective when used in contrast with large areas of natural wood.

Small plaques, often in ivory, with painted portraits, were particularly popular before being largely superseded by photographs.

When painting on wood, a clean line will be achieved by first varnishing the piece to seal the grain.

Paper
Sheet paper, folded using origami techniques, can be made into low cost jewellery in conjunction with base metal findings. Ear rings and brooches are most appropriate, due to the lack of resistance to wear of folded paper. Spraying with clear lacquer or varnish will

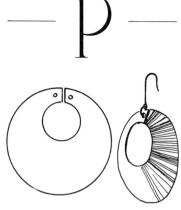

Diag. 191 *Paper shape formed into a three-dimensional shape*

improve the life of pieces formed from normal paper. Coated papers can be much more durable, with a useful life similar to plastics.

Paper spill
A rolled spill of paper folded over at the end is a useful tool for agitating small items being etched and brushing away bubbles in the acid bath.

Diag. 192 *Paper spill*

Papier mâché
Torn paper soaked in water with the addition of a water-soluble glue can be moulded to produce simple shapes such as beads and plaques. When completely dry, such pieces can be sanded, painted and varnished. Papier mâché is primarily used in making low cost short life jewellery. It can also be used as a backing material for supporting foil work in pewter.

Parallel jaw pliers
Pliers with jaws which move together and apart yet remain parallel.

Parcel gilt
Gold plating by electrolysis or mercury amalgam of metal parts, typically silver.

Patination
The surface quality of metal pieces. The term is used to describe both induced patination of metals which produce colour and texture, as well as the naturally occurring changes caused by use and age. Silver, for example, will collect a multitude of fine scratches which impart a unique surface. Copper and copper base alloys will darken naturally from a fresh pink to a rich olive brown.

The quality of patina will vary considerably, depending on the initial surface quality. Indentations created by hammering, engraving, stamping, wire brushing and fusing will hold a surface treatment in different ways, influencing the final effect.

Copper, brass and silver are particularly suitable for treating to produce colour changes to the surface.

The table opposite gives some indications of colours which can be achieved.

Pattern
The master shape used to work from or to create an impression in some casting processes. Patterns in sheet metal or plastic are used to mark out repeated shapes on sheet material.

Base metal	Treatment	Colour
Copper	Boil the piece in a solution containing between 20gm and 100gm of copper sulphate in 1 litre of water.	Dark purple/brown
Copper	Suspend the piece in a sealed container containing ammonia with 20gm/litre of sodium chloride so that the piece is exposed to vapour.	Green or blue green
Copper	Dip the piece in a hot solution of ammonium sulphide.	Black
Copper	Paint on a hot solution of 1.5gm of copper nitrate in 6 litres of water.	Green
Silver	Dip the piece suspended on string or silver wire in a hot solution made from 15mm cube of potassium sulphide in 1 litre of water.	Grey black
Silver	Use the above solution cold.	Golden yellow
Silver	Seal the piece in a steel box containing a knob of sulphur and heat the whole.	Blue
Silver	Dip the piece in a solution of three parts hydrochloric acid, one part iodine and one part water.	Green

Patterned punch

A patterned or textured punch in repoussé work is used to create a background texture after the basic forming process. Such punches can also be used to texture metal pieces produced by other methods.

Patterned rollers (see also Rolling)

Many rolling machines are equipped with extension drives to which can be fitted patterned rollers. These enable strip material to be given a repeat pattern. Such strip is suitable for bangles and rings.

Pave setting

An arrangement of stones set over an area leaving a minimum of the metal exposed. Claws or beading are used to set the stones.

Pearl drilling (see also Peg setting of pearls)

Cultured pearls, where the base is formed from shell, are easily drilled with normal engineering high-speed drills. Where the pearl is formed over other base materials, harder drills may be required.

The pearl must be securely held and a folded plate with a range of holes will secure the pearl.

Pebbles

Pebbles, such as can be collected on the beach or in gravel pits, can be polished by barrelling and incorporated in jewellery. Semi-precious pebbles, such as carnelian and agates, may also be sawn, ground and polished.

Peening

A form of riveting. The flat cross piece of a ball pein *hammer* is used to spread the rivet.

Peg cap

Used to mount half-drilled pearls and other stones. The peg cap is fixed to the stones with adhesive.

Peg setting of pearls

Pearls are set on pegs when they are fixed to a piece. The pearl is drilled from one side to three-quarters of the diameter. A peg is

Diag. 193 *Simple peg*

Diag. 194 *Peg with indentations*

Diag. 195 *Split peg with wedge*

soldered to a piece of sufficient strength to support the pearl, and it is convenient that a shallow seating is also provided for the pearl to sit in. This can be as an indentation of the piece or as a sheet metal cup.

With modern adhesives, it is no longer necessary to use split pegs and wedges as was previously employed, unless a water-soluble adhesive is used, and it is anticipated that the pearl will need to be removed.

It is necessary for the hole in the pearl to be larger than the pegs in the basic diameter. Using round-nose pliers, indentations set at right angles will give a secure keying for the pearl.

Epoxy resin will permanently bond the pearl to the peg. Care is required to avoid getting any of the adhesive on the surface of the pearl.

Pegwood

Softwood sticks used in finishing processes to hold abrasives. The abrasive, dry or damp, is placed in a shallow container and the open grain end of the wood dressed by pushing it into the abrasive. The loaded stick is worked over the area. The wood can be shaped to reach difficult corners.

Pendant

A form of jewellery where a decorative element is suspended on a chain or thong for wearing around the neck.

Pendant drill

A really indispensable tool for the jeweller. It consists of an electric motor, hung up high in the work area, from which extends a flexible drive shaft and hand piece with chuck. The speed of the motor is generally governed by foot control. The designs of chucks vary in the size of tool which can be held and the method of securing. Right angle hand pieces are also available.

Perspex (see also Plastics)

The trade name used to describe a brand of acrylic sheet. Acrylic sheet is a form of thermoplastic material.

Pewter embossing

Sheet pewter is soft and yields easily to burnishing from the back.

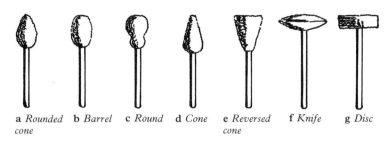

a *Rounded cone* b *Barrel* c *Round* d *Cone* e *Reversed cone* f *Knife* g *Disc*

Diag. 196 *Pendant drills – mounted felt*

Diag. 197 *Pendant drills – mounted grind stones*

a *Reversed cone* b *Small cone* c *Point* d *Ellipse* e *Small round* f *Large round* g *Cylinder*

Fig. 37 *Pendant drills*

The sequence of operation is similar to repoussé work, except that less force is necessary to shape the material.

Photo etching (see also Etching)

An etching process in which the resist is produced photograph-ically. Silver is particularly suitable. Two containers are needed, one containing the etching acid and one with clean cold water for washing tools and the etched piece. Etching should be carried out on a clean bench with a covering of newspaper to absorb any drips. A supply of paper handkerchiefs is also useful.

The acid needed is a 33 per cent solution of nitric acid in water. This is a very corrosive fluid and should be handled with care, taking particular precautions to protect hands and eyes. Always add the acid to the water. The water should not be hot as this will encourage spitting.

The cleaned surface of the silver is treated with a coating which hardens on exposure to ultraviolet light.

The design is laid out in black on white, the black being the part which will be left, while the white is etched away. A photograph is taken and the film developed. The negative is projected onto the sensitised surface. Screened images will interpret toning better. Where the light is transmitted through the negative, the coating will harden, forming the resist. The unhardened coating can be washed away, and the piece etched in the normal way. Kodak supply KRP-3 resist, KOR developer. An instruction book is also available for fuller details of the process. Anyone experienced in developing and printing film should have no difficulty.

The prepared piece of silver can now be slid into the acid, avoiding splashing. To handle the piece once in the acid, a simple home-made wooden slice and stick are effective, and can be washed in the water container.

The first sign of etching taking place will be a small build-up and stream of bubbles from the exposed silver. Any bubbles coming from a resist-covered area may indicate an area not adequately covered.

If the bubbles remain on the surface, the etching process has slowed. The bubbles should be tickled away with a feather or paper spill. The degree of etching can be felt with a wooden toothpick. Deep etching tends to eat away under the edge of the resist,

enlarging the etched part of the design. When it is deep enough, the piece is removed and washed to remove all trace of acid.

The resist can either be removed with spirit, or burnt away with a torch. The etching process can be repeated, giving three-dimensional effects as one design overlaps another.

Photoresists
Resists used in etching which harden under ultraviolet light. A solid or screened negative set over a photoresist-coated sheet will allow the ultraviolet light to harden it. The unhardened resist is washed off and the piece etched.

Pickle and pickling
The general term to describe the liquid used for cleaning flux and oxides from precious metal jewellery after processes involving heat.

The liquid is mainly acid-based, although less dangerous safety pickles are available based on alum and sodium hydrogen sulphate.

The piece to be cleaned is placed in a container capable of resisting the acid and of being heated, and covered in pickle. The pickle is raised to a temperature of about 65°C to 75°C. Higher temperatures, although very effective, produce vapour harmful to the operator. Whatever the temperature, adequate ventilation is essential.

Pyrex cooking ware, reserved for pickling use only, is very suitable for holding the pickle.

The time taken will depend on the degree of contamination, the strength and temperature of the acid. The acid used to make up the pickle is selected, depending on the metal being pickled. The following table lists suitable solutions.

Diag. 198 *Quenching in pickle*

Metal	Pickle solution By volumes
Silver	10% sulphuric acid 90% water
Gold	Between 10% and 20% nitric acid in water
Platinum	Between 10% and 20% hydrochloric acid in water
Copper	10% sulphuric acid 90% water

When mixing pickle *always add acid to water*

After pickling, the piece must be thoroughly washed in clean water or water with a pinch of neutralising bicarbonate of soda, and dried in boxwood sawdust, or on disposable tissues, or in warm air.

Piercing (*see also* Sawing)

The penetration of a sheet material. A number of methods are available depending on the effect required.

Drilling, drilling and sawing, punching and press tool work will produce a clean edge to the cut out. Piercing with round or shaped punches on to a resilient surface will form the edges over with a tear, which can be incorporated into a design.

The traditional hand method is, having marked out the shape, to drill a hole inside the shape, near

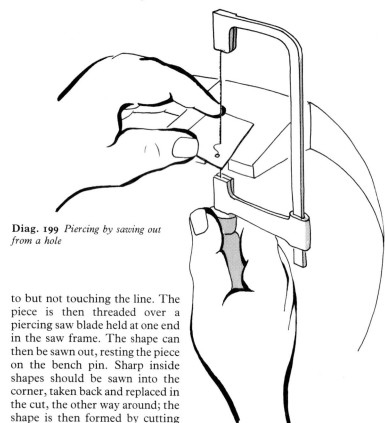

Diag. 199 *Piercing by sawing out from a hole*

to but not touching the line. The piece is then threaded over a piercing saw blade held at one end in the saw frame. The shape can then be sawn out, resting the piece on the bench pin. Sharp inside shapes should be sawn into the corner, taken back and replaced in the cut, the other way around; the shape is then formed by cutting out from the sharp corner.

Pile die

A two-part die for hand-forging blanks, creating a pattern on both sides. This design was used in ancient times for producing coins.

Pin chuck

A small hand-held chuck and handle used to hold tools and pieces. A range of sizes is available covering the range zero to 4.5mm.

Pin chucks are particularly useful for holding tools such as broaches and hand burrs, as well as pieces being worked, such as the straight wires of ear rings.

Pin protector

A cap made for fitting over the end of a simple pin. Generally constructed as a closed end tube of

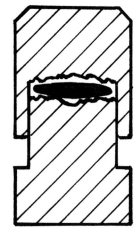

Diag. 200 *Section of a pile die for double-sided production from a blank*

metal into which is fitted a rubber or plastic tube with a fine centre hole. The end of the metal tube is swaged to retain the flexible tube.

Pins

Pins for fastening brooches and for separate use require care in the design and construction to ensure effective functioning.

Simple pins should be formed, when practical, to grip the material between the shank of the pin and the head. Twisting the shank, which is preferably of square section, after hard soldering will both provide resistance to slipping out and also work-harden it, making it more springy.

Brooch pins can be formed from the material of the brooch itself. Where the brooch construction has involved hard soldering, then the pin element will require to be work-hardened by twisting, forging and stretching.

With larger pieces, a pivoted pin (which need not be silver) is necessary. The essential parts are a pin, pivot block, pivot pin, stop and catch.

Pivot blocks, pins and catches can be purchased or made. The pin must spring from the stop, and must be strong and flexible. Steel

Diag. 201 *Pin chuck*

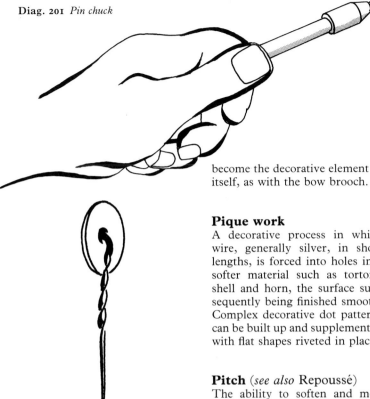

Diag. 202 *Simple pin*

or hard brass are popular materials.

The geometry is important, particularly the relationship between the hole in the pivot block and the height of the stop, which in combination determine the degree of spring.

One variation is to incorporate a formed spring coil around the pivot, which dispenses with the need for a stop.

For larger pieces, a double pin will give better support and reduce twisting. Flat-backed pieces tend to hang forward, which can be unattractive. A hollow-backed piece with the pin assembly inside will hang much better.

Brooches can be attached with decorative pins for use on coarse materials, as with the traditional penannular design, or the pin can become the decorative element in itself, as with the bow brooch.

Pique work

A decorative process in which wire, generally silver, in short lengths, is forced into holes in a softer material such as tortoise shell and horn, the surface subsequently being finished smooth. Complex decorative dot patterns can be built up and supplemented with flat shapes riveted in place.

Pitch (*see also* Repoussé)

The ability to soften and melt pitch at low temperatures, yet still allowing it to harden to give a firm support, presents many applications for jewellery making.

Mixed with tallow and plaster, it is used for repoussé work. Poured into tubes, it allows them to be bent, minimising kinking. Poured hot on a block of wood, it will hold a piece for engraving. Pitch has also been used to set stones in mosaic arrangements since ancient times.

Pitch bowl

A heavy cast metal bowl of hemispherical shape which sits in a circular collar and is filled with a pitch-based mixture. The collar allows the angle and rotation of the bowl and worked piece to be adjusted.

Pitch bowls are used to hold sheet metal pieces while they are being worked. Repoussé work and engraving are typical.

To hold a piece, the surface of the pitch is warmed and, when tacky, the piece is set gently on the surface. The pitch is allowed to cool and harden before being used.

Pivot drill

A small drill bit with the shank of a larger diameter than the bit. The bit part is either flat with two cutting edges or a fluted twist. The name derives from its use in clock-making for drilling pivot holes for gear wheel bearings.

Plaiting (*see also* Braid)

The combining of threads and cords by alternate overlapping. In its most simple form, three elements are joined together at one end. With the pieces under light tension, the left and then the right outside elements are bought to fill the gap between the other two.

Planishing

A finishing process using hammers to smooth the surface of raised and formed sheet metal. The face of the hammer must be polished and free from dirt. The piece being planished is supported on a metal dolly or stake. The action of the hammer is light with a slight sweeping action and the blows are spread uniformly all over the surface.

Planishing hammers have slightly convex faces and come in a variety of weights.

Plaster of Paris

Sold in powder form, plaster of Paris is made from baked gypsum finely ground. When mixed with water it forms a pourable slurry which quickly sets hard, although it takes much longer to dry out completely.

Plaster of Paris can be cast to make simple, low cost pieces of jewellery which can be coloured with water-based paints and finished with matt or gloss varnish.

Diag. 203 *Planishing*

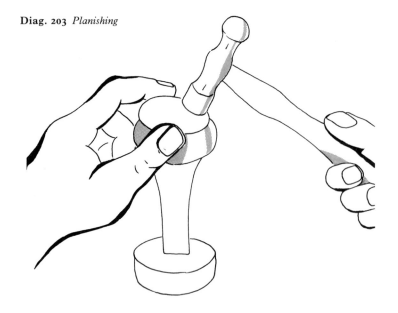

Mixing is best carried out in a plastic bowl. The bowl is half filled with water to which the plaster is added by sifting it evenly over the surface until it settles just above the level of the water. It can then be mixed either by hand or with a plastic spatula. The action should be side to side rather than stirring, which will introduce an excessive number of bubbles. If this occurs, the bubbles can be induced to rise to the surface by lifting and dropping one side of the bowl.

Do not dispose of unwanted plaster down the sink, as it will rapidly block the drains.

Plastic beads (*see also* Beads)

Plastic beads of the simple type cut from tube or individually moulded offer a low-cost method of introducing colour into jewellery. They can also be used to form the base of more elaborate beads with the addition of other materials.

Plastic sheet forming

Thermoplastic sheet can be form-ed by bending and stretching it when heated to a plastic condition. The two principal methods are by the use of formers and by vacuum forming using a suction pump.

Heating can be by simply placing the jigged piece of plastic in a domestic oven or low temperature kiln. Electric hot plates, fires and bands of electric elements can also be used. Hot air guns offer convenience and are effective in reaching particular areas.

To create a simple bend, one area of the sheet is clamped between pieces of plywood. The projecting plastic, particularly that area where the piece is to be bent, is heated and, using a block of wood, the projecting plastic is pushed down and held until it sets.

Container-shaped pieces can be formed by clamping the plastic sheet in a frame. When heated it can be stretched over a former. Greater definition is achieved in the corners by using a shaped frame which is pressed over the formed sheet after initial stretching.

By mounting the former on a vacuum table so that when the frame of plastic is lowered a seal is formed, greater detail and definition can be achieved. Polystyrene is a particularly suitable material for forming. Effective display stands can be formed from plastic sheet.

Plasticine

A reworkable putty-like material. It has a number of uses in jewellery making. It can be used to produce three-dimensional models of designs. Used as a fillet, it will seal a frame being filled with plaster or investment. Moulds can be made by pouring plaster over a plasticine master, and, as it takes impressions well, plasticine can be used to check the impression created by punches and other tools during their making.

Plastics

Plastics may be divided into three groups.

Thermoplastics

These plastics soften with heat. PVC, nylon, polystyrene and ABS are typical. These plastics are typically used for injection moulded components and for powder coating metal items.

Thermosetting plastics

Typically compression moulded, these plastics resist heat and will not easily soften with heat. Bakalite is typical of this group.

Resins

Either hot or cold curing resins may be produced by one or more components. Polyester and epoxy are typical.

Plating

A process of electrolysis in which the piece and an anode of the plated material are suspended in a fluid, the electrolyte. Passing an electric current through these three elements causes material from the anode to become deposited on the piece, the cathode.

Pleating

Alternate folding of thin material. An effective way of producing fan shapes when one side of a piece of pleated material is gathered together.

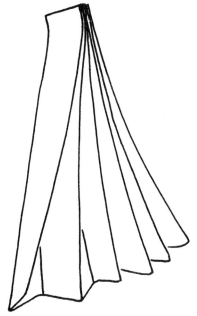

Diag. 204 *Pleating*

Pliers

In hand-made metal jewellery most of the forming and holding of the piece is done using pliers. These come in with a variety of shaped jaws. There is little variation in general design between the various makes other than quality of material and finish. The major alternatives are in the design of the joint. This is either a simple lap joint, as is used on scissors and shears, or the more rigid box joint.

Unless distressing of the surface is desired, all pliers should have smooth jaws which should be kept polished.

Plique a jour enamel (*see also* Enamelling)

The most dramatic form of enamelling, it is similar to cloisonné except that there is no backing and all the beauty of transparent and

Diag. 205 *Pliers*

a *Side cutting*

b *Bending*

c *End cutting*

d *Forming*

e *Holding*

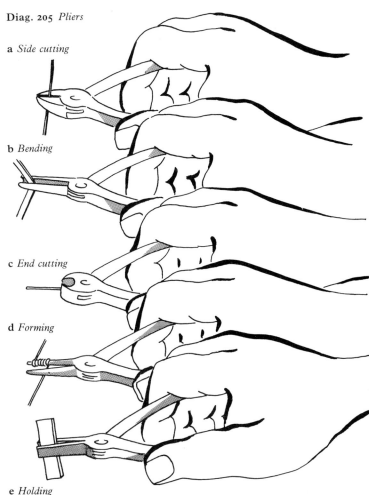

Diag. 206 *Types of jaw sections*

translucent enamels is revealed when light shines through.

Plywood

A laminated material from two ply upwards consisting of glued layers of wood veneer. Its use in jewellery making is primarily limited to painted wood pieces with metal findings. Outline shapes of animals and everyday objects varnished and painted or simply faced with paper and coloured with felt-tip pens or water-colour paints make good jewellery for young children.

Polishing

The alternative to burnishing is polishing with progressively finer

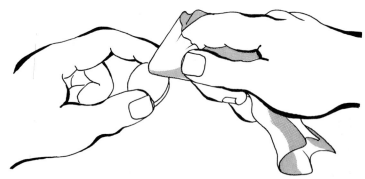

Diag. 207 *Finish polishing by hand
with a cloth*

polishing abrasives. In practice,
two grades are normally satisfactory: initial polishing with lustre
and final polishing with rouge.
Lustre and rouge are available
mixed with a bonding agent in
stick form. They are used to dress
or coat the polishing surface.

Hand polishing

Flat surfaces can be polished by
stretching several layers of linen
over a smooth flat face, which is
dressed with the polishing
medium. The material is held
down firmly and moved in a figure
of eight over the surface. More
complex shapes are polished by
covering sections of wood with
linen or felt, as is done with
abrasive papers. For polishing the
inside of through holes, stretched
cotton threads dressed with the
polishing medium are threaded
through the hole and the piece
moved up and down.

It is absolutely critical to the
final polishing that all traces of
lustre are removed before rouge is
used. Any carry-over will prevent
a good final finish.

Washing the piece, and your
hands, in hot detergent and water
should be sufficient to remove the
polish.

Mechanical polishing

Hand polishing is very time-
consuming, and the use of rotating
polishing mops will produce an
acceptable finish more quickly. I
would also suggest that in final

finishing with rouge there is a
burnishing action, due to the
speed of the mop, not easily
achieved by hand.

The wheel is dressed by holding
the stick of lustre or rouge, one for
each wheel, with the machine at a
mid-speed; an even coating will
result. The piece to be polished is
held in a similar way, and moved
around so that all faces are
polished. Small mops for working
inside confined spaces and powered by a pendant drill are used in
a similar way.

After the initial polish, the
darker grey streaks of fire stain
may appear. If these do not polish
out quickly, it is necessary to go
back to fine abrasive cloths or
water of Ayr stone.

Small pieces of flux still remaining prior to polishing will not be
removed as quickly as the metal,
and if the attempt is made to
remove them by polishing, they
will remain as high spots.

Silver is a soft metal, and after
rouge polishing should be handled
with gloved hands. A final polish
with a soft treated cloth will bring
out the brilliance. It is, however,
only after all the minute scratches
of use produce the classic patina of
silver that the full qualities of the
metal are revealed.

Polishing cloth

Cloths for final polishing contain
a finely dispersed polishing
medium and are used to bring out
the final finish on precious metal
pieces.

Polyester resin (*see also*
Plastics)

A two-part resin suitable for
producing simple cold cast
shapes, encapsulation and infilling. It is water clear but can easily
be coloured in a wide range of tints
and shades both translucent, opalescent and solid.

The maker's instructions must
be followed, but typically a measured amount, as specified, of two
liquids are mixed together and
used immediately. Hardening will
start to take place quickly and only
enough material should be mixed
for the work in hand.

The set piece can be sawn,
drilled, filed and polished, much
as with other rigid plastic materials.

Polystyrene

A plastics material generally formed into components by injection
moulding. In its expanded form it
becomes a very lightweight material, easily shaped by hot knife
and wire tools. Because of its low
density it is suitable for making
masters which, when coated with
conductive paints, can be electroplated or electroformed. The
expanded polystyrene core is
easily eliminated by heat.

Polystyrene cement

A cement used for bonding polystyrene but not generally suitable
for expanded polystyrene.

Polythene

A lightweight thermoplastic material of milky or watery transpar-
ency.

Pounce bag

A small draw-string bag made
from layers of close woven cotton
cloth and filled with powdered
chalk. It is used when marking out
sheet metal to dust a wax surface,
improving the contrast between a
scratched line and the general
surface.

Precious metal testing

Simple testing, generally suitable for craftsmen, can be carried out with a touch stone and a selection of acids. The acids are formulated to react with precious metals in such a way as to determine approximately a minimum content of gold, silver and platinum.

A more precise method is by cupellation, as used by assay offices.

Precious metals

Gold, gold alloys, silver and platinum are defined as precious metals and, with certain exceptions, are required to be *hall-marked* before being sold and described as gold, silver or platinum.

Press

Presses are pieces of machinery designed to create a downward force on a tool which acts on the material. Designs of press vary, depending on the function to be performed.

Fly press

A weighted cross bar rotates in a horizontal plane to drive the ram down via a screw. Fly presses are very versatile and can perform most pressing operations used in jewellery making.

Drop hammer press

A mechanical version of the blacksmith's forging hammer, this is used to impart a heavy impact blow in operations such as forging and coining.

Hydraulic press

The ram is forced down by hydraulic pressure from either a motor or hand pump. Slower in operation but very suitable for drawing operations.

Arbour press

The ram is cut with a rack and driven down by a pinion. Suitable for light forming, punching and such operations as broaching and light riveting.

Toggle press

A lever-operated toggle drives the ram. Pressure increases dramatically in the last stages of the stroke. Suitable for most jewellery work.

Pneumatic press

Powered by a source of compressed air and with a wide range of pressures, they are very suitable for all jewellery operations, being generally adjustable in stroke length and speed.

Press fit

Also called an interference fit, this is a method of joining two pieces of material, generally where one is a pin or shaft and the other has a hole in it. The sizes are critical and require precise measurement and manufacture. It is good practice to achieve the hole size by reaming, and turning or grinding the pin to a measured size very slightly larger. The actual difference depends on size and material. Forcing the pin in the hole can produce a permanent bond.

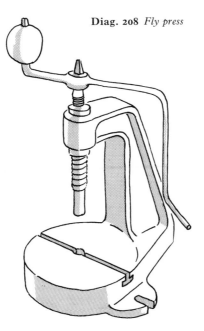

Diag. 208 *Fly press*

Fig. 38 *Hand press tool*

Fig. 39 *Arbour press*

Pressure die casting (*see also* Casting)

Used in the production of costume jewellery, pressure die castings are produced in expensive matching steel tools. Zinc alloys are popular materials for casting, and pieces are generally plated to give a more acceptable finish.

Printing

Printing techniques can be employed to produce repeat patterns on most materials. Custom-made rubber stamps can be supplied by specialist companies at low cost from simple art work.

Using printing techniques with a resist will enable complex repeat patterns for etching to be produced. As an example, a simple repeat swirl, star or similar shape is capable of producing infinite arrangements. These are more difficult to produce by hand painting.

Profile die

Also called a *draw swage*, it consists of a small metal frame into which profiled, two-part dies are fitted. The lower die sits at the bottom of the frame and a screw adjustment adjusts the top die down towards it.

Used in a similar way to a draw plate, the profile die is used for shaping narrow strips of sheet into shaped sections.

Prong

A slender projecting metal element generally used as part of a setting to position and hold a stone.

Protractor

A measuring device for setting and measuring angles.

Pumice

A coarse abrasive used in the early finishing stages of metal jewellery.

Punch and die

A form of tool used to create holes and or shapes in and from sheet materials. The punch and die may be housed in a die set, which keeps the two elements aligned, or set and aligned separately in the press. Some simple forms of punch and die are available for round holes and blanks which cut with the force of a hammer blow.

Punches and dies are primarily used in the commercial production of jewellery, although a simplified system, the RT Blank-ing system, puts the production of a punch and die system within the capability of the jeweller. Full details of this system are contained in report No. 12E/1 published by the Worshipful Company of Goldsmiths, London.

Punching

The process of driving a punch into or through material. Punching can be used to indent the surface, create holes and produce punched out blanks. The design of the punch will vary depending on the job to be performed, although different functions can be carried out with the same punch. The type of support used will also vary the effect of the punch.

Probably the most widely used punch is the centre punch, the working end of which is conical. Its principal use is to indent the material where a hole is to be drilled, creating a small hollow to

Diag. 209 *Punch and die*

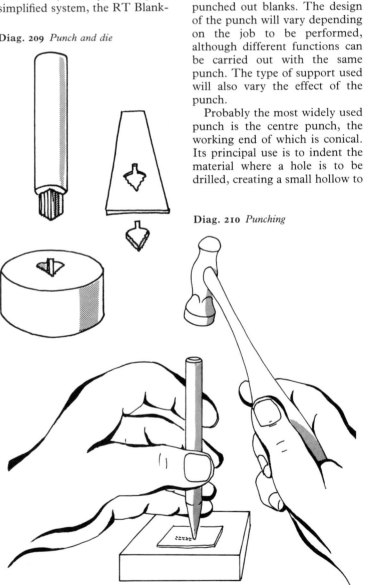

Diag. 210 *Punching*

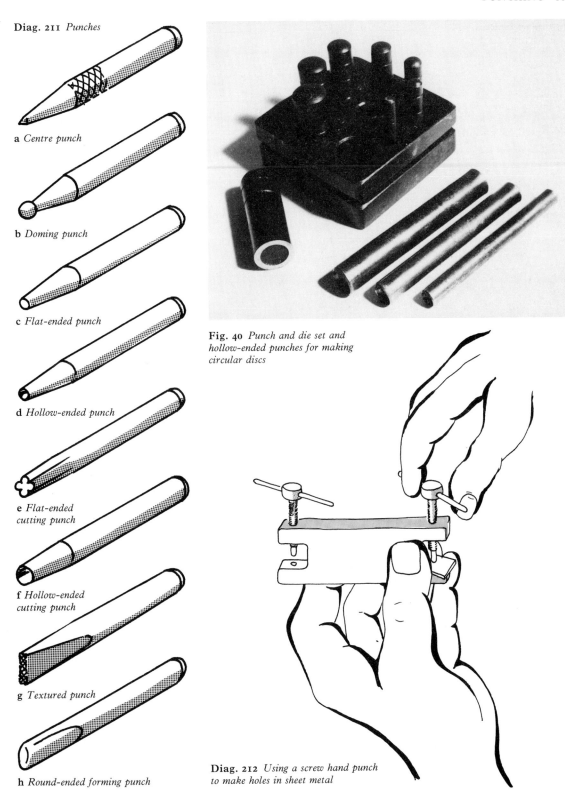

Diag. 211 *Punches*

a *Centre punch*

b *Doming punch*

c *Flat-ended punch*

d *Hollow-ended punch*

e *Flat-ended cutting punch*

f *Hollow-ended cutting punch*

g *Textured punch*

h *Round-ended forming punch*

Fig. 40 *Punch and die set and hollow-ended punches for making circular discs*

Diag. 212 *Using a screw hand punch to make holes in sheet metal*

Diag. 213 *Dome punch and block*

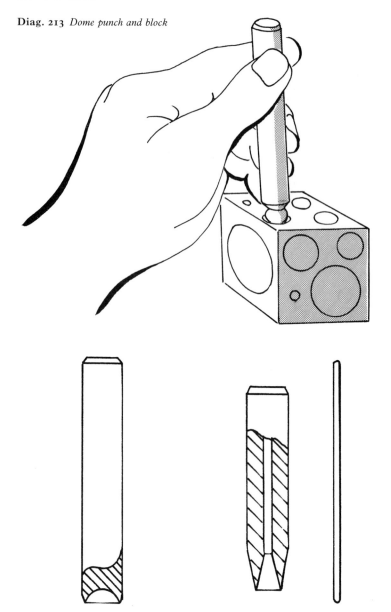

Diag. 214 *Standard sharp edge cutting punch*

Diag. 215 *Hollow sharp edge cutting punch with rod to assist in pushing out cut piece*

unpredictably ragged. If a distorted hole is part of the design, then shaping the point to a sharp-edged pyramid will, on piercing, raise small triangular flaps.

It is possible to use these flaps to hold to another piece of material, with a hole in it which fits over the flaps. The flaps are then formed down, holding the pieces together.

The same punch with a hemispherical end will create domed indentations.

Surface decoration and forming of sheet metal is described under the process of repoussé.

Hollow punches with sharp cutting edges can be used to make holes in thin sheet metal and other materials softer than the punch material. More frequently, such punches are used to produce blanks. Round punches are available and these can be modified by forging to create other shapes. Alternatively, shaped cutting punches can be made from steel bar. This work is intricate and time-consuming and an alternative is to use sharp-edged flat-ended punches.

Pushers

Pushers are used in *stone setting* for deforming the claws (prongs) or the bezel onto a stone.

Bezel pushers have flat or very slightly curved end faces. Prong pushers have a groove to prevent slipping. Both types consist of a short shank fitted into a graver or file type handle.

Putty resin (*see also* Plastics)

A two-part epoxy-based material. It is supplied in two sticks which, when kneaded together, create a chemical reaction causing the material to set hard. Putty resin can be used to form simple shapes or for back filling repoussé and other hollow pieces.

guide the drill. It can also be used decoratively, singly or in repetition to create patterns. For simple indenting, the work is supported on a solid non-yielding surface. Deeper indentations are achieved in sheet metal by supporting the material on a resilient surface such as a lead cake, pitch bowl or pad of cardboard. The

simple centre punch is driven into the material with a hammer. Spring-loaded self-driving punches can be quicker to use one-handed.

The use of heavier blows on a resilient surface will drive the punch right through thin material. The edge of the hole will be

PVC

Polyvinylchloride. A plastics material of the thermoplastic type. It can be supplied both hard and flexible.

PVC sleeving

Small-diameter plastic tube manufactured for insulating electrical wiring. It is particularly effective in low-cost jewellery because of the wide range of vivid colours available. It is easily cut with a knife and can be stretched with the application of heat.

One variation of electrical insulating sleeving will shrink with the application of heat, gripping any irregular shape inside. This should have application in jewellery making.

Skeining, weaving and macramé techniques are all possible with this material.

R

Rabbit's foot brush

A brush made from a rabbit's foot and used for dusting lemel and other powders because of its clean action.

Raising

A process more applicable to silver smithing but with some limited application to jewellery. The process is used to raise a hollow form from a disc.

The process is started by doming the disc in a doming block, lead cake or sandbag. Radial creases are then formed from a central area which will become the base. This bending process starts raising the edge away from the base. With a raising hammer, and resting the piece on a cylindrical mandrel, the creases are compressed. This thickens and extends the material. After annealing, the process is repeated using, where necessary, different mandrels to help create the shape. The hammered surface may be left or planished smooth.

Raising and reducing gold quality (see also Assay)

Gold used in jewellery making is alloyed with other metals to reduce the amount of gold employed and improve some qualities such as strength.

Diag. 216 *Raising*

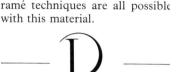

On occasions, it is necessary to reduce the gold content to a known carat value. It is convenient to weigh the piece and, knowing the carat rating, the value of gold content can be calculated. This can be stated in the form: a piece of 9ct. 2gm non-gold material + 0.75gm gold = 2.75gm 9ct gold. By adding non-gold material or gold material to the two component parts, the total weight can be recalculated and, knowing the gold content, the carat value of the total piece can be calculated.

Q

Quenching (see also Hardening metals)

In the hardening of metal, sudden cooling is necessary after heating. Quenching baths must be substantial with adequate capacity. Galvanised steel tanks are satisfactory.

Rasp

A coarse file used for heavy removal of material and surface roughing on wood, leather and similar materials.

Reamers and reaming

Holes can be enlarged and accurately sized with reamers. There are two principal types: tapered reamers for enlarging holes, particularly in sheet metal, and parallel reamers for producing a hole of specific size and with a good finish.

Engineering reamers with ground and shaped cutting faces are available in both forms. For very small holes, jeweller's reamers are used. These are typically four or five sided and tapered. A wide range of sizes is available.

Reamers can be used dry, although a light cutting fluid is preferable. All reaming requires a pilot hole just smaller than the finished hole. Reaming requires a slow cutting speed and, for jewellery work, is best done by hand, holding the reamer in a pin chuck or, for larger reamers, a tap holder with V jaws.

Refractometer

An instrument for identifying precious stones by measuring refractive index. Transparent material will refract or bend a beam of light, depending on the materials refractive index. The refractive index of gemstones generally decreases with decreasing hardness.

Gem-stone	Refractive index	Hard-ness
Diamond	2.42	10
Corundum	1.77	9
Beryl	1.58	7.75
Quartz	1.55	7
Obsidian	1.5	6

Fig. 41 *Milling cutters, centre drills and reamers*

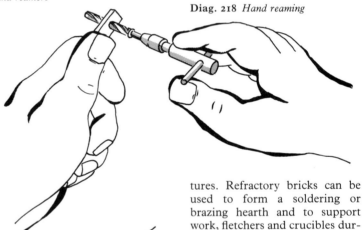

Diag. 218 *Hand reaming*

Diag. 217 *Pin chuck holding reamer for enlarging holes*

tures. Refractory bricks can be used to form a soldering or brazing hearth and to support work, fletchers and crucibles during heating operations.

Refractory metals

Metals with high melting points. Those used in making jewellery are chosen because of the ability to induce a wide range of bright colours on the surface.

Their prime disadvantage is the inability to employ many of the common methods of fabrication. Joining is only practical by riveting and adhesives. They can be sawn and drilled but not bent or swaged with any success.

Titanium, niobian and tantalum are those suitable for jewellery.

Refractory bricks (see also Brazing hearth)

Bricks made of refractory material and hence capable of resisting suddenly-applied high tempera-

Repairing jewellery

There can be no simple guide to repairing jewellery. Jewellery wears out, sometimes beyond repair. Pieces are abused and some older pieces have been modified or repaired in the past. The following notes are offered as a checklist.

1 Examine the piece to determine its general condition and construction.

2 Determine the materials used.

3 Check the type and settings of any stones.

4 Check the condition of any chain or links by exposing to view the touching faces.

5 Check the condition of any non-soldered joints such as open jump rings.

6 Clean the piece

7 Determine the nature of the necessary repair, if this is possible.

8 Advise the customer of the proposed action, the risk, the anticipated result and the cost.

9 Proceed with the customer's agreement.

Repoussé and chasing

The initial stage in shaping sheet metal is repoussé, the second stage being chasing. Correctly, repoussé is the technique of pushing the design forward from the back of the sheet. Chasing is the crisping up of this design from the front.

Repoussé work changes the level of the surfaces of sheet. It is more associated with silver smithing, but has its application to jewellery. It is necessary to use soft or annealed sheet for repoussé work, as the metal will work harden. This might cause the piece to split. If the degree of forming is extensive, then annealing at intervals will prevent splitting.

Before starting, the design must be established and, since it is raised, it is helpful to do this in three dimensions. After initial sketches, a thick layer of modelling clay (plasticine) or wax rolled out on stiff card can be modelled into the design. This is used for visual reference during forming. As the design is formed from the back, and therefore in reverse, it can be helpful to take a plaster cast of the model for visual reference, to reduce mental gyrations.

Diag. 219 *Matting punch*

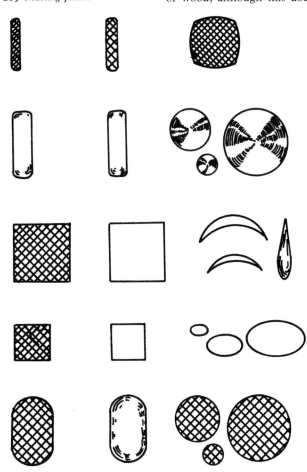

Diag. 220 *Repoussé and matting punches, working faces textured flat and rounded*

To form the sheet, the two principal requirements are suitable punches or formers and a support.

Supports

Pitch blended with tallow and plaster and contained in a pitch bowl will support the sheet, keep it from sliding about, and yet yield to the indentations of punches. Pitch bowls of cast iron are hemispherical in shape to contain the pitch and sit in rings of leather or rope, allowing easy positioning. The total weight gives solid resistance to the hammer blows. For very small work, the blended pitch can simply be melted onto a block of wood, although this does not give the same freedom of movement.

The exact proportions of pitch, tallow and plaster depend on the hardness required, and the working temperature in the workshop. More tallow makes a softer support. A good basic mix is six parts pitch, six parts plaster of Paris (dental plaster), one part tallow. The pitch can be Swedish or Burgundy, and linseed oil may be substituted for tallow.

The mixture is prepared by slowly melting the pitch in an old saucepan, avoiding burning. When this is fully melted, the plaster is stirred in thoroughly. Finally, using a clean stick, the tallow or linseed oil is added and mixed in. When thoroughly mixed, it is poured into the pitch bowl, filling it to the brim, or onto the piece of wood. It takes quite a long time to cool, so do not rush to use it, as the middle may still be soft. As a mixture, it never turns fully solid, and even when cool will flow out of the pitch bowl if it is left at an angle.

For simple shallow repoussé work, a lead cake or even a piece of hardboard (masonite) will suffice. These substitutes will not give the adhesion, and hence solid feel, of pitch.

Punches

Simple repoussé can be done with the ball end of a hammer, and for shallow gentle designs this can be quite effective. Traditionally, however, repoussé and chasing work is done with punches of seemingly endless variety. These range from doming type, rounded chisels, flat-ended in square, round and triangular section, to textured and hollow punches. One catalogue lists 63 basic designs. For starting, one spherical doming punch, one well-rounded chisel and one flat-ended tear drop will cover most requirements, but as in many tooling situations, you never seem to have enough.

Shaping

Having been allowed to cool, the surface of the pitch should be smooth and flat, and at or only just below the level of the top of the bowl.

With a soft flame, the surface of the pitch is warmed until it becomes sticky but not too runny, and the sheet of silver, which should fit easily inside the diameter, is just placed on the surface. Now wait for the pitch to cool and harden. If not already done, the design can now be marked out in pencil and lined in with a scribe.

Shaping can start with a well-rounded punch pushing the design forward, remembering that the visible face is on the back of the piece.

The blow should feel very solid and dead. If it does not, then the silver is not well set and may have air pockets, in which case it should be removed and reset.

The punch is held between the thumb and first two or three fingers, with the little finger or little and next fingers the same side as the thumb. The end of the punch is held just clear of the surface. Held at a slight angle, it will travel forward creating a smooth continuous depression.

When sufficient depth is achieved, the piece is removed with a sharp blow on a round-nosed chisel-shaped punch between the sheet and the pitch. The front shape can now be seen. Excess pitch can be removed by heating and an annealing operation which both softens and cleans. If there is insufficient depth, the operations are repeated.

The design can now be made crisp by chasing.

The back of the piece must be filled with hot pitch mixture, making sure that all the cavity is well filled. This is then set on the levelled hot surface of the pitch bowl and allowed to cool.

The well-rounded inside corners can now be punched sharp where required, and any other indentations formed down.

This process of repoussé, anneal and chase is repeated until a satisfactory piece is achieved. When complete, the design can be sawn out and finished.

Jewellery work which is repoussé, chased, pierced and engraved can be extremely effective, and complex hollow pieces can be assembled from a number of individually produced pieces.

Resins

Two-part resins are used for embedding, inlaying and as an adhesive. Epoxy resin and polyester are the two types most used: epoxy as an adhesive and inlay, polyester for embedding and inlay.

Resists (see also Etching)

In the process of etching, those areas to be protected from the action of the mordant, the acid, are coated with a resist. Proprietary resists with suitable thinning agents are available and are generally applied by brush.

Asphaltum blended with wax and thinned with turpentine is a popular resist. Nail-varnish used with nail-varnish remover is effective but very quick drying. A recent innovation developed in the electronic industry for the production of prototype printed circuit boards is available in a pen dispenser which allows fine lines and easy control.

As an alternative to a painted-on resist, some of the self-adhesive plastic films can be used either by applying cut shapes or by cutting the pattern from a single sheet.

Rubber stamps can be used to apply a liquid resist where repeat designs are required.

A simple home-made resist can be produced by submerging crushed sealing wax in methylated spirit. Left for a few days, the sealing wax will form into a paintable resist.

Reticulation

Particularly suitable for producing a texture for silver, reticulation is a surface effect produced by heat.

High surface temperatures will disturb the surface, which will then cool with a texture. A sheet of cleaned silver heated evenly all over will form an orange peel effect at red heat. A very high temperature flame can be used to induce waves and ripples.

The process can be extended to include the fusion of filings and small shaped pieces which will be drawn into the surface.

The opposite face to the one being worked will also change in character. It can also reflect the shapes of fused pieces.

Ribbon

Commercially produced coloured ribbon can be used singly or plaited as thongs and also incorporated in non-precious jewellery pieces. Its use is particularly appropriate to textile jewellery.

Riffler (see also Files)

A type of file where the cutting surface is restricted to the end that is curved away from the axis. This curvature allows the cutting face to reach down below the general surface of a piece and into difficult-to-reach places. Rifflers have a particular application in tool making.

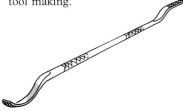

Diag. 221 *Riffler*

Ring buff

A buffing mop, cylindrical and tapered in section, for attaching to a buffing machine and used for polishing the inside of rings.

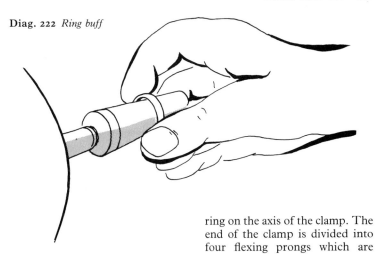

Diag. 222 *Ring buff*

Made from felt, ring buffs can be solid felt or mounted on a wooden core.

Ring clamp

A holding device generally made from wood for holding rings and other small items during finishing, shaping and decorating operations.

The traditional design is shaped like a split cylinder and tapered at one or both ends. The two pieces are loosely linked at the centre and a wedge fits in the non-clamping end. Bone examples of Viking ring clamps survive, identical to modern designs.

Other variations exist. In one variation the two pieces are linked at the non-clamping end and the two halves clamped together with a central screw and nut.

Another design, sometimes referred to as an engraver's clamp or bottom screw clamp, holds the ring on the axis of the clamp. The end of the clamp is divided into four flexing prongs which are expanded to grip the inside of the ring by pulling through, by an end nut and screw, a circular tapered wedge.

Ring clips

Small metal clips fitted inside rings to give a tighter fit. Generally unsatisfactory, they can be useful when the knuckle is much larger than the finger where the ring fits.

Ring cutting pliers

Plier-shaped cutting tool fitted with a small rotatable cutting saw and back guard. Used to remove, by cutting, rings which cannot be pulled off.

Ring gauges (see also Measuring)

The infinite range of finger sizes requires a system of measurement for fingers and rings.

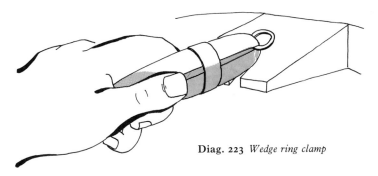

Diag. 223 *Wedge ring clamp*

Diag. 224 *Engraver's ring clamp*

the metal is the most straight-forward method. Ring stretching tools can be of the roller type or mandrel type. Ring rolling tools enable the shank of the ring to be rolled thinner, hence longer, using a selected roller. Rings can also be stretched on a triblet. The method with a solid triblet is either to stretch the shank by hammering

Rings are measured by sliding them over a calibrated tapered mandrel. Fingers are measured by selecting the desired fit from a selection of calibrated rings. These are available in two patterns, wide for band rings and narrow for other rings. The calibration differs between the USA and UK (see table below).

Ring punch

Punch used to mark the ring with a maker's mark as part of a hallmark, or an identity mark showing the quality of the material. Ring punches are characterised by having a cranked body to clear the ring shank when in use.

Diag. 225 *Ring cutting pliers*

Ring sizing

One of the difficulties with rings is the frequent necessity to adjust the size to suit a particular finger. There are various ways of adjust-ing the size of a ring, depending on if it is to be made larger or smaller, the amount of change and the construction of the ring.

It is generally easier to *increase* the size of a ring, and stretching

Most popular ring sizes

English sizes	J	K	L	M	N	O	P
Inside diameter (in)	0.6145	0.63	0.646	0.661	0.677	0.692	0.708
(mm)	15.6	16	16.4	16.8	17.2	17.6	18

USA sizes							
Size	5	$5\frac{1}{2}$	6	$6\frac{1}{2}$	7	$7\frac{1}{2}$	8
Inside diameter (in)	0.618	0.634	0.650	0.666	0.682	0.698	0.714

Diag. 226 *Ring punch*

Fig. 42 *Ring stretching tools*

or to drive the ring up along the tapered triblet, with a hammer and drift.

Split mandrels with a mechanism for opening the triblet offer a quick method. With all the methods using a triblet the ring should be reversed on the triblet to ensure stretching is symmetrical.

Plain rings, particularly high carat gold wedding rings, can be reduced in size by driving the ring into a tapered hole. A doming block can also be used. The ring must be protected from hammer blows by a flat metal drift.

Some split mandrel ring stretching tools also incorporate cavities for ring reduction.

Stretching and shrinking are suitable for size changes of up to about three sizes, depending on the material. Work-hardening takes place during stretching and this can cause soldered joints to fracture. Where a large change in size is necessary, the shank must be cut and a piece removed or added and the joints soldered.

For rings set with stones, care must be taken to ensure that the distortion caused by stretching does not disturb the setting.

With gemstone rings, the decision has to be made whether to remove the stones for the soldering operations or to protect them from the heat with a barrier material. Both methods have their disadvantages. Stone removal risks breaking a setting claw, and heat protection may not be effective.

Ring stick

A measuring device used to gauge the inside diameter of rings. It consists of a tapered metal tube and handle. The outside is marked with a scale of ring sizes. Rings, of circular section, slid over the stick will stop opposite their internal size.

Riveting

Probably the earliest technique for joining pieces of metal together, riveting can be simple, visible and decorative, or near invisible.

In jewellery, rivets are made from annealed wire, and fitted cold. The wire must be a snug fit in the holes in the parts to be joined. It is probably easiest to size the holes with a broach rather than draw the wire to suit the holes.

If a level surface is required, then the holes need to be countersunk, that is increased from the small diameter of the wire rivet to a larger diameter at the surface. A small parallel portion at the larger diameter eliminates any feather edge to the rivet head.

A raised head requires no countersinking. To rivet pieces together, wire is cut to project sufficiently far that there is enough material to fill the countersink, plus a little surplus. It is important that the ends of the wire

Diag. 227 *Rivets*

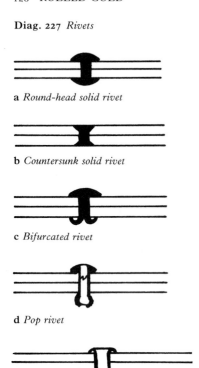

a *Round-head solid rivet*

b *Countersunk solid rivet*

c *Bifurcated rivet*

d *Pop rivet*

e *Hollow rivet*

rivet are filed square or an uneven rivet results. Riveting is done with a small riveting hammer on a hard polished anvil.

Setting the rivet centrally and turning the assembly over frequently during hammering will result in a sound symmetrical joint which can be rubbed down with water of Ayr stone and subsequently polished.

For a raised head, it is necessary to use a riveting dolly and punch. Shaped dollies may be employed to produce a decorative head. It is, of course, practical to combine countersunk and raised heads.

An interesting rivet for free jointing can be made by beading the ends of a wire rivet. In a simpler version, the ends are flattened and finished in a decorative form.

For other materials, hollow rivets and eyelets can be both functional and decorative.

Rolled gold

A composite material in which an outer layer of gold is backed by a less precious metal. This composite material is then rolled to reduce the section.

Rolling

The process of thinning and shaping wire sheet and strip by passing the material between hardened and polished steel rollers. Rolling is used to reduce open cast ingots to flat sheet and square wire. The square wire may subsequently be drawn down. Drawing will both change the cross section and improve the surface finish.

The process of making square wire from an ingot is as follows. The ingot is squared up by filing to both shape it and remove base metals and oxide which have migrated to the surface.

The roughly shaped ingot is then passed through the double V rollers of the mill so that flats are produced just at the high spots. The piece is then rotated about its axis by 90 degrees and passed through again at the same mill

Fig. 43 *Rolling sheet*

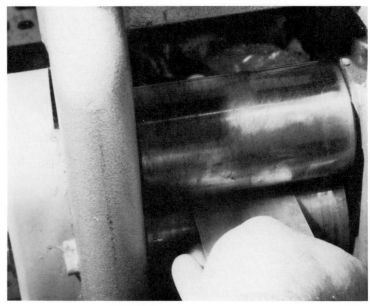

setting. It should then be annealed, washed and dried.

The mill is then set a little lower or the next size down, grooves are selected and the piece passed through again. Annealing, washing and drying should be repeated.

This sequence is repeated, although less frequent annealing is required as the section reduces. Attempting to reduce too quickly and failure to anneal adequately will cause cracking, which renders the material useful only for melting.

Sheet product is treated in the same way. It is critical that the rollers are adjusted parallel, or banana-shaped sheet will result.

Rolling mill

Motor or hand driven rolling mills are used for reducing the section of metal wire, sheet and strip. The rollers of hardened polished steel are linked by gears in a substantial frame. Very small ones can be directly driven, but it is more normal to incorporate a gear reduction to reduce the input torque.

Parallel rollers are used for reducing sheet and strip in one direction. Paired rollers with V grooves will reduce wire to square section.

Some mills are equipped with one flat and one half-round grooved roller to produce half-round sections.

Extension shafts fitted to some mills will accept paired rollers with engraved patterns for producing patterned strips, such as are used for making bangles.

Rope chain (*see also* Chainmaking)

A form of chain construction which gives the impression of a twisted rope. The design typically consists of a repeated pattern of three interlocking links.

Rosin

Soluble in turpentine, rosin can be used as a resist in acid etching.

Rotary files

Also called burrs.

Rotton stone

Also called Scotch stone and *water of Ayr*. It is a soft slate-like material available in square sticks in sizes from 3mm to 15mm ($\frac{1}{8}$in to $\frac{5}{8}$in) square.

It is used wet as an abrasive to smooth the surface of precious metal. Its unique property is that, as it is rubbed over a surface, it wears quickly to the profile of the surface. With care, it can be sharpened like a pencil to reach difficult places. The stick should be repeatedly dipped in water to form a slurry which takes away the tiny pieces of waste.

Rouge

A very fine polishing compound made from iron oxide. It is used in the polishing of precious metals and stones. It can also be used as a barrier to prevent the flow of solder in selective soldering, or as a dry powder, with water or in cake form, for dressing wheels.

Type	*Application*
Red	Precious and base metals. Solder inhibitor.
Crocus	A coarser compound of red.
Green	Chromium oxide based and used on platinum and stainless steel.

Streaking can occur during polishing on a wheel and this is best removed with paraffin.

Rouge stains absorbent materials and is very penetrating. After polishing, all traces must be removed.

Rough rock

Pieces of precious or semi-precious stone as mined or quarried.

Round nose pliers

Pliers used for forming and holding with tapered circular jaws. The shape of the jaws is particularly useful for forming jump rings.

Router

A high-speed cutting tool similar to a milling cutter, but typically shaped to produce a complex cut such as a moulding. Normally used on softer materials such as wood.

Rubber

Silicon and latex rubber is one of the more recently introduced materials for jewellery pieces. These rubbers have the advantage of being easily moulded in simple moulds as well as being used for making moulds for lost wax castings.

Cold cure rubbers will cure at room temperatures within 24 hours, although heating to 60°C will reduce this time to just a few hours. Vulcanising rubbers are cured only by heating.

To produce a vulcanised mould, the metal master is surrounded by pieces of un-vulcanised rubber sheet in an open mould frame. Frames are used singly or in pairs. Sprue pins, if not incorporated in the model, may be either fitted in single frames or clamped in a groove in double frames.

The filled frame is lightly clamped between plates and the whole assembly is put in an oven for 15 minutes at 150°C. The assembly is fully tightened and the rubber fully cured for 45–60 minutes.

After it has been removed and allow to cool, the clamp is detached and the mould taken out of the frame. Great care is now required to cut along the centre line with a sharp scalpel. A slightly irregular cut will aid location, which can also be ensured by not cutting all the way through and leaving a hinge at one end.

Before use, the mould should be brushed with release agent and lightly clamped between two suitable flat plates. It is now ready to be filled with wax. A commercial wax injector is the most satisfactory method, although syringes and similar devices can be adapted.

S

Safety catch (*see also* Brooch)

Simple brooch catches can be made more secure by incorporating a central concentric swivel element, which can be rotated after entering the pin, thus preventing it coming free.

Safety chain

A short length of chain with jump ring and bolt ring used to duplicate a chain fastening.

Safety pickle (*see also* Pickle)

A less hazardous form of pickle frequently based on alum.

Salamander (*see also* Melting)

A type of crucible, tall with a pouring lip. Sizes are described by the amount of brass which they can hold, and range from 0.07 to 17kg ($\frac{1}{4}$lb to 37$\frac{1}{2}$lb).

Sand

Coloured sand, layered and enclosed in glass containers, has been incorporated in jewellery.

Sand, made damp, in a small container will form an infinitely adjustable support for repair work in particular rings. The damp sand will also give some protection for set stones.

Sand bag

Flat circular leather bags filled with sand provide a yielding support for items being worked on. Engraving and light-forming processes are currently carried out on sand bags, which provide non-damaging support for irregular

Diag. 228 *Brooch safety chain*

Diag. 229 *Sand bag*

shaped pieces which could be damaged if set on a bench or bench pin.

Sand blasting

Components can be finished, particularly after casting, by directing a jet of air-blown particles over the surface of the piece. The operation is carried out in a cabinet with viewing window and fitted gloves to hold the piece and direct the jet. A compressed air source is required.

The particles used vary, depending on the material being finished, the type of finish required and the condition of the piece.

For small-scale needs a similar effect can be obtained by pouring the abrasive material from a height of 3–4m (10–13ft) onto the piece supported on a coarse grid.

Satin finish (*see also* Glass brush)

A uniform finish achieved by wire brushing or blasting with abrasive.

Saw bench

Used for cutting sheet and section to length, the metal working saw bench can cut at right angles to the length or at other pre-set angles, but only in straight cuts.

Lapidary saws are fitted with diamond saw blades with a continuous flow of coolant.

Both versions consist of a rigidly mounted motor with arbour

for mounting the blade which projects through a slot in the saw table above. The saw table is equipped with guides and stops. Some models employ a sliding table or vice which allows the piece being cut to be fed into the saw.

Saw frame

The jeweller's essential tool with replaceable blades used for cutting shapes from sheet metal. Jeweller's saws are all of a similar length but vary in depth. Shallow frames are easier to control, particularly for fine work. They have the disadvantage of not being able to reach into larger sheets of material.

A comprehensive arrangement is for the jeweller to be equipped with two frames, one fitted with a coarse blade, one with a fine blade and one deep saw frame with a medium blade.

Some saw frames are of fixed length, some adjustable. Adjustable frames are able to make use of broken blades, but the real economy of this is doubtful.

Saw types

Saw blades may form an integral part of the saw or be replaceable when worn. They are described by the pitch of the teeth.

Diag. 230 *Band sawing*

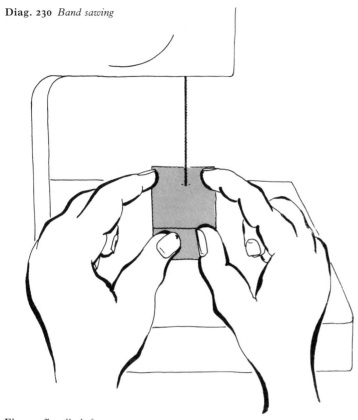

Fig. 45 *Jeweller's frame saw*

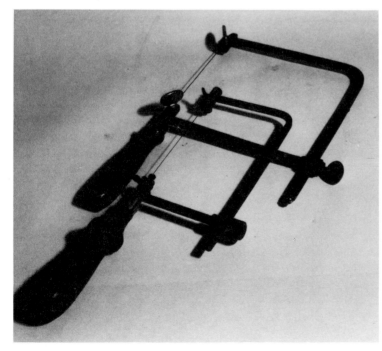

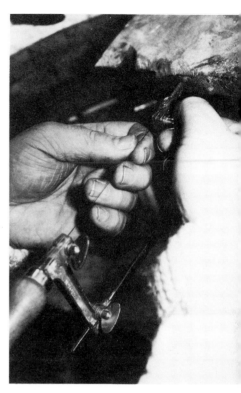

Fig. 44 *Setting the blade in a jeweller's saw*

Replaceable blades typically fit frame saws and are small in cross section relative to length. Blades which form part of the saw tend to be of wide section. Jeweller's saws, hacksaws, junior hacksaws, and fret saws typify the frame types. Woodworking hand saws are typical of the integral type. Between these two categories are flat wide blades used for parting off, which can be interchanged.

Machine-powered saws form another category.

Sawdust

Boxwood sawdust is a convenient medium for drying by absorption components which have been worked.

A tin box is half-filled with sawdust. The component is put in, the lid closed and the contents shaken. After use, the lid is removed and the box is stored in a warm place to allow the sawdust to dry.

Sawing and jeweller's saw

The process of cutting materials using a saw. The individual teeth of a saw blade each remove a small shaving of material which then falls away from the cut, producing sawdust. The blade should be used for most of its working length. In general, the load on the cut is provided by the weight of the saw – all the effort being put into moving the saw back and forth. If the piece being sawn is not securely held, then much of the energy will be used in moving the piece to the detriment of the cutting.

The blade or saw must be selected to suit the material type and the material thickness. A blade is fitted into the saw frame with the blade teeth pointing towards the handle. With very fine blades this direction is not always easy to see, but can be felt with a finger nail. The blade is clamped at one end with the frame sprung lightly against the bench, and the other end of the blade clamped. The degree of tension is judged from experience: too slack and the blade will not cut well, and also break easily; too taut and, being

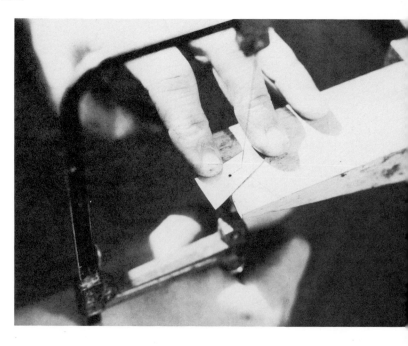

Fig. 46 *Sawing out from a hole*

over-stressed, it will have a short life. Gentle plucking with the thumb will verify the correct degree of tension.

For heavy gauges a light rub with a block of beeswax will give a sweeter cut. If a blade gets twisted or becomes blunt, replace it immediately. A twisted blade, in particular, can easily ruin a piece by not cutting in a straight line.

An adjustable frame allows short lengths of broken blade to be used, but, because the blade has already failed, this economy is seldom worthwhile.

Before cutting, it must be decided whether the cut is to be made inside, outside or on the line.

The sheet, suitably marked out, rests on the bench pin. Assuming right-handed operation, the sheet is held down firmly with the left hand, with the saw in the right hand and the start of the cut facing the jeweller. The saw is lightly held with the blade resting on the sheet. The sawing action, vertically up and down, is a smooth continuous operation using almost the full length of the blade. Little or no pressure is necessary; the right-hand grip on the saw should be light and not forcing. During any cutting, withdrawing or turning action, the up and down action must be continued or the blade may break.

Curves are made by a combination of slightly changing the angle of approach of the saw, and at the same time turning the sheet with the left hand. Sharp changes

Piercing saw sizes and applications

Blade size

Blade reference number	Thickness in inches	Width in inches	Teeth per inch	Suitable for material thickness
M4/0	0.006	0.018	80	up to
M3/0	0.007	0.019	80	0.015 in
M2/0	0.008	0.021	60	0.016in to
M1/0	0.009	0.023	60	0.030in
M0	0.010	0.025	60	
M1	0.011	0.026	52	0.031in to 0.045in
M2	0.012	0.027	44	0.016in to
M3	0.014	0.030	44	0.060in
M4	0.015	0.032	32	0.016in to 0.092in
M5	0.017	0.036	32	over 0.061in

of direction are made by keeping the vertical up and down movement and, without moving the blade forward, turning the sheet. What happens is that the side of the blade cuts into the sheet, pointing the cutting edge in the new direction.

Where a very sharp change of direction is required, it is necessary to withdraw the saw, and then feed the blade in backwards. At the end of the cut, the blade can then cut out a sharp angle.

Heavier materials are best held in a vice. For jewellery making a hacksaw and junior hacksaw will be suitable for most applications.

Scale

Heating metals in a normal atmosphere can cause a scale to form on the surface. Typical of this is the effect of high temperature on the uncoated face of a piece of copper during enamelling. A fine black oxide scale will form which will contaminate the surface if not removed. This is one good reason why copper supports cannot be used in a kiln.

Scalping

When scrap is cast in ingots for rolling or drawing surface impurities are removed by scraping or filing. The process is termed scalping.

Scissors

Hand-cutting tools for soft materials. Scissors are available in many designs and should be selected for the specific purpose.

Score bending

Sheet metal and plastics materials of thick section can be more easily bent into a sharp corner by scoring the inside bend line. Scoring tools with a 90 degree cranked end can be pulled along the line guided by a straight edge. The cut should be taken almost through the material

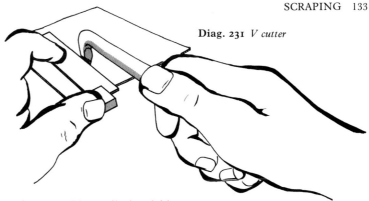

Diag. 231 *V cutter*

to leave a thin easily-bendable section.

When box-making, the scoring should be made along the box corners and across the vertical corners, the waste pieces subsequently being cut out. This provides chamfered corner joints.

Scorper

An alternative name for a *graver* or burin.

Scotch stone

Also called *water of Ayr stone*.

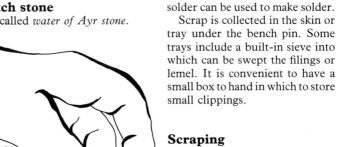

Scrap (*see also* Lemel)

Precious metal scrap from sawing, filing and failures should be recovered.

All cutting processes produce scrap, either in the form of clippings of sheet and wire or filings. The clippings can safely be melted into ingots or beads. Alternatively, they can be collected and sold or traded with a bullion dealer.

Filings need more care. Provided no solder is included, filings can be washed in detergent and hot water and included in the melting pot. If solder is included, or if the scrap is the sprue of a casting and hence has a higher degree of impurity, then trading in or selling it to a bullion dealer is the best move. If this lower grade scrap is reused, then there is a danger that the piece will fail an assay.

With care, scrap containing solder can be used to make solder.

Scrap is collected in the skin or tray under the bench pin. Some trays include a built-in sieve into which can be swept the filings or lemel. It is convenient to have a small box to hand in which to store small clippings.

Scraping

Metal can be removed from flat and curved faces by scraping. The method is used to remove small

Diag. 232 *Scraping the inside of a ring*

amounts of metal such as when sampling metal or sizing a ring.

Scraper designs vary, but for jewellery work a three-sided type is suitable. Scrapers can be made from worn-out files which are first softened by annealing, then hardened and tempered after filing to shape. Scrapers need to be kept sharp, and to protect the cutting edges it is convenient to store them with a cork pushed over the end.

Scrapers are used with a paring action. A decorative effect can be achieved by varying the direction of the cut, thus creating a mosaic pattern.

Scratch brushing
Scratch brushing is used to give a matt or frosted finish to metal parts. The process can be by hand or machine. Various types and grades of brush are used. One widely practised technique is to use a powered rotating brass wire brush with a stream of water to lubricate and wash the face. For small components, the same process can be used with a hand brush under a running tap.

Standard steel wire machine brushes tend to be too coarse for jewellery components, but one design of brush is employed. It consists of a plastic hub on which are set pivoting wire bristles. Available in a number of grades, they produce a predictable range of graded frosted finishes.

Screw clasp (see also Findings)
A form of clasp used on chains and neck pieces in which a freely revolving nut and screw join the ends of a chain.

Screw plate
Also called a die plate, it consists of a range of threaded holes formed with cutting edges in a small steel plate. It is used to cut threads on rods for the smaller

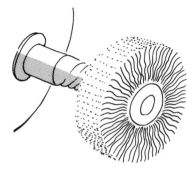

Diag. 233 *Scratch brush*

Diag. 234 *Satin finishing wire brush*

Fig. 47 *Precision screwdrivers*

sizes of thread where normal dies are not available.

Screw types
Screws are described by the diameter, form and length of the thread, the type of head and the material. Head types are illustrated in Diag. 235.

Screwdriver
Screwdrivers to suit the variety of head types available come in a wide range of shapes and sizes. For jewellery work, a set of jeweller's screwdrivers will fit the many small slotted screws generally used.

Screws
Small screws and nuts can be used to hold jewellery components together; and screw heads can give a decorative effect.

Various head designs are available, and thread diameters of less than 1mm upwards are available, the very small sizes being obtained from a horologist supplier. A wide range of thread forms exist; metric sizes are preferred.

Special screws, and screws in precious metals, can be made on a lathe and using dies. Screws either fit into threaded holes or are secured with a nut.

Scribe

A sharp pointed steel rod used for scribing lines when *marking out* material for cutting and drilling.

Scrimshaw

The practice of incising a design using a pointed tool on ivory and bone. The incised design of fine lines is filled in with lamp black or other contrasting medium.

Other materials such as hard wood, nuts and steel have been used. The practice of scrimshaw was particularly popular with sailors in the days of sailing ships.

Scroll (*see also* Findings)

The small spring-retainer used on stud ear rings.

Sealing wax (*see also* Etching)

Traditional red sealing wax, which can be dissolved in methylated spirit as well as softened by heat, can be used to make an effective resist.

Sealing wax can also be used to make simple beads as well as a medium for back filling sheet repoussé work.

Seed pearls

Naturally occurring pearls, approximately round in shape, and from 1mm to 1½mm in diameter.

Sequins

Small flat shapes, frequently circular, of a highly reflective material with a central hole. Supplied for dress decoration, they can be incorporated in non-precious

Diag. 235 *Screws*

a *Cheese head*

b *Round head*

c *Pan head*

d *Countersunk head*

jewellery, particularly when made from or incorporating fabrics. Sequins can also be used in conjunction with beads, particularly small glass beads, and incorporated in wire threaded constructions.

Setter's wax

A malleable wax used for holding components and stones.

Setting punch

Hollow-ended punch, shaped to fit over and form the bezel over a stone. The use of such punches is typically applied to production jewellery.

Diag. 236 *Scribe*

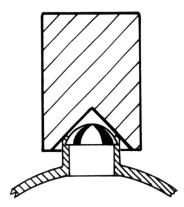

Diag. 237 *Setting punch*

Setting tools (*see also* Stone setting)

A small range of hand tools are used to set stones in claws or bezels.

Initially the bezel or claw is deformed with a pusher. Subsequently a burnisher is used to flow the material to give closer contact and a smooth finish. A notched tool is used to straighten claws and, with some settings, to induce a better grip of the claw on the stone.

Small bladed tools are used in some settings to raise a shaving of metal, forming a simple claw. The same tools can be used to lift claws and bezels when removing stones. Seating burrs are used to cut the face on which stones sit. Sized burrs are used to create the setting for the stone, whilst gravers and graining tools are used for other settings.

Settlement tank (see also Lemel)

A tank introduced in the drainage system of a workshop to collect the heavier precious metal washed from components.

Sewing

Sewing or thonging can be employed as a technique for joining jewellery components. The technique can be employed for its decorative and imitative qualities, particularly when pierced metal components are held together with metal wire. Threading can be made easier by using multi-strand twisted wire.

Sgraffito

The process of scratching a line to produce a mark or design, in particular when breaking through one surface to reveal a contrasting surface below.

One application is enamelling. The component is given a layer of enamel which is fired. When cool, this fired face is coated with a thin layer of gum on which is sifted a second contrasting layer of enamel. Prior to finishing, the design is scratched through this second layer revealing the first surface of enamel. The piece is then fired for a second time, fixing the design.

Shading tool (see also Engraving)

A graver with grooved working face creating multiple cuts. Shad-

ing tools are described by the width of the tool, the number of grooves and the distance between the lines cut. Tool widths range from .625mm to 2.25mm with six, eight or ten rows or lines.

Used as a graver, shading tools produce multiple cuts over an area and are used to provide a background texture and to add emphasis to an engraved line.

Shank

The main part of a ring. The term is also used to describe the part of a tool away from the cutting end.

Sharp-edged punches

Thin sheet material can be cut with sharp-edged *punches*. Made from steel rod, punches for cutting circular blanks are readily available.

Punches can be made for cutting other shapes by a combination of drilling and filing. For complicated shapes it is helpful to make the punch hollow, so that a

Diag. 238 *Sgraffito design being scratched on an enamel plaque supported on a stainless steel trivet*

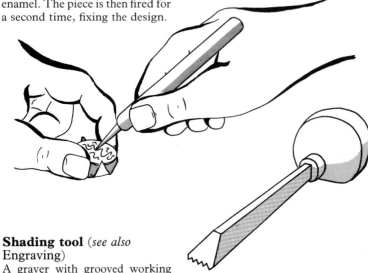

Diag. 239 *Shading tool*

rod can be inserted to remove the blank. Punching should be done on a yielding surface to protect the cutting edge of the punch.

Sharpening tools

Cutting tools require to be kept sharp for efficient cutting. The angles of the cutting faces must be retained and any grinding should not generate heat which draws the temper.

Drills, chisels, lathe tools and the like are sharpened on a powered grinding wheel. Frequent dipping of the tips in water keeps the temperature down. The final edge may be achieved using a hand-held carborundum stone.

Small hand tools, such as gravers, are best shaped with a hand carborundum stone or, if excessive, on a wheel and finished with an *Arkansas* stone.

Gravers are easily checked for sharpness by testing them on a thumbnail.

Shears

Hand or bench shears are used to cut sheet metal. Two blades are brought together by pivoting about a point, as with scissors. Bench shears are also called guillotines. Hand shears are also called snips and are available with straight or curved blades.

Sheepskin apron (see also Jeweller's bench)

The traditional leather apron used to catch lemel when working at the bench. The apron can be worn as a normal apron and hooked to the bench or, more usual today, fixed to the bench and draped over the knees of the worker.

Sheepskins have been used in retrieving gold from streams to trap the fine particles and are the basis of the Golden Fleece of Greek mythology.

Sheet

The term used to describe flat material of uniform thickness.

Shell

The wide variety of sea-shells provides a wealth of shape, colour and texture. Abalone, awabi and mother of pearl are popular, being available in thin wafers as well as flat cabochons.

Shell can be worked with normal steel tools such as drills, burrs, gravers and files. Tungsten-tipped tools offer the advantage of longer life but are not essential. Shell can be finished easily with abrasive papers and stone polishes such as aluminium oxide.

Cameo carving, exploiting the coloured layers of shell, is a traditional shell technique.

Shell, because of the ease of drilling and sawing, is a suitable base for inlay work.

Shot (*see also* Granulation)

Shot can be formed by dripping molten metal from a height, causing it to cool and solidify on the way down, where it is collected.

Shot from precious metal can also be formed on a charcoal block. The process is simple. Small clippings of metal are placed on the charcoal block and heated to above melting point. Surface tension will cause the metal to form into a bead. A tiny flat will form on the bottom, its size dependent on the size of the bead. A little flux will assist the process. Larger beads tend to contain a small air pocket which can hold pickling acid if this is not washed out. The small flat can be reduced or eliminated by pressing a small hemispherical indentation, the size of the intended bead, into the surface of the charcoal.

Beads, thus produced, can be finished by simply barrelling them against themselves in a soap solution.

Side cutters

Cutters with the cutting jaws in line with the handles. One variant has the jaws at 45 degrees to the line of the handles.

Silicon carbide

A cutting medium used loose, on abrasive paper and cloth, as grinding wheels and in a rubber-like mix in blocks and wheels.

Silicon rubber

A flexible rubber available in single or two-part mixes which can be poured or trowelled into place. It is very suitable for making moulds, particularly for making wax models for lost wax casting.

Because of the ease with which the single component form can be extruded from a tube, silicon rubber can be used to create non-precious jewellery. Large tubes in neutral, black and white are sold by builder's merchants, and a wide range of colours are available in smaller tubes, also from builder's merchants, and sold for sealing gaps between baths, basins and wall tiles.

Silk

The fine, naturally produced textile and thread. Twisted silk thread makes effective cords and decoration.

Silver conductive paint

(*see also* Electroforming)

Lightweight hollow complex components can be made by electroforming. To make the solid master conductive, it is covered in a layer of conductive paint with a high density of silver.

Silver foil

Very thin sheets of silver can be shaped and incorporated in transparent and translucent enamel to give a reflective face.

Silver gilt

The term used to describe silver items which are wholly or partly gold-plated.

Silver plate

Base metal, frequently brass or other copper-based alloy, electroplated with silver.

Skin (*see also* Jeweller's bench)

The traditional addition to the jeweller's bench is, in effect, a fixed apron. It is used to collect lemel, to hold tools and catch dropped items. The alternative is a rigid metal tray, which has the advantage of better resistance to hot items and acid splashes, although less resilient for dropped items.

Sleepers (*see also* Findings)

The term used to describe small simple ear rings such as are worn after the ears have been pierced and when the piercing is needed to be kept open with a minimum decorative effect.

Slip casting

A moulding technique used to shape ceramic pieces. A two-part mould is cast over a master using plaster of Paris. When dry, a liquid slip mixture is poured in, swirled around and tipped out. The absorbent nature of the mould takes moisture from the slip, producing a hollow ceramic form within the mould. When the slip has dried, the mould is separated and the piece finally dried and fired.

The process is suitable for making large ceramic beads.

Smith's anvil

The traditional anvil used for forging. Sizes are determined by weight, a typical range being $\frac{1}{2}$cwt, 1cwt, 1$\frac{1}{2}$cwt and 2cwt.

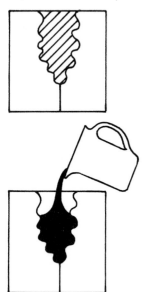

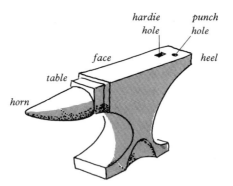

Diag. 241 *Anvil*

Diag. 240 *Slip casting*

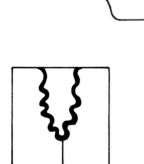

Smith's mandrel

A large, tapered, round, mandrel used primarily in silver smithing.

Soap

Barrelling components with steel shapes in water requires a soap to

lubricate the surfaces to give a good burnished finish. The soap flakes used also give a fair measure of protection against rusting of the steel shapes.

Soft soldering

Low melting point solder, tin-based and used with a soldering iron, is used for joining brass, copper and steel components. Solder is available with a core of *flux* or the flux may be applied

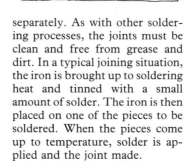

separately. As with other soldering processes, the joints must be clean and free from grease and dirt. In a typical joining situation, the iron is brought up to soldering heat and tinned with a small amount of solder. The iron is then placed on one of the pieces to be soldered. When the pieces come up to temperature, solder is applied and the joint made.

Solder

Solder is a metal alloy used to join metals which will melt at a lower temperature than the metals being joined. There are essentially two types of solder: low temperature solder, tin-based, used on non-precious metals and applied using a soldering iron, and high temperature solders which require temperatures from around 600°C to 800°C, used for precious metals and where a very strong joint is required.

Soldering

Soldering is the principal method employed to join pieces of silver together or to make a joint when forming a piece back onto itself, as when a ring is made from a length of wire or other section.

Diag. 242 *Soft soldering*

A well-made joint will only result if the mating pieces are a good fit, the surfaces to be joined are clean and free from grease and dirt, and solder of the right grade is correctly applied.

In essence, soldering is a process in which an alloy – the solder – with a melting point lower than the metal of the components is melted by the heat from the component parts. It is essential to use hallmarking-quality solder on precious metals.

Soldering is essentially a very hot activity and some of the operations are in acid. It is good practice to handle the piece and the solder with tools rather than fingers at *all* stages.

It is necessary to support the piece during soldering, and various materials are used, each with its own particular characteristics. Charcoal, either natural or compressed, is a good general-purpose support. Natural, although more expensive, lasts longer and burns less readily. Its low specific heat means it does not take much heat away from the piece and, since it is carbon, there is less tendency for the silver to oxidise. In some assemblies, vertical pieces of wire can be supported by drilling holes in the charcoal block. Charcoal can also be carved to shape where special support is required.

In other soldering operations, small pieces, or paillons, of solder are placed on the joint. These are cut from the strip, and this is most easily done with snips. The end of the strip is pushed onto the index finger of the left hand, while being held between the thumb and second finger. The face of the snips rests against the index finger. This technique prevents the cut solder from flying about and being lost. By varying the pressure of the solder against the index finger, the length of the solder paillon can be varied. For very small pieces from wide solder, strips should first be cut lengthwise; then each cross cut will produce a number of paillons.

Solder is also available in powder form, either plain or mixed with a flux. This form is particularly suitable for soldering filigree work, where it can be applied with a brush or stick to the joints prior to heating.

For some joints, particularly with repetition work, preformed pieces of solder shaped to fit the joint can help achieve uniformity.

To ensure acceptance for hallmarking, the amount of solder must be kept to a minimum. No part of the piece can be made of solder, and solder can only be used to make a joint. Extra easy solder is low in silver content, and excessive use can cause rejection.

Like any silver alloy, silver solder will oxidise. It is, therefore, preferable to cut only such solder as is necessary for the job in hand.

Only composition blocks specified as suitable for soldering should be used. Some heat-resistant boards can explode when heated. As with other asbestos products, safety precautions must be observed. Composition boards can be drilled and shaped to support pieces. Being a more uniform, man-made material, it is particularly suitable for larger structures. Although suitable for soldering, it is not suitable for melting silver on as the silver sticks to the surface.

Ceramic

Purpose-made ceramic blocks and shapes as used in pottery firing can be used to form a bed in which to support pieces.

When it is necessary to heat a piece from underneath, a discarded piece of gas fire element – the type with many small projections – forms an excellent support. A proprietary perforated ceramic block for soldering is also available.

Metal supports

The traditional jeweller's wig of compressed iron wire with wire handle gives the operator a high degree of mobility in moving the piece in relation to the flame.

Full heating from underneath is best accomplished with a stainless steel mesh on a tripod.

A stretched nichrome or iron wire can be used to support formed wire and other lightweight pieces.

Protective supports

A small metal container of wet sand is useful for supporting small pieces where some parts of the piece must not become hot, the stone in a ring being typical. Although a useful technique, it cannot be guaranteed, and greater

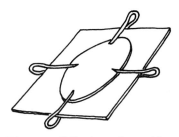

Diag. 244 *Split pins used to position pieces for soldering*

Diag. 245 *Wire soldering tweezers*

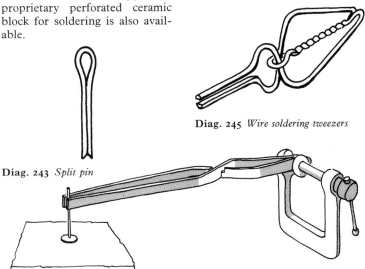

Diag. 243 *Split pin*

Diag. 246 *Self-grip soldering tweezers set in a G clamp as a third hand* than normal heat is required to raise the temperature of the exposed part.

Holding devices for soldering

Some pieces can be soldered on a support without need of further supporting or positioning devices.

In many cases, however, pieces must be accurately held in position during soldering. Iron binding wire, available in various diameters, is probably the most versatile material. It withstands soldering temperatures and generally does not adhere to solder. Parts can therefore be bound together and soldered under and through the binding wire. Engineering split pins are also very versatile, particularly in holding flat sheets together.

Soldering tweezers come in a variety of forms from simple crocodile-clip type, to elaborate double-ball joined arms. For positioning one piece down on another, as when fitting an earwire to an ear ring, a pair of spring soldering tweezers fitted with a small G clamp (to keep them from falling sideways) gives more freedom than a ball joint.

The cleaned carbon rod from an exhausted single-cell torch battery can be filed to shape, and, with flats on the ends and resting on the ceramic blocks, makes a useful ring support. Purpose-made tapered carbon rods are available for supporting rings.

Besides having rigidity and thermal resistance, all supports should aim to take the minimum amount of heat away from the piece.

Solder does not always melt and flow as intended. To persuade it, a poker is a useful and versatile tool. This is easily made from a length of steel or iron wire set in a simple wooden handle. The end of the wire should be filed to a point with some 10mm ($\frac{1}{2}$in) bent at right angles. Such a poker will be found useful in positioning paillons of solder and finely positioning pieces. It can also be used for pick soldering.

Preparation

The precious metal parts to be joined must be clean and free from oxide, dirt and grease. The parts must fit well, the solder only making the joint and not forming a component part. The most reliable cleaning method is to heat the parts and plunge into pickle, rinse and dry. Alternatively, boil in pickle, rinse and dry.

Flux

Before heating, flux must be applied to the area of the joint to prevent oxidisation. Flux is available in a variety of forms. The traditional method is to use a borax cone and tray. With a little water in the tray, rubbing the cone produces a cream which should be applied either with a splinter of wood or a small borax brush of quill and bristle, but no metal.

Proprietary fluxes, in powder form for mixing with methylated spirit or water, or fluid fluxes, offer advantages over the basic borax. In particular, they are easier to remove after soldering.

Hot application of solder

For joining pieces where the joint requires only one or two paillons, the solder can be applied to the heated assembly. This method has the advantage that the heat to melt the solder comes from the piece and not the flame, which minimises oxidisation and degrading of the solder.

Cold application of solder

Where an assembly requires more than a few paillons, it is preferable to apply these to the fluxed assembly prior to the application of heat. The application of heat causes the flux to bubble, which can cause the paillons to move out of place. When this occurs, and during the heating, the paillons should be pushed back into position with a poker.

Pre-soldering

Where small pieces are positioned on large pieces, particularly if the small part is on a flat, well-finished area, it is desirable not to have an excess of solder. This can be

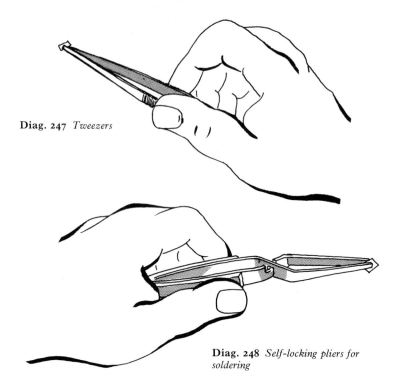

Diag. 247 *Tweezers*

Diag. 248 *Self-locking pliers for soldering*

achieved by pre-soldering the small piece, allowing the solder just to melt and adhere to the surface, without flooding over too large an area. After pickling, rinsing, drying and refluxing, the piece is positioned and both parts heated. Care must be taken not to overheat the smaller piece. At soldering temperature the two pieces will join, and, aided by capillary attraction, the solder will stay between the parts and not flood the surface.

Sheet soldering
It is sometimes necessary to join two or more sheets together, for example when one has a raised or pierced surface decoration and needs a backing. Simply building up thickness by soldering sheets together is not good practice, and could be rejected by the assay office.

On one of the cleaned and fluxed sheets, paillons of solder are positioned regularly over the surface and heated just to the point of fusion. After cleaning, the tops of the solder are filed flat. The pieces are then refluxed and wired together. The method of heating must ensure that both pieces, and not just the top piece, reach soldering temperatures.

Pick soldering
There are some awkward jobs where a small paillon of solder has to be positioned in a nearly inaccessible place.

If the solder is melted on a piece of charcoal and touched with the end of a poker, it will adhere and can be picked up and carried to the heated joint. There is some danger that the repeated heating could degrade the solder, but the technique is valuable for some awkward jobs.

Filigree
Where a multitude of joints require soldering, and particularly where the parts are delicate, powdered solder is applied to the fluxed joints with a small brush.

The temperature must be carefully regulated, and a small kiln is preferable to a flame, to prevent overheating of the pieces.

Long joints
The melted solder will always tend to flow to the hottest part. This characteristic can be used to 'pull' the solder along a joint.

Chain
Wire for making chain commercially has a core of solder which allows automatic soldering when heated, without the additional application of solder. This material is used primarily on automatic machines.

Applying the heat
The essence of soldering is that the heat which melts the solder, in whichever process, comes from the metal being soldered rather than from the torch. The heat from the torch, therefore, needs to be aimed at the piece in total rather than just at the area of the joint. This is particularly so when there is a wide variation in cross section. The greater the mass of precious metal, the more heat is required to raise the temperature a given amount. In the soldering of a small bead on to the end of a taper, if the heat were directed at the joint, two things would happen: the small bead would melt, because its small mass would cause a high temperature rise, and the thin neck would less easily come up to temperature, as all the heat would be drawn into the larger mass at the end. The result would be failure.

If, instead, the large mass is heated and, just short of soldering temperature, the torch is moved along the joint, then both the thin section and the bead will come up to soldering temperature at the same time.

A similar situation occurs in soldering straight ear wires to ear rings, and the heat should principally be directed at the heavier decorative element rather than the wire.

Once the joint is made, heat can flow between the pieces, which will tend more nearly towards the same temperature. It is quite practical to draw solder along a joint by moving the torch around, causing the solder to flow to the hottest part.

If the piece being soldered is clean, then the capillary effect will draw the molten solder into the joint. On some occasions, it needs a little persuasion, and a poker or fiddle tool to assist.

In selecting the torch to use, the mass of precious metal to be heated must be taken into account. A needle flame will solder a single jump ring but will not have enough heat to solder the same jump ring onto a heavier piece. Generally, if in doubt, a larger, softer flame is better than a smaller, harder one.

Precious metal solder
It is essential to use solder described as hallmarking quality. Engineering quality silver solder will not pass the assay test because of its lower silver content.

Hallmarking silver solder comes in five recognised grades, offering a range of melting points to suit the application (see p. 142). Where joints are made sequentially, it is not always necessary to use different grades, although repeated heating can degrade previously made joints if the piece is reheated to the same temperature.

Where more than two soldering operations are performed, it is generally preferable to start with hard and complete with medium solder. If the piece is delicate, then starting with medium and completing with easy solder will help prevent overheating.

With a range of solders it is essential to keep them separate and identified. To assist identification, solders are produced in different sections. If in doubt, try a piece of the solder on a scrap piece of silver or gold.

When large heavy pieces are being soldered, the solder can be

Silver solders

Type	Melting temperature °C	Principal use	Usual cross section
Extra easy	667–709	Last stage and delicate joints	2 × 0.5mm
Easy	705–723	Last stage joints	0.3 × 0.5mm
Medium	720–765	General purpose	1.5 × 0.7mm
Hard	745–778	First stage joints	5 × 0.6mm
Enamelling	730–800	Joining pieces subsequently to be enamelled	1.5 × 1mm

Gold solders

Type	Carat range	Typical melting temperature °C
Extra easy	6, 9	640–700
Easy	9, 14	720–750
Medium	9, 14, 18, 22	750–880
Hard	9, 14, 18, 22	750–800

stick fed; that is, the piece is heated to the melting point of the solder, which is touched onto the joint, where it melts and flows to form the joint.

Soldering irons

Soldering irons used for *soft soldering* such metals as brass, copper and tinplated steel are available in a range of sizes and should be selected to suit the job. The function of a soldering iron is to heat the piece to be soldered to the melting temperature of the solder. The size of the iron is therefore determined primarily on the weight of the piece being soldered. Flame-heated irons can be used, but electrical heating is more predictable, giving a more constant amount of heat.

Soldering jigs (see also Soldering)

The accurate positioning of components to be soldered together can be facilitated by using appropriate jigs. In the design of the jigs, it is important to minimise the mass of the jig, which would otherwise take too much heat away from the components. Iron binding wire can be twisted and formed into simple jigs for short-run operations.

The perforated ceramic soldering tables now available provide a

matrix of holes, ideal for locating pins and pegs. More lasting jigs can be moulded in fired clay or other fired ceramic material.

One technique for the pro-

duction of location jigs is to mould the shapes from clay, allow them to dry and low fire them at about 650°C. After cooling, these low fired parts can easily be shaped with simple hand tools to incorporate faces, holes, V guides and other locations. These jigs can then be fired to a higher temperature and, although some shrinkage will occur, the essential features will remain.

Sorting tray

Simple grooved trays to facilitate the sorting and grading of stones and beads.

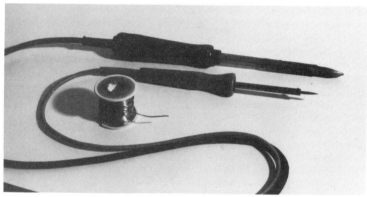

Fig. 48 *Electric soldering irons and reel of soft solder*

Diag. 249 *Iron binding wire used to jig a wire to a plate for soldering*

Diag. 250 *Simple two-level soldering jig*

Diag. 251 *Perforated ceramic base used to hold pins for soldering*

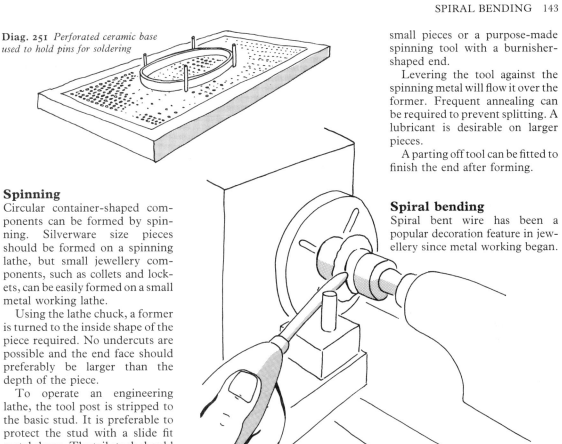

Spinning

Circular container-shaped components can be formed by spinning. Silverware size pieces should be formed on a spinning lathe, but small jewellery components, such as collets and lockets, can be easily formed on a small metal working lathe.

Using the lathe chuck, a former is turned to the inside shape of the piece required. No undercuts are possible and the end face should preferably be larger than the depth of the piece.

To operate an engineering lathe, the tool post is stripped to the basic stud. It is preferable to protect the stud with a slide fit metal sleeve. The tail stock should be fitted with a revolving centre. A cap is made from metal to fit over the revolving part of the centre, providing a flat smooth end face to match the diameter of the former.

A disc of annealed maleable metal, whose diameter is equal to twice the depth plus the base diameter of the piece, is placed against the base of the former. The tail stock with capped revolving centre is bought up in contact and locked in place. The tail stock screw is turned to give a firm clamping of the material, yet not so much as to overload the bearings. Spinning can now commence.

The cross slide is adjusted to position the post just to the right of the rotating disc. A round-ended forming tool is held between the post and the piece so that the working face is at the diameter of the base of the former. The tool can be a large hand-burnisher for small pieces or a purpose-made spinning tool with a burnisher-shaped end.

Levering the tool against the spinning metal will flow it over the former. Frequent annealing can be required to prevent splitting. A lubricant is desirable on larger pieces.

A parting off tool can be fitted to finish the end after forming.

Diag. 252 *Spinning*

Spiral bending

Spiral bent wire has been a popular decoration feature in jewellery since metal working began.

Diag. 253 *Spiral winding in a vice*

A jig is required, to keep the forming flat and allow for even forming. The jig consists of a central peg fitted in a base in which is drilled an anchor hole adjacent to the peg.

If annealed wire is used, the spiral will remain tight after forming. If hard or half-hard wire is used, the coils will tend to open up after winding.

To wind a coil, the jig is firmly held either by clamping it to the bench or in the jaws of a chuck. The end of the wire is bent at 90 degrees and inserted in the hole. One hand is used to wind the wire around in increasing diameters, and the other is used to keep the winding flat. A steady load on the wire will ensure an even wind.

An improvement on the jig is to thread the peg and clamp the wire with a disc. The back of the jig can also be fitted with a spigot, allowing it to be held in a lathe chuck. The winding can then be done in the lathe.

Spirit lamp

A simple glass- or metal-bodied lamp with an adjustable wick. Useful for warming wax-working tools, spirit lamps are also capable of giving enough heat for delicate soldering when used with a mouth blow lamp.

Spit stick (see also Engraving)

A form of graver, burin or scraper of V shape with curved sides, also described as onglette in shape.

Split pins (see also Soldering jigs)

An engineering component which has various uses in jewellery making. As its name implies, it is a pin with a split body joined at one end, and normally used to retain a nut or washer by being pushed through a cross hole in a shaft when the ends are opened, securing the pin.

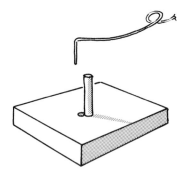

Diag. 254 *Spiral winding jig*

Diag. 255 *Spirit lamp*

A very wide range of sizes are available. The smaller ones, frequently copper-plated, can be incorporated in non-precious jewellery. The larger ones are useful in soldering processes to hold components together or support pieces.

Spray-etching (see also Etching)

A more uniform etching can be achieved using a bath in which the etching acid is sprayed on the material. Commercial spray-etching baths are available, being produced for the electronics industry.

Spring steel

Carbon steel, hardened and tempered to give a hard but flexible material.

a *Compression spring*

b *Tension spring*

c *Leaf spring*

Diag. 256 *Springs*

Springs

Springs can be formed in various ways. Coil springs can operate in torsion compression or tension. Leaf springs deflect under load either as a cantilever or simply supported at the ends. Doubled over leaf springs operate under compression as a coil spring, yet without material directly between the load and reaction points.

Steel is the most widely used material for springs and is permitted in pieces for hallmarking. Precious metals such as standard silver and low carat gold in hard form can be formed as springs.

Very small coil springs of steel are incorporated in bolt rings to return the bolt. Small leaf springs are built into swivels as used on watch chains. Small safety pins, such as those incorporated in safety chains, are formed as a single coil torsion spring.

Sprue

That piece of metal in a casting which joins the reservoir of metal to the piece.

Sprue cutters (see also Casting)

Hand cutters with short strong jaws used for cutting the sprues from the cast piece.

Square (see also Marking out)

A square, try square or steel square is used for checking adjacent faces for squareness and for marking out lines at right angles to an edge. One of the arms is thicker than the other, allowing it to be run along the datum edge. Squares can also be used on face plates for marking vertical lines, or setting pieces vertical prior to marking out. A 75mm (3in) square is suitable for most jewellery work.

are required. Normal fabric dyes are suitable for most other materials. Those sold for nylon fabric are effective to a degree on solid nylon and other plastics, but experimentation is required.

Stainless steel

A tough steel with the ability to resist corrosion. It can be sawn, filed and polished. Joining is best achieved by welding, although it is possible to braze, but this will leave a colour band.

Free cutting material should be selected as it is easier to work.

Stake

A shaped steel block on which sheet metal components are formed using a range of hammers.

Stakes come in a variety of round, square, oval and tapered shapes. The polished working face is fitted with a square shank which can be held in a vice, or in a vice-held cranked bar called a horse.

Combined stakes with three or

four working shapes have a flat-faced centre section enabling it to be held in a vice. Specialised stakes are available for shaping spoons.

Standard mark

The part of a hallmark indicating the type and quality of the metal.

Standard silver

Also called sterling silver, it is required to contain not less than 925 parts per 1000 of pure silver to conform to hallmarking requirements. Standard silver is the common material for jewellery making. It melts at 893°C, compared with pure silver which melts at 960°C, gold at 1063°C and copper at 1083°C.

Standard wire gauge (see also Measuring)

A measuring system used to define the size of wire diameter and sheet thickness; the abreviation swg is used. Other systems such as Birmingham wire gauge, Brown and Sharp are also used.

Diag. 258 *Steam casting*

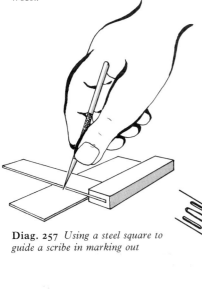

Diag. 257 *Using a steel square to guide a scribe in marking out*

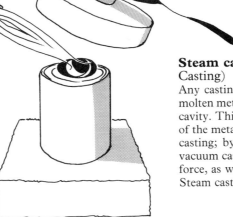

Staining (see also Dyeing)

Absorbent materials such as wood, textiles and some plastics can be coloured with stains and dyes.

Wood stains are obviously suitable for wood where wood colours

Steam casting (see also Casting)

Any casting process requires the molten metal to be forced into the cavity. This can be by the weight of the metal itself, as with gravity casting; by air pressure, as with vacuum casting, or by centrifugal force, as with centrifugal casting. Steam casting is a simple process and relies on the generation of steam from a damp pad, to force the molten metal into the cavity.

A model is made in wax, sprued and invested. The wax is melted out and, in a shallow recess, enough material to well fill the cavity is set. The whole is set on a porous fire brick. The pad is formed from a fibrous material, traditionally asbestos but more recently an asbestos substitute. This pad is set in a shallow lid and fitted with a file handle as shown.

A little flux is added to the material, and this is melted with a flame until it is fully fluid. Without removing the flame, the wet pad is bought down smartly on to the top of the molten metal, sealing the escape of steam around the edge. As soon as it touches, the flame is removed.

As soon as all hissing stops, the pad is lifted away and the whole flask is dropped in a metal bucket of water. The sudden contraction will cause the investment to break up and fall away from the cast piece, which is finished in the normal way.

Steam cleaning
High pressure steam generators provide a controlled jet of steam which will effectively clean pieces of jewellery.

Steel
This basic industrial material is primarily used for the construction of tools rather than products. Silver steel, capable of being hardened and tempered, is readily available in rod and sheet form.

Steel, is a suitable material for jewellery but suffers from its tendency to rust. This can be overcome by the use of stainless steels. To minimise rusting in normal steels, a high polish finish and blueing in oil will assist.

Steels are available in a vast range of types and should be selected carefully to suit the function.

Steel shot
One of the forms of steel shapes used in *barrelling*, steel shot is used for open areas without intricate corners.

Stencil
Repeat shapes can be marked out on a flat material with stencils. Common shapes such as ovals, circles, squares, crosses, letters and numbers are readily available.

Sheet metal is best marked with a fine sharp scribe. Stone slabs are easily marked with an aluminium scribe which gives a fine metallic mark.

Sterling silver (*see* Standard silver)

Sticky wax
A form of wax used in the spruing of wax models. Its sticky quality enables components to be easily joined.

Stirring rod (*see also* Melting)
Stirring rods of graphite or carbon are used when melting metal for the production of ingots or castings. The choice of material prevents contamination of the alloy.

Stone cutting
Precious and semi-precious stones can be cut, shaped and polished. Starting with rough rock, cabochon stones are first sawn into slabs, typically about 6mm ($\frac{1}{4}$in) thick. On the sawn face,

Diag. 259 *Grinding a stone to shape*

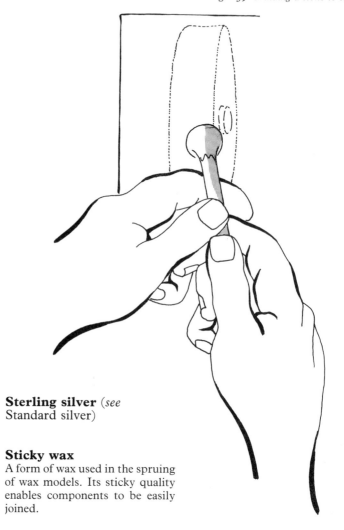

the shape of the stone is marked using an aluminium stick pencil and also, generally, a template. Radial saw cuts at right angles to the outline will form spokes which can be broken off, leaving a rough shape which can subsequently be ground and polished.

Precious stones, generally cut in facets, may be cut into smaller stones by sawing or splitting. They are then ground to sit in a dop stick for facetting.

Sawing is carried out with a diamond saw used with a lubricant.

Stone moulds (see also Casting)

Gravity casting of small precious metal components can be carried out in stone moulds. Tufa stone or tuff stone is one example being used by Navajo American Indians, and many early civilisations have made moulds from the soft stones for gravity casting. The process is essentially the same as cuttlefish casting.

Stone saws

Diamond chips embedded in steel saws are used for cutting the harder stones. The saws used for jewellery are of circular saw design but without cutting teeth.

Stone setting (see also Setting tools)

The process of fitting stones into metal jewellery. This involves the preparation of the seat or face on which the stone rests, and the final shaping and forming of the metal parts which will grip the stone in place.

The two most common methods of setting stones are by *bezel* and by *claws*.

Stone setting pliers

Hand pliers with shaped jaws which provide a seating face on one of the jaws, enabling the other

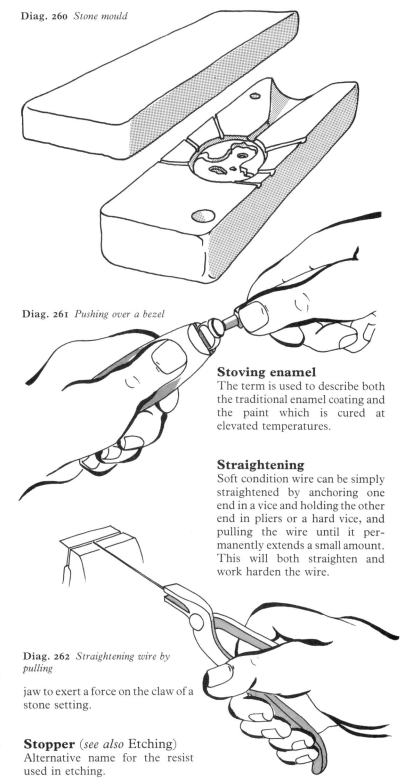

Diag. 260 *Stone mould*

Diag. 261 *Pushing over a bezel*

Diag. 262 *Straightening wire by pulling*

Stoving enamel

The term is used to describe both the traditional enamel coating and the paint which is cured at elevated temperatures.

Straightening

Soft condition wire can be simply straightened by anchoring one end in a vice and holding the other end in pliers or a hard vice, and pulling the wire until it permanently extends a small amount. This will both straighten and work harden the wire.

jaw to exert a force on the claw of a stone setting.

Stopper (see also Etching)

Alternative name for the resist used in etching.

Strapwork

Strapwork is the general term used to describe the construction of pieces by braiding or plaiting.

The three-wire braids are the most simple and widely used. The individual strands may in themselves be made from a number of strands, either simply laid side by side or woven or braided together. Round wire can be used, but the particular appeal of strapwork is the use of flat strips which are bent over rather than round, to change the direction of the strand.

Main braids can be divided out and the multiple strands themselves be braided. Many of the techniques used for textile braid work and macramé can be applied to metal strapwork.

Strapwork is also possible with other materials from paper to leather and plastic, all of which can have their application to jewellery.

Straw

Corn dollies and the technique of forming can be used to produce jewellery items.

Streak testing (see also Assay)

Simple testing of precious metals. The reaction to specific acids is observed by producing a streak of the material on a matt black stone, the touch stone.

Stretch forming

The technique of forming metal or softened plastic sheet in which the material is stretched and reduced in thickness to follow the shape, rather than being allowed to nearly retain its thickness by drawing from a surrounding area of material, as in deep drawing. One feature of stretch forming is the minimising of creasing which can occur with other forming techniques. The penalty is the greater risk of tearing the material.

One application to jewellery is illustrated in the stretch forming of a back piece for a pendant. The frame is soldered to a piece of sheet and the outside trimmed off. A steel die is cut in the desired relief, the outside of which locates in the inside of the frame. A drop press or hand hammer forces a yielding material, such as lead or layered paper, onto the sheet, stretching it to follow the form of the die without distorting the frame.

Stringing beads

Silk or nylon thread is used to string beads. Lengths of stringing material can be obtained fitted with a twisted wire needle to facilitate the threading. Sorting trays with grooves allow grading of the beads prior to threading.

Beads can be threaded to touch one another or the thread can be knotted between each bead.

Stripping

The surface of jewellery components can be removed by electrolysis in a plating bath or by quick immersion in an aqua regia acid solution.

Studs

Simple decorative ear rings consisting of a decorative head in metal or with a stone, with a short straight ear wire secured in the ear with a keeper or scroll. Studs can also be used and described as sleepers.

Sulphuric acid

Used diluted with water, sulphuric acid will form a pickle which will remove flux and oxides on silver and other metals. Sulphuric acid is highly corrosive and will burn on contact with the skin and clothes. When mixing with water, always add the acid to water, and do not use hot water. Adding water to the acid and/or using hot water can cause violent action of the liquids, resulting in splashing.

Surface plate (see also Marking out)

A cast steel plate with an accurately machined flat face. It provides a flat datum face for marking out components using height gauges, scribing blocks, square, V blocks and slip gauges.

Swage block

A metal block, generally steel, constructed with a range of grooves into which sheet metal components can be formed using hammers and punches.

Swaging

The forming and flowing of metal. Typically the term is used in describing the forming over of an edge of metal, as in stone setting. It is also used to describe the shaping of sheet material into tubes and sections using a swage block.

Swage blocks, with their multiplicity of recesses, allow a piece of sheet metal to be formed progressively into tubes and open sections. They can also be used for forging a section from, for example, round to half-round.

To produce a cylinder, a piece of sheet is cut to the length required and of a width equal to the mean circumference of the tube. The piece is laid in a large semi-circular recess and formed down. This can be done by hammer, or by using a hammer on a cylindrical forming drift, such as a piece of dowel or rod. This process is repeated using progressively smaller recesses and drifts until the ends of the sheet meet. After the first few forming operations, the piece should be rotated to give equal forming all around.

Pieces longer than the width of the swage block can be formed by moving the piece back and forth during forming.

Swage blocks of both half-round and V section can be used to forge solid wire and rod. The most

Diag. 263 *Swage block*

Diag. 264 *Swaging*

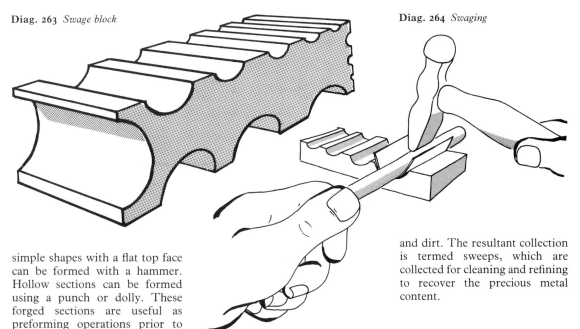

simple shapes with a flat top face can be formed with a hammer. Hollow sections can be formed using a punch or dolly. These forged sections are useful as preforming operations prior to drawing.

Swansdown mop

A soft mop used for final *polishing* on a polishing machine.

Sweeps (*see also* Lemel)

The shavings, filings and scrapings which fall to the floor are collected along with other dust and dirt. The resultant collection is termed sweeps, which are collected for cleaning and refining to recover the precious metal content.

Syringe

Redundant medical syringes are useful for washing out pickle from intricate and hollow metal components, using a water and bicarbonate of soda solution.

Tab fastenings

Tab or tab and slot fastenings can be employed to secure components together when soldering or claw fixing is inappropriate. Tabs have the advantage that they can be secured by the user. This

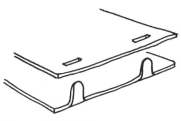

Diag. 265 *Tab fixing*

enables such items as photographs to be fitted in lockets and frames. Tab and plate construction has the advantage of spreading the clamping over a larger area, such as when fitting precious metal pieces to fabrics and leather.

Tantalum

A relatively new metal, discovered in 1802, it is ductile and can be worked with normal metal working tools in a similar way to steel. Its usual colour is bluish but, like titanium, its main attraction for jewellery is the wide range of bright colours which can be induced by heating it to tempera-tures above 300°C. Fabrication by welding or soldering is outside the processes normally used in jewellery manufacture and is best incorporated in one of the other more common jewellery materials by riveting or burnishing. There are restrictions relating to its use with hallmarked pieces, and current regulations should be referred to.

Tapping

Threaded holes can be made by drilling and tapping. After marking out and centre punching the position of the hole, a hole just slightly smaller than the root or core diameter of the thread is drilled in the material. Tapping drill sizes for threads are listed in engineering tables or can be measured on the tap of a screw of the same thread.

Taps come in three forms for

Diag. 266 *Tapping a threaded hole*

each thread size: taper, second and plug. The taper tap has a long tapered lead in and is used to start the thread. The second has a short lead, and the thread on the plug tap goes almost all the way to the end in full form. It is frequently possible to use only a second tap and plug tap or just a taper tap and plug tap. If the material is very thin, then a taper or second tap used alone may suffice.

For hand tapping, the tap is held in a tap holder allowing sufficient grip for cutting. Very small taps can be held in a pin chuck. When cutting threads in the end of a piece held in a lathe chuck, the tap can be held in the tail stock chuck.

A thin lubricant such as paraffin is generally desirable. To cut, the tap is entered into the hole and, with a little end pressure, rotated about one third to half a turn, and then reversed back, clearing any swarf. This turn forward, turn back process allows cutting for up to a turn before clearing swarf and reduces the chance of taps breaking. When a full thread part of a tap has passed through the material, the thread is complete and the tap can be removed.

Making threaded holes in solid material requires a hole to be drilled deeper than the thread length required, as the tapping

cannot go all the way to the bottom of the hole. Through holes are always preferable.

Tassel
The natural form resulting from a knotted multi-strand thread with the cut end teased out. The shape can be simulated in metal and other materials and used to terminate or decorate edges.

Tempering
Part of the process of bringing steel tools to the required hardness.

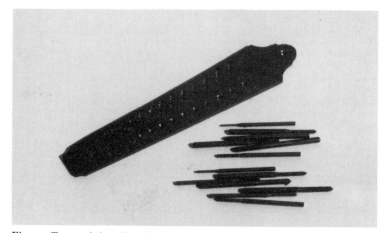

Fig. 49 *Taps and threading plate*

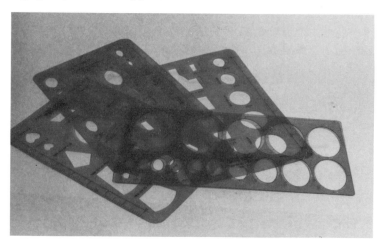

Fig. 50 *Templates*

Templates
Where a sheet material shape is required to be repeated and the method of production is by cutting to a scribed line, then a template will ensure accuracy of repetition. Sheet aluminium is a

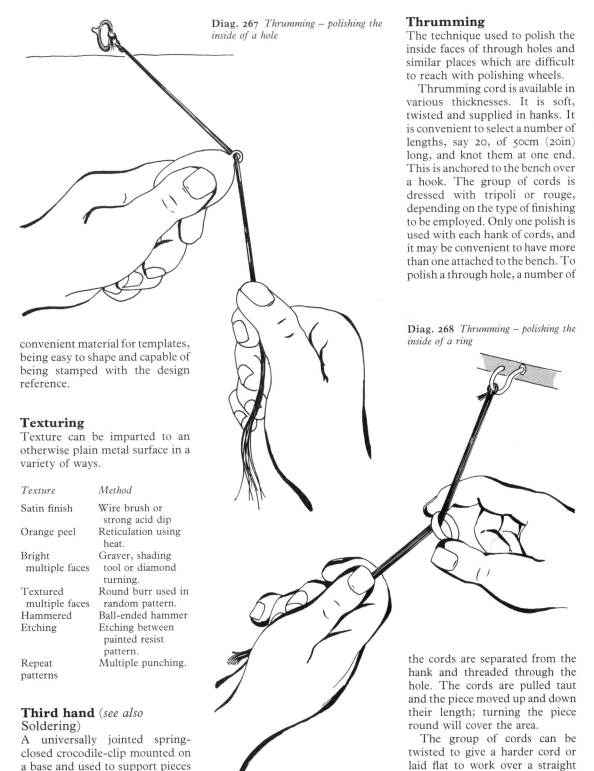

Diag. 267 *Thrumming – polishing the inside of a hole*

Diag. 268 *Thrumming – polishing the inside of a ring*

convenient material for templates, being easy to shape and capable of being stamped with the design reference.

Texturing

Texture can be imparted to an otherwise plain metal surface in a variety of ways.

Texture	Method
Satin finish	Wire brush or strong acid dip
Orange peel	Reticulation using heat.
Bright multiple faces	Graver, shading tool or diamond turning.
Textured multiple faces	Round burr used in random pattern.
Hammered	Ball-ended hammer
Etching	Etching between painted resist pattern.
Repeat patterns	Multiple punching.

Third hand (*see also* Soldering)

A universally jointed spring-closed crocodile-clip mounted on a base and used to support pieces during soldering.

Thrumming

The technique used to polish the inside faces of through holes and similar places which are difficult to reach with polishing wheels.

Thrumming cord is available in various thicknesses. It is soft, twisted and supplied in hanks. It is convenient to select a number of lengths, say 20, of 50cm (20in) long, and knot them at one end. This is anchored to the bench over a hook. The group of cords is dressed with tripoli or rouge, depending on the type of finishing to be employed. Only one polish is used with each hank of cords, and it may be convenient to have more than one attached to the bench. To polish a through hole, a number of the cords are separated from the hank and threaded through the hole. The cords are pulled taut and the piece moved up and down their length; turning the piece round will cover the area.

The group of cords can be twisted to give a harder cord or laid flat to work over a straight edge.

Thrumming can cut through metal very quickly and the piece must be moved around to prevent cutting an unwanted groove.

Tin lid moulds

A simple moulding technique for making split moulds in plaster of Paris. A redundant tin lid or box at least 30mm (1¼in) deep is filled to a depth of about 10mm (½in) with plasticine. On this face is built up a half model of the piece. In the flat face, cone holes for location can be cut. The walls are lined with plasticine to create a tapered face and allow easy removal of the casting. Plaster of Paris is poured in the mould and allowed to set. The face of the mould is then waxed. The resultant cast mould is set in a similarly lined tin and the hollow filled with and built up to form a full three-dimensional model. This is then cast over with more plaster and, when dry, both moulded parts are removed and thoroughly dried.

Gas vents are scored in the faces and, if not already moulded in, a sprue hole is carved in the faces.

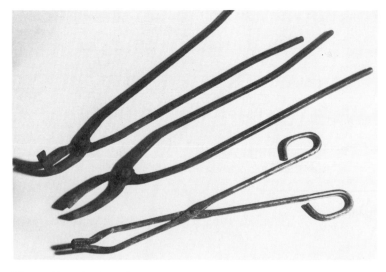

Fig. 51 *Tongs for hot metal and acid*

Diag. 269 *Tin lid mould being filled with plaster of Paris*

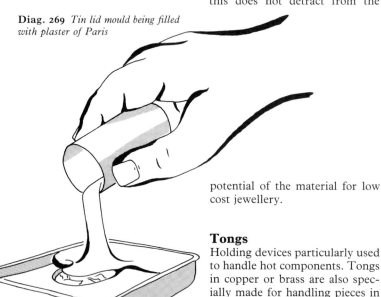

Tin plate

Steel sheet coated with a thin layer of tin. Tin plate is the traditional material for food cans. It has the advantage of resistance to corrosion, ease of cutting, punching and soldering, and, if recovered from discarded cans, is free. These attributes have led to its use as a material by poor craftsmen in underdeveloped countries, but this does not detract from the potential of the material for low cost jewellery.

Tongs

Holding devices particularly used to handle hot components. Tongs in copper or brass are also specially made for handling pieces in and out of acid baths.

The principal variable part in the design of tongs is the gripping jaws. Particularly applicable to jewellery making are those tongs used to grip hot flasks and crucibles. For forging tools, a pair of tongs with straight grooved jaws will hold rods securely which would more easily slip out of flat-faced jaws.

Tool steel

Very hard steel, capable of being shaped only by grinding and used for making lathe tools and other cutting bits.

Tortoise shell

Shaped and finished using the same methods as horn; tortoise shell has more attractive markings. There are many very good imitations of tortoise shell. These are most easily detected by burning a tiny sample or sticking a hot pin in the material. The difference between a cellulose-like plastic smell and the natural material smell, not dissimilar to that experienced when teeth are drilled at a dentist, is easily recognised. A similar test applies to testing ivory.

Touch stone (*see also* Streak testing)
The black matt finish stone used to streak a sample of precious metal for acid testing.

Trace chain (*see also* Chainmaking)
The most simple form of chain, comprising oval links set at 90 degrees to each other.

Tracer punch
A smooth-ended punch used to set wire inlay.

Trailed wax
A technique used to build up wax models in natural formation for lost wax casting. The wax is ejected from a gun in a soft condition and is trailed onto a flat surface, such as glass, to build up the model. Wax trailing can be used to add a decorative feature to moulded wax models.

Transferring designs (*see also* Marking out)
The need frequently arises when a design on paper has to be transferred onto metal. A number of techniques exist, but in general the process involves the transfer of a mark which is subsequently reinforced by scribing.

One method is simply to use carbon paper under the design, having prepared the surface of the metal with white poster paint or a similar receptive coating. The outline is traced over with a ballpoint pen or similar smooth blunt tool. Covering the back of the design with soft pencil marks produces a similar effect.

A second method is simply to prick through the design, producing a series of fine points which can be joined up to complete the design.

For repeated use, the design is cut out as a template and the design scribed around.

a *Round*

b *Round with gemstone cut out*

c *Oval*

d *Square*

e *Hexagonal*

f *Cushion square*

g *Tear drop*

Diag. 270 *Triblet sections*

If the design is made on a self-adhesive label, this can be fixed directly to the piece and the design cut to shape.

Treblet
A large triblet or tapered mandrel used for forming sheet and wire into large curves. A bench treblet can be 500mm (20in) high with diameters of 75mm to 300mm (3in to 12in) and weight 40kg (88lb).

Triblet
The tapered steel tool used to form rings and other pieces to shape. Triblets are available round, square, oval, triangular and rectangular for chain making. Triblets can be used in increasing the size of rings. It is important when sizing rings only to allow the hammer to strike the ring and not the triblet. Rings need to be reversed so as not to induce a one-way taper.

Fig. 52 *Round, square, oval and chain triblets*

Triplet

The three layered construction of a cabochon or other cut stone in which a thin layer of precious material, typically opal, is sandwiched between a crystal cap and a backing stone.

Tripod

Steel tripods with woven metal tops enable pieces to be supported when the heat has to be applied underneath. The use of a tripod is appropriate when soldering small items to a plate where the application of enough heat to raise the temperature of the plate would melt the small items. The mass of the mesh and tripod will take a significant amount of heat from the piece.

Tripoli

An abrasive material used for coarse cutting on a polishing mop.

Tube cutter

A simple jig device used to grip small-diameter tube and provide both an end stop to set the length of the tube being cut and guide the saw.

Tube making

Tube in a wide range of sections can be purchased. It is solid drawn and without a seam. Alternatively, tube can be made.

If all scrap can be recovered, then it is economical to produce short lengths of tube by drilling rod in a lathe. The more practical method is to form it from sheet.

A strip of the required gauge is marked out and cut to a width equal to the mean circumference of the tube. This is calculated by multiplying the average of the inside diameter and outside diameter by π (3.142) that is $\dfrac{(\text{o.D} + \text{i.D})}{2} \times 3.142$. For thin sheet the inside diameter multiplied by π can be used.

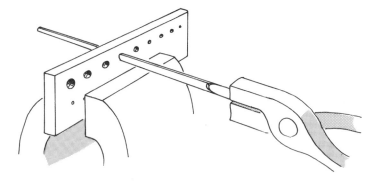

The corners at one end are snipped off and, with a half-round swage block and rods, the sheet is progressively formed from flat to half-round to round using a soft-faced mallet. The use of a mandrel of the final inside diameter is essential to bring the edges of the sheet together. If the strip is not held square in the swage block, a twisted joint line can result, but this is not necessarily unacceptable. The edges can be joined by soldering.

The tube can be reduced in size after annealing or soldering, using a draw plate. A knife edge or tapered mandrel is needed to keep the joint square and prevent the tube from collapsing. The removal of the corners of the sheet before forming will enable the tube to be gripped by draw tongs more easily.

Tufa casting

A form of *gravity casting* using soft tufa stone. A very similar process to cuttlefish casting.

Tumbled stones

Stones or pebbles, generally of the semi-precious type, which have been smoothed and polished by tumbling them in a barrel with grit and polish. Shapes are unpredictable and need careful selection for use.

Tumbled stones can be used in preference to rough rock, being already partly shaped for grinding to special shapes.

Diag. 271 *Drawing tube*

Turning (*see also* Cut off tool)

The process of shaping circular pieces on a lathe. In simple turning, the material is held in the chuck and rotated at a speed which is dependent on the material type and size. A cutting tool set in the tool holder on the cross slide is moved by rotating the control handles of the cross slide and carriage. This action brings the

Fig. 53 *Tripod with mesh for heating*

tool tip in contact with the material and, with appropriate settings, will remove the desired amount of material. A chuck mounted in tail stock will hold drills which, by locking the tail stock to the bed of the lathe, can be fed into the work by rotating the feed screw handle on the tail stock. The rotation of the piece must be stopped for the component to be measured.

When the basic shape has been formed, it is parted from the other material using a narrow parting off tool. The component thus formed can be complete or may then be reversed in the chuck and have further turning work done. An alternative method of parting

off in bead work is achieved by turning the outside shape and breaking through to the end of the bead nearest the chuck by drilling the centre hole. Small collets can be economically made by turning, provided all the swarf is recovered.

Tweezers

Spring-holding devices available in a variety of shapes and sizes for different jobs.

It is well worth buying the best quality available and keeping each pair for a limited function, such as stone handling, soldering, acid bath use and handling small findings.

Straight pointed tweezers in stainless steel will suit most functions. For handling stones, grooved and cross-grooved tips will help prevent stones slipping.

Twist drill (*see also* Drilling)

The established drill design used for most general engineering hole drilling. The twist or flute allows the metal which the tip has cut away to move up the length of the drill, allowing cutting to continue.

Twist drills are suitable for jewellery work on precious metals. The very small sizes are available with larger diameter shanks to fit the chucks of pendant

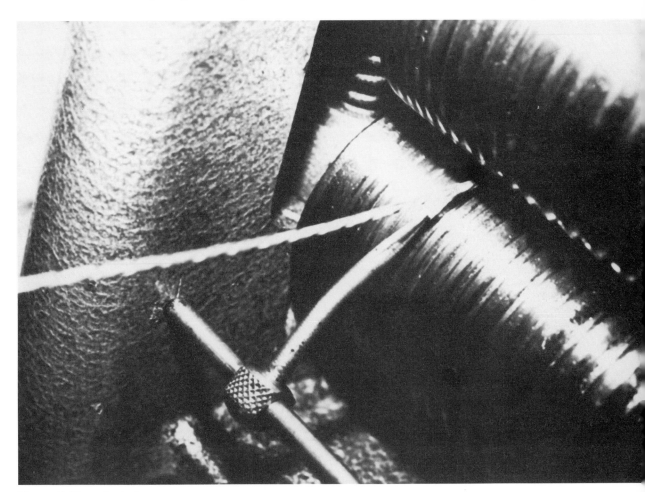

Fig. 54 *Rolling twisted wire to a square section*

drills. Although not theoretically correct, they do work well in jeweller's drill stocks where the drilling action reverses.

Twisting jump rings

Jump rings should be opened by twisting rather than pulling the joint apart, as the latter will distort the shape.

Twists

Twisting wires together can produce a wide range of effects for use as bangles, neckpieces, edgings, rings and many other decorative components. In his book on metalworking and enamelling, Herbert Maryon lists and describes 72 different twists.

The most simple twist is with a square section wire giving a screw thread-like effect. This twisting can be continuous or spaced with untwisted lengths. Another simple twist is with two round wires. These can be left as twisted, slightly flattened by passing them through a rolling mill, given a more round section by drawing through a round hole draw plate, or given flat facets by drawing through a square hole draw plate.

Combinations of a plain wire and a pair of twisted wires can produce a very elaborate section, with a beaded effect contrasting the slow twist of the plain wire. Pairs of twisted pairs set in an opposite twist will produce a solid section with the appearance of rope chain.

One essential for successful twists is to use only fully-annealed wire which is uniform in softness over its full length. Any changes in hardness over the length of the wire will cause uneven winding.

Pairs of wire or single sections are most easily twisted by gripping one end in a bench vice and holding the other end in a geared hand drill. If soft material, such as a piece of leather or pad of paper, is wrapped around the end held in the vice, then the change from twisted to plain is more gradual and the chances of fracture reduced. The chuck of the drill can be fitted with a strong hook over which to hook the wire. A screw cup hook is convenient.

Twists should be annealed after twisting, unless the springy quality resulting from the twisting is required.

Ultrasonic cleaning

Jewellery components can be cleaned by the removal of unwanted particles using an ultrasonic cleaning bath.

A cleaning tank is typically fabricated from stainless steel and fitted in a sheet metal enclosure. Fitted to the outside base of the tank is a transducer which oscillates at high frequency. The electronic circuitry to control this is also mounted below the tank, with the controls mounted on the enclosure.

The tank contains a cleaning fluid which can also act as a deoxidisation medium. It is essential that the unit is only switched on when there is fluid in the tank or the transducer can be destroyed.

The effect of the high-frequency activation of the fluid in

Fig. 55 *Ultrasonic cleaner*

the tank is complex. It appears that the action is the creation of sharply divided areas of pressure which free and float away the unwanted bodies.

Cleaning is most effective when the piece is suspended in the fluid rather than being sat on the bottom of the tank. Various methods of suspending the pieces are employed including baskets, hangers and suspended containers.

— V —

V cutter

To produce a sharp inside and outside corner on folded sheet material, it is necessary to cut a 90 degree groove along the fold line. For sheet metal work a hand draw tool with a V cutting end set at right angles to the shaft is used, by drawing it along a straight edge towards the operator. The cutting face and backing faces are sharpened as with a graver to produce a clean cut.

Vacuum casting

Molten metal can be persuaded to flow into a lost wax created cavity by reducing the air pressure beneath the flask so that normal atmospheric pressure acts only on the top of the metal. One feature of casting investment is that it is microscopically porous and allows for the flow of air.

In vacuum casting, a flask is invested in the same way as for steam casting or centrifugal casting, but with a recess in the top of the investment connected to the sprue hole and hence to the cavity.

The heated flasks are set on a base with sealing washers and the metal is melted using a torch on the top face of the flask. When fully molten, a vacuum is applied quickly to the base, creating a near zero pressure at the base of the flask. With normal atmospheric pressure on top of the metal, it is quickly forced into the cavity and, when the flow is complete, the vacuum can be removed. All other operations are as for lost wax centrifugal casting or steam casting.

Vacuum pump

An air pump arranged to pump out air from a container. It has two prime uses in casting jewellery components: evacuating a bell-jar with freshly poured investment to remove air bubbles, and evacuating air from beneath a flask when vacuum casting.

Varnishing

Used on wooden jewellery in matt or gloss finish both to finish the components and to seal the surface prior to painting.

Veneers

Thin slices of selected wood used for covering a plain base. Inlay in the form of marquetry can be employed in wooden jewellery.

Vernier gauge (see also Measuring)

A measuring tool in which a sliding cursor traverses a scale indicating the distance from the reference face or anvil. The cursor is divided into less divisions than the major divisions and, by noting lines of coincidence, a more accurate reading can be made.

Vibrating table

Air bubbles trapped in *investment* will cast as small spheres, spoiling the casting. By placing the flask on a vibrating table after pouring and vibrating the investment before pouring, the bubbles will be released and allowed to rise to the surface.

Tables can be worked by an electric motor fitted by a crank, an eccentric or by a solenoid.

Vibrator engraver

Mainly employed for marking tools rather than for decorative effect, the vibrating engraver has a point which, through a solenoid action, vibrates at a variable frequency and amplitude. The point will produce a series of fine indentations in the material and can be used like a writing implement.

Vice

A basic holding device. Vices can be divided between bench-mounted and hand types.

Bench-mounted vices are described by the width of the jaws. Variations include quick action release mechanisms, swivelling bases and interchangeable jaws. When fitting a bench vice, it must be securely bolted with the face of the fixed jaw just projecting forward of the front face of the bench, to enable long vertical pieces to be held. Some models incorporate an anvil piece and, although useful, is always something of a compromise.

Hand vices range from simple wedge-locking ring clamps to tiny vices mounted on a handle. Pin vices can be of the chuck or sprung-jaws type with a side screw. One design available em-ploys a tapered screw handle which closes the jaws and has the advantage of not having a projecting side screw.

Vitreous enamels
The true enamels which fire at high temperatures.

Vulcanising press
A heated press used to vulcanise rubber moulds for lost wax casting. The press clamps the frame containing the metal master and rubber compound.

W

Water of Ayr stone
A soft slate-like stone, it is used wet for smoothing metal surfaces which show file or other marks and for very light shaping of metal. Water of Ayr is available in sticks from 3mm ($\frac{1}{8}$in) to 25mm (1in). It wears away slowly in use, forming an abrasive slurry and forming itself to the shape of the piece. Frequent dipping in water cleans away the slurry and waste metal. A soft stone, it can be carved and filed to shape for reaching awkward corners. It is not suitable for use in revolving chucks.

Waxes
A range of waxes is available for the creation of wax models used in lost wax casting. Descriptions vary between manufacturers, but the following is typical: wax wires, perfect purple wax, carving wax, pattern wax, casting wax, spru wax, sticky wax, injection wax, profile wax, stippled wax sheet, modelling wax, hard, medium and soft carving wax, filing wax.

Weaving
All materials with a measure of flexibility can be used in variations of fabric-weaving techniques.

Diag. 272 *Finishing – removal of file marks with water of Ayr stone*

Materials can be combined to give contrast and colour and a woven element can be decorated by the introduction of beads. Silver is a convenient material.

Although silver wire lacks the flexibility of traditional weaving threads, many of the techniques of weaving and basket making can be applied to silver.

Fine solid wire can be used for designs with very simple turns, but, where tighter turns are needed, silver thread made from a twisted pair will weave more easily. Whatever the thread form, the material must be in a fully annealed state.

Simple but very effective is a braid plaited from three strands.

A wide variety of finished pieces can be achieved by tight or loose plaiting, and by using some of the many twisted patterns for each of the three individual strands.

The ends of the three strands need to be anchored, and it is worth soldering them together, which can also add to the finished design. The end can either be held in a vice, or held by a nail or screw to the bench.

Two strands of fairly heavy gauge can be linked together by forming around pins nailed in a block of hardwood, but care must be taken not to kink the wire.

Strands can be linked by single or multiple twists, and, starting with an even number of strands, a simple diamond fish-net is formed quite quickly. Simple patterns can be achieved by making the 'diamond' shapes long or short. This can be enlivened by threading small beads of various shapes between the cross-overs.

Basket weaving has developed to cope with the characteristics of cane and willow. These characteristics are not dissimilar to those of silver wire, and most of the techniques can be applied on a very small scale to silver jewellery.

Weaving is not limited to round or twisted wire. Sheet material cut comb-like will accept similar or fully cut pieces, which can be fixed by bending over the exposed ends. Alternatively, sheet and wire can be interwoven.

Knitting a tube of wire over nails in a drilled wooden block or cotton-reel will, with care, produce a flexible chain suitable for necklaces and bracelets.

A simple loom made with two sets of nails in a wood block enables simple weaving to be produced, but great care is needed to prevent kinking of the weft.

The uniformity of this approach can be departed from, and free patterns formed around and within a circle or square of pins. Cross-overs, if not twisted, can be joined with a separate twist of wire and, as with previous techniques, the introduction of through beads or other shapes will enliven the design.

Welding

A joining process for metals. The process consists of heating the area of the joint to or above melting point. This is done with an electric arc or high-temperature gas flame. Into this heated joint a rod of the same material is fed where it puddles and unites with the material of the body.

Variations of the process are spot welding and projecting welding.

For jewellery work, a high-temperature gas flame of oxygen and hydrogen is used, but a high level of skill is required to create neat joints.

Some base metal components are designed for projection welding for high-volume production.

Wheel engraving

The technique of engraving particularly applied to *intaglio* work on gemstones. The wheel, an abrasive loaded copper disc, rotates in bearings with a supply of coolant on the cutting faces. The piece to be engraved is held against the wheel.

White metal

A tin alloy used for casting low cost costume jewellery.

Whiting

A chalk compound used in the same way as yellow ochre for a solder resist. It also has properties for cleaning metal components.

Wig (*see also* Soldering)

The jeweller's wig is a close compressed bun-shaped mass of iron wire with a wire handle on which small components can be hand-held while soldering.

Wire

A piece of metal, with its length large compared to its section, in a long continuous length.

Wire rolling (*see also* Rolling)

Rolling mills can produce square section wire from ingots and D section wires, sometimes using extension rollers. Both square and round section wire can be further shaped by passing them through the flat rollers producing rectangular and rounded-edge rectangular wire. Twisted wire can be further shaped by passing it through rollers.

Workshop

The layout of the workshop is important for the efficient production of jewellery. Areas should be set aside for hot, dirty and clean working. Adequate controlled ventilation and lighting are essential.

Yellow ochre

A natural earth which, when mixed with a little water to a slurry, can be used to paint parts prior to soldering over areas where no solder is required.

Appendix

Suppliers	Stock
UK	
J. Gordon Parks and Partner 193 Wardour Street London W1V 4LP tel. 01-439-2347/8/9	*Tools, stones, findings*
Charles Cooper (Hatton Garden) Ltd Hatton Wall Hatton Garden London EC1N 8JJ tel. 01-278-8167	*Tools, findings*
H.S. Walsh & Sons Ltd 12–16 Clerkenwell Road London EC1 tel. 01-253-1174/5 *also at* 243 Beckenham Road Beckenham Kent BR3 4TS tel. 01-778-7061 and 01-778-9951	*Tools, findings*
Thomas Sutton (B'ham) Ltd 37 Frederick Street Birmingham B1 3HN tel. 021-236-7139	*Tools*
USA	
Allcraft Tool & Supply Company Inc 100 Frank Road Hicksville New York 11801 tel. (516) 433-1660 and (212) 895-0686 *also* 22 West 48 Street (Room 506) New York, New York 10036 tel. (212) 246-4740 *also* 204 North Harbor Blvd Fullerton California 92632 USA tel. (714) 870-8030 and 870-8031	*Tools and supplies*
C.W. Sommers & Co., Inc Room 509 387 Washington Street Boston Mass. 02108 USA	*Tools, findings*

Bibliography

ABBEY, S., *The Goldsmiths' and Silversmiths' Handbook*, The Technical Press, England, 1952

AREM, J., *Gems*, Bantam Books, 1975

BLAKEMORE, K., *Management for the Retail Jeweller*, Iliffe Books, London

BRITISH MUSEUM, *Jewellery Through 7000 years*, The Trustees of the British Museum, B.M.P., 1976

DIVIS, J., *Silver Marks of The World*, Hamlyn, 1976

EDWARDS, R., *The Technique of Jewellery*, Batsford, 1977

EMERSON, A.R., *Handmade Jewellery*, Dryad Press, England, 1953

GEE, G., *The Silversmith's Handbook*, Crosby Lockwood & Son, London, 1885

GRAHAM-CAMPBELL, J. and KIDD, D, *The Vikings*, The Trustees of the British Museum, B.M.P., 1980

GOODDEN, R. and POPHAM, P. *Silversmithing*, Oxford University Press, 1971

HARRIES, J., *Your Business and The Law*, Oyez Publishing Ltd, London, 1975

HIGGINS, R. *Jewellery from Classical Lands*, The Trustess of the British Museum, B.M.P.

MOURNEY, G., *Art Nouveau Jewellery and Fans*, Dover, 1973

NEUMANN, R. VON, *The Design and Creation of Jewellery*, Sir Isaac Pitman & Son Ltd, 1962

SHOENFELT, J., *Designing and Making Handwrought Jewellery*, McGraw-Hill, 1960

TAYLOR, G and SCARISBRICK, D., *Finger Rings from Ancient Egypt to the Present Day*, Ashmolean Museum, Oxford; Lund Humphries Ltd, London

UNTRACHT, O., *Metal Techniques For Craftsmen*, Robert Hale & Co., London, 1969

WICKS, S., *Jewellery*, MacDonald Educational

WILSON, H., *Silverwork and Jewellery*, Pitman, London, 1948

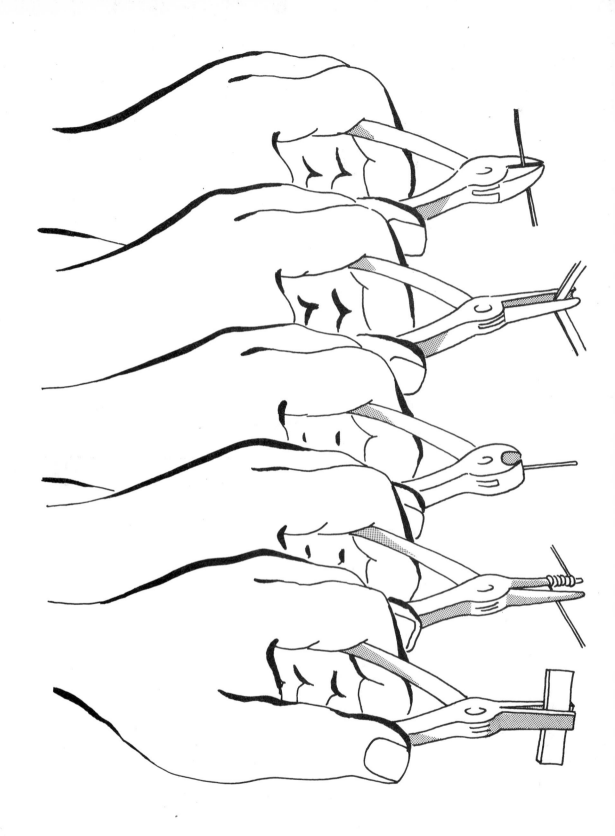